Essays on Modern India

History and Culture Series

ESSAYS ON MODERN INDIA

Edited by
Dr. Raj Kumar

2003

DISCOVERY PUBLISHING HOUSE
NEW DELHI-110002

First Published-2003
Reprint : 2012

ISBN 81-7141-690-X

Published by

DISCOVERY PUBLISHING HOUSE
4831/24, Ansari Road, Prahlad Street,
Darya Ganj, New Delhi-110002 (India)
Phone: 23279245 • Fax: 91-11-23253475
E-mail:dphtemp@indiatimes.com

Printed at:
Dynamic Printers

Preface

In this short collection of essays on modern India we do not claim to present to our readers complete history of the period. Effort, here, has been made to compile the essays which could interest, inform and inspire our readers, so that knowledge of the past could enliven our present and brighten our future.

This collection of essays will be useful to the students, teachers and all those who undergo competitive examinations. Our general reader will, ofcourse, enjoy reading it.

Raj Kumar

Acknowledgements

Collection of these essays was a great learning experience. Writings of Professors S. Gopal, Bipin Chandra, S. Bhattacharya, Sheikh Ali, A.R. Kulkarni, S. Khedirval, Ravindra Kumar, Suranjan Chatterjee, R.J. Moore, N.S. Bose, V.N. Dutta have inspired and educated me, I am indebted to them.

I have frequently discussed these topics with my colleagues and friends during national and international conferences, I am grateful to them.

I am grateful to the staff and librarians of various institutions and universities, especially ICHR, USI, NMML, Banaras, Madras, Jabalpur, Pune, Bombay and Calcutta for their help and assistance.

Last but not the least my publisher Shri Tilak Wasan deserves blessings best wishes of our readers for facilitating its prompt publication in its present form.

Raj Kumar

Contents

CHAPTER - I

INTRODUCTION

ADVENT OF THE EUROPEANS

Vasco da Gama landed at Calicut, sailing via the Cape of Good Hope in 1498. This marked the beginning of the European era in Indian history. The lucrative trade in spices of Malabar in modern Kerala—had tempted the Portuguese and inspired the search for a sea route to the Indies. The Portuguese had already established their colony in Goa by the first decade of the 16th Century but their territorial and commercial hold in India remained rather limited.

In the next century, India was visited by a large number of European travellers—Italians, Englishmen, Frenchmen and Dutchmen. They were drawn to India for different reasons. Some were traders, others adventurers, and quite a few fired by the missionary zeal to find converts to Christianity. Among them was Francois Bernier, the French doctor who enjoyed the confidence of princes and nobles and was in a uniquely privileged position to observe the functioning of the Mughal court. His account is a valuable source of information for historians.

These travelogues aroused European interest in India, and prompted in course of time, the colonial intervention. England, France, the Netherlands and Denmark, floated East India Companies. Chartered as trading companies by their respective governments, their primary commercial interest was in Indian textiles, both silk and cotton, indigo and at times, other sundry merchandise.

During the late 16th and the 17th Centuries, these companies competed with each other fiercely. By the last quarter of the 18th Century the English had vanquished all others and established themselves as the dominant power in India. The military campaigns of Robert Clive and the administrative enterprise of Warren Hastings (1772-1785) contributed significantly to this achievement.

BRITISH COLONIALISM

The British administered India for a period of about two centuries and brought about revolutionary changes in the social, political and the economic life of the country. Most Indians who came in their contact could not perceive the strategic threat posed by the East India Company. The British from the beginning followed a policy of divide and rule. Diplomacy and deceit were used to gain control of revenue collection in the province of Bengal. This gave the foreigners effective control of administration. The Marathas, the Sikhs and the rulers of Mysore could never unite to confront the foreign enemy and fell one by one. By the onset of the 19th Century there was no local power that could cope with their onslaught.

Once the British had consolidated their power, commercial exploitation of the natural resources and native labour became ruthless. It is true that there were a few benevolent Governor Generals who initiated social reforms and tried to render the administration more efficient and responsive, but they were exceptions. By the middle of the 19th Century arrogant exploitation of the people had tried the patience of the Indians to the limit.

The British had, to serve their own purpose, set up educational institutions that imparted western education and had established a vast network of rail-roads and telegraph lines. This united the country in an unprecedented manner. The Indians, exposed to western ideas of responsible and representative government, began to yearn for liberty and equality. There were many who looked back to the nation's glorious past and strove to rekindle the sentiment of patriotism. Foremost among them were Raja Ram Mohan Roy, and Ishwar Chandra Vidyasagar. The 19th Century is often referred to as the age of national resurgence in India.

The flash point was reached in 1857 when the British introduced a new rifle and cartridge in the British Indian Army. The bullet offended the religious sentiments of both the Hindus and Muslims, as it allegedly contained pork and beef tallow. Soldiers at Meerut were the first to rebel and reaching Delhi proclaimed Bahadurshah Zafar the sovereign ruler of India. The revolt soon spread like wild fire all over north India and could only be put down after great difficulty and bloodshed. Nationalist historians have seen in it the first Indian war of independence.

The six decades between the end of the "mutinous" war of 1857-59 and the conclusion of First World War saw both the peak of British imperial power in India and the birth of nationalist agitation against it.

THE FREEDOM STRUGGLE

With increasing intrusion of aliens in their lives, nationalist feelings began to be articulated by an increasing number of Indians. The Indian National Congress (1885)—a society of English educated affluent professionals—to seek reforms from the British was founded. The British did not respond adequately to the legitimate demands of the Indians and this resulted in growing resentment against them.

By the last decade of the 19th Century a younger, more militant generation of Indians had begun to assert their birthright to independence. The Indian National Congress inevitably changed under the constant pressure exerted by men like Bal Gangadhar Tilak from Maharashtra. In Bengal too, there was a fiery group of revolutionaries who maintained that violence was the only language the foreigners understood.

The partition of Bengal announced by Lord Curzon in 1905, triggered a political earthquake—people rose in revolt en masse and forced the withdrawal of the ill advised plan. The mass movement brought out the widespread love for India and things Indian—Swadeshi—and reinforced communal harmony. Foreign produce was boycotted and a bonfire of imported clothes became the characteristic feature of protest.

The anticolonial struggle became truly a mass movement with the arrival of Gandhi in 1915. Mohandas Karamchand Gandhi (1869-1948) had suffered great humiliation in South Africa due to the policy of racial discrimination and was committed to rid his motherland of the ills of foreign rule. While practising as an attorney in South Africa, Gandhi had read widely and contemplated deeply. After having acquainted himself with the ground reality in India he devised a unique strategy for India's freedom struggle. Laying equal emphasis on the ends and means, he told his compatriots to accept non-violence as their creed and civil disobedience as their invincible weapon.

Gandhi was a uniquely gifted as well as a charismatic personality. It was not long, before he galvanised the masses in the fight against the British. Almost all the major leaders in the national movement accepted him as their mentor. He conceived and led the Non-cooperation Movement in 1922, the Salt

Satyagraha in 1930 that climaxed in the Dandi March and the Quit India Movement in 1942 with its stirring battle cry—Do or Die—shaking the roots of the British empire.

Even revolutionaries like Bhagat Singh and Chandrashekhar Azad, who disagreed with the philosophy of non-violence, respected him. Netaji Subhash Chandra Bose, who organised the Indian National Army (1943) in South East Asia during the Second World War to liberate India, also sought his blessings before starting his military campaign. Jawaharlal Nehru, Maulana Azad, Jaiprakash Narayan, Vallabhbhai Patel followed Gandhi's commands as disciplined soldiers of the Congress party.

After a long and arduous round of constitutional negotiations and in the face of the determined struggle of the Indian people, the British agreed to transfer power on 15th August, 1947.

But with freedom came the division of the country—a partition that brought in its wake unprecedented death and devastation. Undeterred, millions of Indians continued their endeavour to build the nation.

—RAJ KUMAR

CHAPTER - II

INDIA'S AGONY

Coming to a country desolated by famine, one might have imagined that the first care of Warren Hastings would have been to nourish back into life the apparently dying industry of Bengal. He held a position unprecedented in its power either for good or for evil. By an Act passed through Parliament in 1773 the British Government—under Lord North—had claimed supreme authorit in Hindustan. The East India Company was permitted to carry c its business as before, but the new dependencies were no long to be severally governed from Calcutta, Madras, and Bombay, each being ruled by its own Council, subject only to the Board of Directors in London; the Presidencies were to be controlled by Governor-General, resident in Calcutta, holding his post for fiv years, and assisted by a Council of four.

The first Council which thus ruled the British conquest in Hindustan consisted of General Clavering, Colonel Monson, Mr.Francis, and Mr. Barwell, and the first Governor-General was Warren Hastings, appointed President of Bengal by the Company in the preceding year. Unprecedented either for good or for evil was Warren Hastings' position. Unhappily, both for India and for England, he chose the evil, not the good. His ability none can challenge; his deceit, his treachery, his far-sighted craftiness none can deny. He was at once most able and most unscrupulous; no means were too cruel or too base for his using, provided only that they led to the predetermined goal.

Warren Hastings' first important act as Governor-General would be enough, if it stood alone, to stamp his name for ever with irredeemable infamy. At the very commencement of his authority he had treated in most friendly—and most dishonest—fashion with Surajah Dowlah, Soubahdar of Oudh. He had taken back from the Great Mogul the districts of Allahabad and Corah—ceded to him in exchange for a debt shortly before—and had sold the stolen property to the Prince of Oudh for some £500,000; Surajah Dowlah was enormously wealthy; Hastings wanted money for his employers. Surajah Dowlah was troubled with no scruples.

Hastings rivalled the Soubahdar in his freedom. Having bought from the Company two districts belonging to the Great Mogul, Surajah Dowlah next bid for another district on his frontier, over which the Company had as little right as over Corah and Allahabad. In the vales and mountains of Rohilkhand dwelt an industrious and valiant people; they were diligent, agricultural, cultured and harmful to none; they dwelt in peace within their own borders, so long as they were left unmolested; but were of Afghan blood, and if foe overtrod their boundary, 80,000 fair-haired Rohillas rose to beat back the aggressor.

Industrious in peace, they were also valiant in war, and so bold-hearted and loyal were they that when in 1772 the Mahrattas menaced Oudh, and offered large gifts to the Rohillas if they would give them safe passage through their mountain lands, they steadily refused to do so, exposing themselves to the wrath of the terrible Mahratta cavalry, because they had made a treaty with Oudh—pressed thereunto by the Company—and would not break their faith. The Mahrattas swept over Rohilkhand in 1773, destroying as they went; the brunt of their attack fell on the gallant Rohillas, and they were ultimately repulsed by the troops of Oudh, aided by the British arms.

So grateful was Surajah Dowlah for this brave service that he immediately took steps to incorporate the country of the free Rohillas into his own domains, and in 1778 we find him writing to Warren Hastings, asking his assistance to subdue his late defenders. Hastings, by his own confession, encouraged Surajah Dowlah in his basely treacherous design, but the Prince of Oudh feared to undertake the task alone.

These gallant mountaineers, with their free, bold hearts and dauntless independence, were no children to pass under the yoke. The luxurious people of Oudh could not hope to overbear them in battlefield; such an attempt would be foredoomed to failure. But there was one way open to success. There were some troops near Oudh fully equal to match with the warriors of Rohilkhand. If Warren Hastings could be bought over to the views of Surajah Dowlah, the coveted province might be wrested from its rightful possessors.

The bribe was offered, £4,00,000 to the East India Company, and £20,000 to the Governor-General himself, if Hastings would sign a treaty to which was annexed a secret clause, pledging the Company to hire out British troops to the Prince of Oudh to enable him to seize Rohilkhand. Hastings consented, and signed the treaty in September, 1773, the stipulation being added that all the expenses of the war should be defrayed by the Soubahdar.

In April, 1774, the execution of the treaty was claimed by Surajah Dowlah, and the troops of Oudh and of the Company entered Rohilkhand side by side. The Rohillas—their offers of peace being rejected—defended themselves with the courage of despair. "It is impossible," wrote Colonel Champion, commander of one of the brigades of the army of Bengal, "to describe a more obstinate firmness of resolution than they displayed."

They ranged themselves along the hill-sides of their home, and fought furiously for liberty; chief after chief fell, and still the ranks stood firm. The troops of Oudh fled, but against them steadily advanced the invincible European foe, and at last the Rohillas broke, leaving 2,000 men dead on the field of battle. To the mountain fastnesses fled Fyzoola Khan and his still resolute followers.

The valleys of Rohilkhand were ravaged with fire and sword. The troops of Oudh, which had fled from the Rohilla warriors, plucked up heart of grace to seize the Rohilla women. The fair cities were burnt, the fruitful fields were laid waste; a price was set on the head of every Rohilla, and 1,00,000 people fled to the jungles, while British soldiers stood by, holding down the country. Hastings had kept his word; the Rohillas "were exterminated".

The Council at Calcutta—not too squeamish about trifles—protested against the black iniquity perpetrated in the name of the Company. Hastings scoffed at their remonstrances; while he lined his own pockets, he also sent home huge sums of money to the East India Directors, and he felt his seat secure. But the Council persevered in their resistance. Francis, above all, challenged the acts of the Governor-General, until in March, 1775, the Council passed a resolution affirming that "There is no species of peculation from which the Governor-General has thought it reasonable to abstain".

At last the dispute grew too scandalous to be hushed up. There was a Hindu named Nundkumar, a Brahmin, who had held a high position in the Court of Moorshedabad. Here he had met Hastings and had quarrelled with him and the angry feelings between them had been yet further embittered by disputes over the fall of the native Government of Bengal. Nundkumar thought that in the quarrel between the Governor and his Council he saw the way to his revenge. He wrote a paper against Hastings, charging him with receiving bribes, and with selling posts in the public service. Francis read the paper in Council, and demanded on Nundkumar's behalf that he should be brought face to face with the Governor.

Hastings roughly refused to be thus practically put on his trial, and after much tumult he withdrew from the Council hall, followed by a single supporter. General Clavering was elected to the chair, and Nundkumar was called in and heard at length; his testimony concluded, the Council recorded in its minutes that Nundkumar's exposure had thrown a clear light upon the means whereby the Governor-General had made "the large fortune he was said to possess, upwards of 40 lacs of rupees (£4,00,000), which he must have amassed in the course of three years" (April 11, 1775).

Nundkumar was not left long in peace to enjoy his triumph. Just as Clive had not shrunk from forgery to gain his end, so now his worthy disciple did not shrink from murder. Nundkumar was seized and thrown into gaol on the charge of having, six years before, committed forgery. By the laws of England forgery was a capital offence, and those laws had been imposed upon India in 1773; but in 1769, the date of the alleged crime, Nundkumar was not under British rule at all. He was a man of high rank in the native court of Moorshedabad, owing no sort of allegiance to English law.

Forgery only became a capital crime in British Hindustan in 1773, four years after its alleged committal by Nundkumar, and criminal law has no retrospective power; so that—putting aside the injustice of imposing English laws on a country to which they were unsuited—Nundkumar's case was not within either the law of the country or the jurisdiction of the court before which he was dragged. As a Brahmin, his life was sacred to his fellow-countrymen, and nothing could have been more impolitic—even had the punishment been just—than to outrage all native feeling by this sudden attack on the chief of the Brahmins of Bengal.

When to all this we add that Nundkumar was tried, not by his fellow-countrymen, but by an English jury composed of the creatures of Hastings, and that it was never proved that he really committed the crime alleged against him, all honest men will re-echo Burke's passionate cry that Hastings "murdered Nundkumar by the hands of Sir Elijah Impey," the English judge. Nundkumar was publicly hanged on August 5, 1776, solely because of his knowledge of the Governor-General's crimes.

Having thus struck down the enemies immediately around him, and having kept his seat of Governor by quietly repudiating a resignation sent by him to England during the stress of his trouble in Calcutta, Hastings turned his mind to matters further afield; and hearing that a treaty had been concluded between France and the Mahrattas, he dealt his first blows against the new allies, and set his army in motion.

The tidings that war had broken out between England and France gave the Governor an excuse for strong action, and he promptly seized the French factories in Bengal, while his lieutenants strove to break the Mahratta power, and humble the pride of their chiefs, Scindia and Holkar.

In 1780 peace was concluded with the Mahrattas—all territories taken on either side being restored—for a power was threatening Madras which menaced English supremacy with destruction. Hyder Ali, ruler of Mysore, had left Seringapatam in June, 1780, followed by 85,000 men, had swept over the Carnatic, reached the sea-coast, and by the 24th of July was encamped within forty-two miles of Madras.

Hyder Ali's attack had been brought on themselves by the bad faith of the English. In 1769 a peace—ensuing on a war of invasion of Mysore by the English—had been signed under the very walls of Madras by the governor of that city and the triumphant Mysore chieftain. By the treaty the contracting powers bound themselves each to assist the other in all defensive warfare.

In 1770 Hyder Ali was attacked by the Mahrattas, and appealed to the British to fulfil their pledge of help. They declined to assist him, threw the weight of their influence on the side of his enemies, and earned the undying hatred of the betrayed prince

. When war broke out between the English and French, Hyder Ali showed some inclination to side with the French; and when in 1778 the English threatened Mahe, a French town within the territories of Mysore, he warned them that if they succeeded in their attack he would invade the Carnatic. Mahe fell, and the Mysorean ruler kept his word. The conflict lasted for four years, and was fought out bravely and persistently on both sides. Hyder Ali died on December 7th, 1782, and the war was carried on by his son, Tippoo Sahib, until on March 11th, 1784, peace was signed at Mangalore, on the *status quo ante bellum.*

While this struggle was going on in the Carnatic, Bengal and the neighbouring provinces were also writhing helplessly against the ever-weightening British yoke. Warren Hastings was in want of money. The war expense against French, Mahrattas, and Mysoreans pressed him hardly. The Court of Directors at home had to stop complaints with gold. His own pockets needed lining. Whence was money to come? The Mogul could bear no more squeezing. There was no new investment to be made such as the Rohilla loan.

He turned his eyes towards Benares. This city was the shrine of India. Pilgrims crowded its streets. Rich offerings were laid upon its altars. There rich sinners bought absolution, and pious rascals paid diamonds for crimes. There also was a centre of commercial wealth; the trade of Benares floated down the Ganges, and crossed the wide ocean to the capitals of the world. Benares stood forth as the wealthiest prize when Hastings was seeking gold and gems. And yet more, Benares might so easily be plundered. It was under the sway of the Company.

The Vizier of Oudh had by treaty ceded to the Company all his rights over the great religious and commercial centre, and Chait Singh, the Prince of Benares, paid direct tribute to the English traders. In 1778 Hastings called on this prince, in addition to be covenanted tribute to furnish three battalions of native troops for the use of the Company, at a charge of £50,000. The Rajah, being helpless, submitted. In 1779 the same extra charge was paid.

In 1780 the same charge was again demanded; the Rajah pleaded for remission, and offered to Hastings, as a bribe, £20,000. The Governor took the money, and pressed the demand paying over—some time after—the £20,000 into the Company's coffer, and wringing out of the despairing Rajah another £10,000 as fine. It was paid; but Hastings was not yet satisfied, or rather he desired to drive the Rajah into refusal, that he might have excuse for plundering him wholesale. He now demanded that the Rajah should further supply a body of cavalry for the Company's use, and on plea of delay Hastings marched to Benares with an escort of troops.

The unhappy prince offered as ransom for his town £200,000, and meeting Hastings at Buxar, made the most complete submission. Hastings offered to accept £5,00,000, and on the deprecating evasion of the Rajah, he seized him and committed him to prison. He had acted too audaciously, Chait Singh was beloved for his just and gentle rule, and the angry population rose in his defence.

The Company's troops were put to the sword; Chait Singh escaped from his cell by a rope twisted out of the turbans of his friends, and gained a place of refuge. The English troops gathered, and subdued the city. A lad of nineteen years of age was set up as pageant prince, and Benares was added to the territories of the Company.

Chait Singh's wealth, however, fell far short of the Governor's hopes, and his treasury was still empty. A great crime had been committed, and little gold had resulted as reward. Another effort must be made; since Benares, when squeezed, shed so little wealth, it would be well to try Oudh. Here the circumstances were peculiar, and vast sums were to be had in exchange for a shameful crime.

The Vizier of Oudh was the Prince Asaph-ul-Dowlah, and his mother and grandmother were women of enormous wealth. These two Begums of Oudh were under the special protection of the English, and were therefore easily to be reached. Hastings met Asaph-ul-Dowlah at Chunar, and arranged with him to plunder the Begums for their mutual benefit, the money to go to the Company, and to be taken as release for all claims against Oudh; the pretext was to be that these two old women had entered into a conspiracy with Chait Singh. But the conspiracy must be proved.

Impey, the judge by whom Hastings had murdered Nundkumar, was summoned from Calcutta; he held a place worth £8,000 a year, given him by Hastings, and revocable at Hastings' pleasure, so he hastened to the assistance of his patron. The affidavits in support of the charge of conspiracy were in a dialect unknown to Impey, but why should such a trifle be allowed to delay "justice"? A sentence of confiscation of all lands and treasures was passed on the Begums. How was it to be enforced? The princesses dwelt in their palace of Fyzabad—the Beautiful—and woman's home in the East was sacred from tread of man. Small difficulty was such punctilio of courtesy to Warren Hastings. His troops surrounded the palace, and burst open the door.

The two Begums were made prisoners in their own apartments; the two chief officers of the household, both aged men, were seized and fettered; and as no treasures were forthcoming, they were removed to the dungeons of Lucknow, where they were placed under British guard. What tortures they were subjected to, no one can tell; only this we know, that the British resident at Lucknow bade the guard, in writing, let the torturers pass into the presence of their prisoners, "to be permitted to do with them as they shall see proper".

Thick darkness remains over the "corporal punishment" thus inflicted on two helpless old men by British permission. While these horrors were being perpetrated at Lucknow, the Begums and their female servants were being almost starved to death at Fyzabad, until at last, bit by bit, £12,00,000 had been wrung out of their agony. Then all the miserable victims were set free, and the Company's treasury was full at last.

Meanwhile in England a storm was gathering against the crime-stained Governor-General. In 1782 a Select Committee of the House of Commons, moved for by Dundas, strongly censured the conduct of Hastings, and also that of Sir T. Rumbold, Governor of Madras; another Select Committee, moved for by Burke, censured Sullivan, the Chairman of the East India Company's Directors, and Sir Elijah Impey, the legal tool of Hastings. Impey was recalled by the Home Government, but the Directors refused to recall Hastings, and he held his seat until 1785, when he resigned of his own accord. The story of his trial need not be told here; Hastings passes out of the story of India, laden with the curses of the people he had oppressed and destroyed. Let him pass from ours with the final words of Burke's impeachment wringing in our ears :

> "I impeach him in the name of the Commons' House of Parliament, whose trust he has betrayed. I impeach him in the name of the English nation, whose ancient honour he has sullied. I impeach him in the name of the people of India, whose rights he has trodden under foot, and whose country he has turned into a desert. Lastly, in the name of human nature itself, in the name of both sexes, in the name of every age, in the name of every rank, I impeach the common enemy and oppressor of all."

CHAPTER - III

RAMMOHUN ROY

The traditional historians suffering from a 'proimperialist' bias eulogised Rammohun Roy as the 'father of Modern India' for generating progressive social and religious reforms and laying first the foundations of political movement.[1] In the wake of a radical leftist movement in the late 1960s and early 1970s and their condemnation of Rammohun Roy, historians have started questioning the Raja's role. Quite surprisingly, R.C. Majumdar, who was much imbued in Hindu obscurantist ideology, refused to accept Rammohun as the pioneer of such a movement.[2] This initiated further enquiries leading to the emergence of two conflicting interpretations. The liberals argued that in spite of Rammohun Roy's sincere desires for modernisation of and elevation of Hindu society from 'backwardness', he failed to understand the constraints inherent in such movements in a colonial political economy. And hence, we see in Rammohun Roy the contradictions between modern thoughts and 'backward linkages.'[3] Another view labelled him as an agent of colonial rule.[4] Out of these conflicting interpretations, however, new evidences have come to light. The need for another article arises from the failure of above historians to develop an integrated 'world view' of Rammohun Roy and appreciate it in the perspective of his own age and the bearing it still has on the present society. Cristopher Hill had pertinently pointed out : "History has to be re-written in every generation, because although the past does not change the present does ; each generation asks new questions of the past, and finds new areas of sympathy as it relives different aspects of the experiences of its predecessors."[5]

THE POLITICAL ECONOMY OF COLONIALISM

The objectives of the colonial government were to extract the maximum revenue from land and create a class of dependable propertied intermediaries who would serve the colonial power and their objectives as subordinate partners. Considerable time was wasted to discover the most effective means for the above ends. The *izaradari* system had unleashed a wave of violence in the countryside as the new revenue-farmers speculated on profit erroneously.[6] This happens when elements foreign to the requirement of the agrarian economy are given the powers to regulate the economic functions. Fortunately, it was discontinued. Eventually, the permanent settlement of 1793 was seen as the most efficient and effective means of securing both the objectives.[7]

It was hoped that granting of 'the magic touch of property' to the zamindars would rehabilitate agricultural production and secure the 'surplus' for the government. Henry Pattullo had rightly observed that, by the granting of proprietary right the zamindar 'fidelity and attachment would thereby likewise be forever secured against all enemies, in defence of property."[8] In practice, however, the high revenue demand ruined many big and small zamindars. The purchasers of their estates sold by auction were mostly urban and rural moneocrats, whose links with land were either remote or altogether absent.[9]

A new epoch thus began, the epoch of waning interests of zamindars in further productive investment in land. The only difficulty of collecting rents from the peasants was removed by Regulations VII-1799 and V-1812. The government's motives behind 'these regulations were: to give powers to the zamindars over their peasants in matters of rent-arrears, which in effect meant to ensure to governments' absorption of surplus from land; and secondly, such powers and aid to the zamindars would secure their attachment to the state, and would improve the attractiveness of land as a rent-earning asset. The one great advantage of the permanent settlement, Bentinck truly admitted, was its creation of a vast body of rich landed proprietors, "deeply interested in the continuance of the British dominion."[10]

The permanent settlement had failed to improve existing method and techniques of agricultural production.[11] The increasing burden of rent left with the peasantry increasingly less incentive to improve the condition of production with their capital. With rare exceptions the zamindars had become pure rentiers, an estimate of increase in rent between 1793 and 1880 revealed a range between 120 and 180 per cent for several districts of Bengal.[12] The permanent settlement, wrote the Governor-General,

Lord Moira, on 31st December 1819 : "has to our painful knowledge subjected almost the whole of the lower classes throughout these provinces to most grievous oppression—an oppression, too, so guaranteed by our pledge that we are unable to relieve the sufferers."[13] E. Colebrooke, in his evidence before the Select Committee of 1831-32, said : "the errors of the permanent settlement in Bengal were two-fold : first, in the sacrifice of what may be denominated the yeomanry, by merging all village rights, whether of property or occupancy, in the all devouring recognition of the zamindar's paramount property in the soil; and, secondly, in the sacrifice of the peasantry by one sweeping enactment, which left the zamindar to make his settlement with them on such terms as he might choose to require. Government, indeed, reserved to itself the power of legislating in favour of the tenants; but no such legislation has ever taken place; and, on the contrary, every subsequent enactment has been founded on the declared object of strengthening the zamindar's hand."[14] Marshman, one of the editors of the *Friend of India,* also asserted the same thing.[15]

The diminishing involvement in any productive investment coupled with the growing interests in land as only a rent-earning asset, accelerated the process of vertical sub infeudation of landed rights. Such a non-productive process came to be legally sanctioned by the Patni Regulation VIII of 1819.[16] Thus, surplus extracted from the peasantry was distributed over an immense variety of intermediary tenures, the zamindar, and the government. In some districts of Bengal as many as 50 or more intermediate interests were created.[17] Although the zamindars had their wastelands reclaimed almost gratis, whatever capital they expended in settling reclaimers were realised with interest through enhanced rents and various abwabs. Hence, a process of deterioration in the agrarian economy had set in.

Comparative changes also occurred in the industrial sector of Bengal economy. Since the beginning of the 19th century, Britain's relation with her colony reflected an adjustment of mercantile capitalism to the needs of the industrial capitalists at home. The consequences were the control of labour process and production of specific commodities of business interests like indigo and opium and the ruin of many traditional productions. Simultaneously was at work the old principle of mercantilism, plunder and drain of wealth from the colony.[18]

Cotton manufactures of Bengal were the first to receive Lancashire's thrust. Larkins observed: "the weavers finding no employment for their looms, many of them have been necessitated to quit their homes and seek employment elsewhere; most of them take to the plough, some remain in their own districts, while others migrate into distant parts of the country."[19] District towns of Burdwan and Midnapore, like Khirpai, Kharar and Kalna, which were mainly cotton-weaving centres were ruined.[20] Taylor reported the same ruin and impoverishment of Dacca muslim weavers, evident from the decline in *chowkedaree* tax from Rs. 31,500 to Rs. 10,000 between 1814 and 1838.[21] It was the combination of a policy of coercive control over the producers, prohibitory duties adversely related to indigenous commodities, and the obvious superiority of quality and price of Lancashire cotton pieces which combinedly account for such a devastating destruction.[22] Although the silk manufactures of Bengal escaped ruin during the period under scrutiny, Bentinck had correctly foreseen that it would not withhold destruction for too long.[23] During the same period, coercive control over production and marketing of commodities like opium and raw-silk, created much resentment among the producers. [24]

Similar was the plight of the salt manufacturers. The officers of the Salt Department admitted this manufacture to be a source of great misery to the molungis, in particular, as they were forced into Company's service. Being indebted to the Company inextricably and for life, they were virtual slaves.[25] Occasionally, the molungis refused to work for the Company and resisted their control.[26] Rammohun Roy realised the situation, and in his evidence before the Select Committee he pleaded for Company's complete monopoly and import of salt into Bengal.[27] The Government took appropriate steps : the prices of Bengal salt was artificially kept up to the advantage of British producers in a competitive market and ruin native production. As a consequence, approximately 6 lakhs of molungis lost their profession.[28] Lord Dalhousie admitted that this disaster was due to the above policy.[29]

This process of 'de-industrialisation' coupled with an emerging crisis in the agrarian economy, and the new investment policy, had considerable influences over the course of growth of the new Bengali middle-class. Measures had already been taken to increase the attractiveness of landed property as a rent-earning asset. Henceforth, there was no appearance of entrepreneurs willing to risk their capital in small industrial enterprises. The development of industrial capitalism in England sounded the death-knell of the Agency Houses functioning in the colonies as appendages to mercantile capitalism, and in which many early Bengali moneocrats had invested their capital. As for instance, the sudden demand for the House of Cockerell and Trail, the biggest creditor of Palmer and Co., to liquidate immediately half of the debt, in 1830, caused the fall of Palmer and Co.[30] The withdrawal of creditors within the Agency Houses in the new circumstances diverted native trading capital to land and to rural moneylending.[31]

To sum up, in a colonial economy the mechanism of control over the economy is principally political. Control over the production of requisite export-oriented commodities both in its raw and manufactured state, and distribution of home-manufactured commodities in the colonial market were manoeuvered by business houses and various native intermediaries. Through its control over the state machinery the Company effectively aided the entire process of economic control. The permanent settlement, on the other hand, infused new life into the decaying feudalism of Bengal. The granting of proprietary right to land, absolute powers to extract rents from the peasants, and the gradual process of transference of traditional rural responsibilities of the landed proprietors to the government, and the legal recognition of the *patni* system, created a class of unproductive proprietors. Land had become a rent-receiving asset along with the functions of absentee-landlordism, the salient feature of neo-feudalism—the pillar on which the roof of the colonial regime rested. A system which owed its birth to the colonial rule was loyal to the state policies. And that explains why the *bhadralok*-feudals of Bengal never gave due attention to the destructive economic policies of imperialism. Hence, to these neo-feudalists the attraction for an 'alien-consciousness' was a motivated response designed to strengthen the system.

POLITICS OF COLLABORATION AND STRUGGLE

In a caste-class hierarchical society under the aegis of colonial rule, political behaviour in 19th century Bengal was channelised along two diametrically opposite paths : policy of control and collaboration vis-a-vis politics of struggle. The significant characteristics of the period were, the emergence of parasitic neo-feudal class owing its existence and consequently loyal to the colonial government. Secondly, the neo-feudal class, because of its inherent parochial values derived from caste linkages, religious beliefs, territorial and economic factors, were divided among themselves. The internal struggle weakened the strength of the class as a whole and created difficulties for the colonial state to rule effectively, because the neo-feudal class was the only pillar on which the strength of the new regime rested. Lastly, the initial thrust of an alien power and the emergence of a sound imperialist policy had destroyed beyond repair the economic utility of various productive classes. The artisans and peasants were repeatedly in arms, and rural crimes were on the increase. In such circumstances, the attempt of the government was to evolve certain solutions with a view to welding the divided society into a working harmony.

The staunch orientalism of Warren Hastings and his associates to retain the existing social infra-structure and pursue with necessary tolerance the understanding of the Hindu value-system, was on the wane from the last decade of the 18th century. The industrial bourgeoisie of Britain had conquered the land as a market, and consequently diffused a new theory of administrative responsibility. A Calcutta Anglo-Indian wrote in 1829 that the sole British objective should be to improve the condition of the people,[32] which meant a greater intercourse with the Indians. The negation of the orientalist theory of limited assimilation by a calculated deeper assimilation was inevitable in the emerging conditions. H.T. Colebrooke and others had stimulated the notion that the departure of the Hindus from their traditional doctrine had caused their social degradation and that an elevation from this backwardness required English aid and retreat to the past. Educated Bengali *bhadraloks* fell victims to this elusive advertisement, and it was natural in the context of their own social position. The Mutiny at Vellore and an increasing popular unrest in Bengal had confirmed Bentinck that social and administrative reforms were necessary to weld the society and help state control. The Charter Acts of 1813 and 1833 enlightened Bentinck[33]:

> "Our character is no longer the inconsistent one of merchant and sovereign...our future care is that of vast territory cursed from one end to the other by vices, the ignorance, the oppression, the despotism, the barbarous and often cruel customs that have been the growth of ages under every description a Asiatic misrule—rule moral regeneration of this immense mass of our fellow

> creatures—the communication to them [of] the blessings of the European condition, in knowledge, in domestic comfort, in security of person and property, in independence, in morals."

The objective of English education was explicitly stated by Trevelyan. The educated classes would realise the need of acquiring and diffusing European knowledge for naturalising European institutions on Indian soil in the interest of their own stability, and for that purpose they would have to seek government protection. Naturally, this would serve the purpose of the Empire and the beneficiaries of English education.[34] The Christian missionaries were already in the field to implement such a programme.[35] Interference in Hindu society was intended to create tastes and develop values which would feed the manufacturing interests of Britain, and strengthen in Bengali mind the need for the Empire and its partisan liberalism, Secondly, the benefits of reform would be limited to the upper-crust of the Hindu Society.

In fact, the British had stigmatised the whole nation as unworthy of trust, incapable of honourable conduct and fit to be employed only in menial situation. The Cornwallis system was calculated to debase the upper gentry fallen under Company's dominion.[36] These debased neo-feudals uncritically emulated the imperialist doctrine of India's social backwardness and degradation in morals and values.[37]

However, the differences among the neo-feudal class led to the formation of *dals (groups)* and their respective *dalapatis* (group leaders). There were two factors which created the *dals* and accelerated mutual antagonism. First, though European thought had influenced the neo-feudal class, their non-productive activities developed in them a curious culture which was a peculiar blending of parochial feudal values with a veneer of European material and cultural traits.[38] Hence this class of collaborators were culturally, though not politically, alienated from their masters. Caste institutions and orthodoxy were retained. These *dals*, comprising mostly and dominated by the higher castes, were divided along caste lines.[39] Often the dominant castes in a *dal* recruited less inferior castes to strengthen the *dal;* on the other hand, the inferior castes used these *dals* as their vehicles of social elevation. The *Atmiya Sabha*, for instance, was controlled by the Brahmin caste, while the Kayasthas and Vaidyas were in control of the *Dharma Sabha*. Secondly, the government's new policy of interference in Hindu society bred mixed responses, which crystallised into and provided an orientation to the programme of the various *dals*. Radhakanta Deb and his followers were keen on separating their religion from secular activities; he, for instance agreed to work with the School Book Society, provided no religious matter was introduced into their publication.[40]

In point of comparison, the so-called 'conservatives' were no less liberal in matters concerning English education and uplift of the status of women. Bishop Heber observed on Radhakanta Deb that he speaks English well and has read many of our popular authors particularly historical and geographical.[41] He was the Director of the Hindu College and championed the cause of social amelioration of women. Contradistinctly, the so-called 'liberals' were not sincerely devoted to a 'modern ideology.' In spite of the *Atmiya Sabha's* repeated stress on Vedantic monotheism. Prosanna Kumar Tagore performed the family Durga Puja with all traditional celebrities. Similarly, Dwarakanath Tagore and Rammohun Roy donated gifts to the Brahmans, who had maintained the sacredness of their caste, and gave feast to the Chaubeys in Brindaban.[42] The essential difference, thus, lay in necessity and non-necessity of government interference in Hindu religion and custom. We would see later how much traditional was Rammohun Roy who sincerely believed that the organisation of society depended on religion and a solution of which would elevate the society and create a working harmony for the stability of the Empire.[43]

Opposed to both these dominant *dals* were the Derozians. Over a short span of time, Derozio and his pupils came above their caste hankerings and could look down upon Hindu society and represents a 'modern' view.[44] Rammohun Roy and his *dal* were criticized by them for an utterly *confused* stand and *sheer opportunism.*[45] Hindu religion was denounced as vile and corrupt and unworthy of the regards of rational beings.[46] They pleaded for a programme of secular liberal education to uplift the Indians. However, Derozio failed to understand the society and diffuse his *radical* doctrine among the masses and mobilise them for a more wider movement.[47]

The political movements of the lower castes and classes in rural and urban centres were seriously disturbing the peace of the *bhadraloks* or the new feudal class. The strike of the Oriya palki bearers in 1872 for cancellation of their badges and higher wages was viewed by them as drainage of money from Bengal.[48] Similarly, the strike of the washermen for higher wages was a threat to their social comfort.[49] In fact, the *bhadraloks* seriously detested education to the masses for it would enlighten the lower classes and make them more conscious of their rights. Vidyasagar wrote to the government of Bengal :[50]

> "As the best, if not the only practicable means of promoting education in Bengal, the government should, in my humble opinion, confine itself to the education of the higher classes on a comprehensive scale."

The training of the *bhadraloks* in English education and political philosophy under the patronage of the Raj contributed their *indifference* towards the actual conditions of life of the labouring people and their *struggle* for existence. The mutiny of the native infantry at Barrackpore[51]; protest of the artisans against Company's control and injudicious prices[52]; increasing peasant rebellions and rural crimes[53]; formation of new religious sects among the lower classes and their denunciation of 'caste toboos' and struggle for higher social status[54]; and growing crimes in Calcutta[55]—were disturbances in the otherwise peaceful life of the *bhadraloks.*

The political and religious movements were working under certain constraints. In spite of certain common elements in the movements, the zeal to combine was absent. The requisite leadership and ideology were lacking, without which no movement achieve success. Nevertheless, the class-struggle of the exploited masses in whatever form was seriously disturbing the peace of the imperialists and their subordinate collaborators. Government policies emanated from this environment, of which Rammohun Roy was a product and a participant.

Rammohun Roy's stress on 'religion' was not surprising. He understood that, religion and caste were still an important emotional force in either uniting or disuniting the social forces. Religion was his prescription for *strengthening the empire.*[56] The appeal to elevate *self-consciousness* turned out to be an utopia. Only changes in the material world,[57] which generated the parochial values of the society, could transform the existing values.[58]

SOCIAL BACKGROUND OF RAMMOHUN ROY

Rammohun Roy was born into a Radi Kulina Brahmin family of respectability and great religious heritage from both paternal and maternal sides, which combined business with piety.[59]

Brajabinode, grandfather of Rammohun Roy and an influential zamindar, held an important portfolio during the administration of Alivardi Khan and received rewards for his services.[60] The family fortunes, however, sunk after the decline of Nawabi aristocracy, only to emerge again under the Company's farming system. This re-emergence was based on land exploitation in collaboration with the Company and on the destruction of the local political power of the Sadgops and Bagdis—thus, the reformer's *respectability* owed to his family's participation with the Company in the destruction of the old Mughal rural gentry.[61]

In May 1791, Ramkanta Roy, father of Rammohun Roy, took *izara* of the pargana of Bhursoot for 9 years whose annual *sadar jama* was assessed at Rs. 1,01,389.[62] In 1794, an important *taluq* called Harirampur in Chitwa pargana was bought at a revenue sale in the name of Jagamohun Roy, brother of Rammohun Roy.[63] At an early age Rammohun learned the art of estate management in his father's *taluqs*[64] along with the learning of Arabic and Persian languages, which were the requisite qualification for getting state services during the early phase of Company's rule. During this period, Rammohun Roy's attitude towards the Company was an 'aversion'.[65] This feeling changed when business transactions and official engagements brought him closer to the European gentlemen.

Independent of his proprietory interests, Rammohun Roy was engaged in money lending business. In 1797, he left Langulpara for Calcutta to extend his business activities there. Golaknarayan Sarkar carried his work in the city as an appointed clerk. He lent Rs. 7,500 to Andrew Ramsay of the Company's Civil Service.[66] His motive behind moneylending to civil servants, in particular, was that,

> "Natives not having any hope of attaining direct consideration from the Government by their merits or exertions, are sometimes *induced to accommodate* the civil servants with money, by the hope of *securing their patronage* for their friends and relatives, the judges and others having many situations directly or indirectly in their gift; sometimes by the hope of benefitting by their friendly disposition, when the natives have estates under their jurisdiction, and sometimes to avoid incurring the hostility of the judge..."[67]

This statement clearly reveals the real motive of great reformer.

By the *haptam* regulation of 1799, land was steadily becoming an asset.[68] In 1799, Rammohun Roy bought two *taluqs*—Gobindapur in Jahanabad pargana, and Rameshwarpur in Chandrakona pargana—both in Burdwan district, for a total sum of Rs. 4,350. The income from these estates was Rs. 5,500 annually.[69] This thrust for land was continued. Between 1803-04 and 1809-10, four more *patni taluqs*—Langulpara, Birluk, Krishnanagar and Srirampur—were purchased, which combinedly yielded him an annual income of Rs. 5,000 or Rs. 6000.[70] Money was also invested in the Agency House of Mackintosh and Co., and in the purchase of Company's paper.

Two conclusions can be drawn from this part of our argument. First, his caste respectability and strong thrust for property infused into his thoughts a strong property consciousness. This feature caused his indifference when the old gentry collapsed under the racking revenue assessments of the Company government.[71] Secondly, the permanent settlement and the regulations which followed secured his proprietory right and his other businesses. This made him indebted to the British Rule.

The permanent settlement had created tensions in the countryside. Rammohun Roy had witnessed peasant movements against the Company and the zamindars, which seriously disturbed the infant empire of the Company and the neo-feudal class. The members of Rammohun Roy's *Atmiya Sabha*—Dwarakanath Tagore, Prasanna K. Tagore, Kaleenath Roy, Baikunta Nath Munshi, Raja Kali Shankar Ghosal, Kasi Nath Mullick, Hurrchunder Ghose—were all large proprietors. Rammohun Roy's reform movement emanated from the crisis of a class, which was also self-divided due to a sectarian ideology, on which the foundation of an infant empire and the security of a class largely depended. Colonel Young, a disciple of Bentham, observed:

> "For he (Rammohun) is greatly attached to us and our regime... because he considers the contact of our superior race with his degraded and inferior countrymen as the only means and chance they have of improving themselves in knowledge and energy."[72]

From his social position Rammohun Roy realised that reforms were a *necessity* to preserve the alien empire and the security of his class.

PEASANT RESISTANCE AND RAMMOHUN'S REACTIONS

Rammohun Roy thanked God for "having unexpectedly delivered this country from the long continued tyranny of its former rulers and placed it under the Government of the English, a nation who not only are blessed with the enjoyment of civil and political liberty, but also interest themselves in promoting liberty and social happiness, as well as free enquiry into liberty and religious subjects, among those nations to which that influence extends."[73] A gross distortion of reality. Lenin wrote that, "practice is higher than (theoretical) knowledge, for it has not only the dignity of universality, but also of immediate actuality."[74] The more colonialism entrenched in Bengal the greater was the intensity and extensity of peasant violence against the zamindars, moneylenders and their colonial masters.[75]

In 1831, peasants of Barasat and adjoining areas, only 30 miles away from Rammohun's Calcutta residence, led an armed upsurge against the zamindars and the Raj. The peasants knew why and for what they were fighting. To Rammohun Roy, the peasants were utterly ignorant of and indifferent to the past and present system of administration. Only those who had become rich through the business, and others who were enjoying their privileges through the 'permanent settlement' had realised the importance of British domination.[76] Another incident would highlight his involvement. One Ramjoy Batabyal, a resident of the village of Ramnagar near Krishnanagar, was violently deprived of his landed property by Rammohun Roy. He threatened the later's house with 4 to 5 thousand of his followers, threw stones, and filed a suit against him for looting his field and garden. The Hooghly Court found Rammohun Roy guilty and fined him Rs. 2,092.[77] Rammohun Roy perpetrated his various acts of oppression in his own estates through Jagannath Majumdar, his faithful naib. In the section following our purpose is to analyse the reformer's attitude towards indigo cultivation.

Indigo cultivation was not new to Bengal agriculturists, but its extension owed to the demand of the Company. To the Company's servants indigo was the most advantageous mode of remitting their fortunes to Europe, and the textile manufactures' demand for the commodity for 'dyeing' purpose gave them the opportunity.[78] Possessing capital and requisite skill, the indigo planters forced the peasants to cultivate indigo : "the contract for the growth and production of the plant, so far from being voluntary, is forced upon the ryot, who is compelled by more or less of pressure to accept advances; that these advances are rarely given, or are not given in full after the first year or two; that the ryot is compelled to plough, sow, and weed his land, and to cut and cart the plant, at times when he would prefer being engaged in the cultivation of other crops of superior profit....."[79] Turnbull, the Magistrate of Nadia, reported that the contract with the ryot is "frequently insufficiently defined and is generally extremely unfavourable to the ryot."[80] The cultivation of indigo was detrimental to the economic interests of the peasants, because they received *unfair* prices compared to other commodities.[81] The Court of Directors also confirmed this fact : "the ryots are to a great extent oppressed and defrauded, if not by indigo planters themselves, by agents employed by them, acting in their names and for their advantage...... the chief actors in which are hired men, engaged by the planters for the express purpose of enforcing their clams in defiance of the law. These facts are affirmed even by those who have borne strong testimony to the personal good character of the planter."[82] The ryots often complained that they were unable to free themselves from the planters even after clearing all debts and advances.[83] Lord Macaulay admitted that "many ryots have been brought, partly by the operation of the law and partly by acts committed in defiance of the law into a state not very far removed from that of predial slavery."[84] The peasants refused to cultivate indigo :

> "I will die sooner than cultivate indigo—I would rather go to a country where the indigo plant is never seen or sown—Rather than sow indigo I will go to another country, I would rather beg than sow indigo."[85]

Also, the manner in which the indigo-planters settled themselves in the countryside antagonised the zamindars. Tenants were often driven away from the control of the local zamindars for the cultivation of indigo.[86] With government assistance the planters could easily apply force to secure their objectives.[87]

That the extension of indigo culture was pernicious to the peasants in particular was contradicted by Rammohun Roy :

> "As to the indigo planters, I beg to observe that I have travelled through several districts in Bengal and Bihar, and I found the natives residing in the neighbourhood of indigo plantations evidently better-clothed and better

> conditioned than those who live at a distance from such stations. There may be some partial injury done by the indigo-planters; but on the whole, they have performed more good to the generality of the natives of his country than any other class of Europeans whether in or out of the service."[88]

In a letter to Nathaniel Alexander, Rammohun Roy further observed that "the advances made to the ryots by the indigo-planters have increased in most factories in consequence of the price of indigo having risen, and in many, better prices than formerly are allowed to for the plant."[89] The 'advances' to individual peasants may have increased marginally but their conditions did not improve. The growth-cycle of indigo prevented double-cropping with rice.[90] The shift from production for subsistence to production for market forced the peasants to helpless situations : dependence on market for purchasing subsistence commodities at a higher price, and compulsion to sell his own commodity at a dictated price.[91] Rammohun Roy overlooked the actual effects of indigo-culture on the peasantry and failed to correct his assessments, from a study of the indigo-peasants' movements.

Why did he foster such a false notion ? As an 'interpreter' between the ruler and the ruled he should have pointed out the sources of contradiction to the government for a 'check'. His reasons were well calculated. The indigo planters were men of 'capital' and 'energy' and the Bengali comprador entrepreneurs sincerely hoped that colonisation of indigo planters would lead to an import of capital, which might ease the financial crisis of the Agency Houses and the various collaboration companies in Bengal. To Rammohun Roy, *money consciousness* was important and sometime became more important than the objective of reform.

RAMMOHUN ROY ON COLONIALISM

A dinner was given in honour of Rammohun Roy on 6th July 1831 at the city of London Tavern by some officials of the East India Company. Speaking before the select audience Rammohun Roy said :

> "Before the period at which India had become tributary to Great Britain it was the scene of the most frequent and bloody conflicts. In the various provinces of the Eastern dominions, nothing was to be seen but plunder

> and devastation, there was no security for property or for life, until by the interference of this country the great sources of discord were checked, education has advanced, and the example of the British system of dominion had a conciliating effect upon the natives of the east."[92]

In other words, nothing pertaining to the rule of law ever prevailed in Pre-British India; crime as rampant and anarchy was the rule.[93] No researches till date support this view for the eastern provinces upto 1740 after which the Company itself became a participant in the internal struggles. The man who stood 'at the fountain-head of modern thought and life in India"[94] purposely upheld a false notion. The reasons have been explained, and Rammohun Roy himself had clarified the point :

> "I first saw and began to associate with Europeans, and soon after made myself tolerably acquainted with their laws and form of government. Finding them generally more intelligent, more steady and moderate in their conduct, I gave up my prejudice against them, and became inclined in their favour, feeling persuaded that their rule, though a foreign yoke, would lead more speedily and surely to the amelioration of the native inhabitants......[95]

The Bengal Herald owned by his friends explains this above argument. An English educated landed gentry is "placed between the aristocracy and the poor, and are daily forming a most influential class. Previous to their formation, the wealth of the country was in the hands of a few individuals, while all others were dependent on them, and the bulk of the people were in a state of abject poverty of mind and body which will perhaps form a juster reason for the pervading moral bondage of the Hindoos."[96] Again, "whenever such an order of men have been created, freedom has followed in its train."[97] A correct lesson from history. But, these were not the men in whose train freedom could follow. The Company governments' economic and social policies had created enough room for their alienation from actual productive work : these were parasites and an unproductive social force in the nineteenth century society of Bengal. In Europe, things were different and conditions matured differently.[98]

However, the argument of Rammohun and the 'Bengal Herald' exhibits the impact of European liberalism.[99] Their sincere objective was to create an *environment* where *social harmony* would be the supreme law, and only a thorough process of judicial arbitration could create the atmosphere of social harmony. His evidences before the Select Committee of the House of Commons in 1831 bear ample testimony to his argument.

Replying to a question of what *methods* the landed proprietors do adopt for realising their rent arrears, Rammohun Roy said that by applications to the police the moveable property of the peasants was alienated and by the ordinary judicial process the immovable property of the peasant was alienated.[100] The 'Bengal Hurkaru' seriously criticised this observation :

> "How could Rammohun Roy... forget the seventh Regulation of 1799 ?.... How could Rammohun Roy forget to state that it is through, and by, a frightful power (arrest...) and no other, that rents are raised; that Moroosi (hereditary) pottahs are forcibly taken from Kodkhast ryots, and Meadee Pottahs (pottahs for a term of years) substituted for them; so as eventually to make the whole of their tenants almost tenants at will, and enable the Zamindars, through the authority of the gulled Cornwallis Government, who supposed they would 'endeavour to promote the welfare and prosperity of their tenantry, to rack them to their last rupee."[101]

Rammohun Roy's reply was from reality; but his emphasis rested on the importance of the judiciary. He repeatedly pleaded for an effective reorganisation of the rural courts so as to guard against frequent unrests among the peasantry, the khudhasts in particular.[102] He had realised that the peasants were impoverished by the high rents, but pleaded that the burden of land revenue on the zamindars was excessively high and a reduction of revenue would automatically reduce the total rent imposed on him.[103] This was again factually incorrect, but his *money consciousness* prevented him from revealing the truth.[104]

Moreover, he argued that landlords in the permanently settled areas were firmly attached to the government. This could not be said of landlords in Madras or the Conquered Upper Provinces.[105] If the permanent settlement had been extended to all regions and all classes, similar relations would have emerged.[106] Internal and external security would have been assured 'without the necessity of keeping on foot an immense standing army at an enormous cost.'[107] The example of Ireland was given in the *Mirat-ul-Akhbar*, were the evils of absenteeism and the injustice of maintaining Protestants clergymen out of revenues wrung from the Roman Catholic inhabitants had caused much discontent.[108] To the *reformer*, the key to the consolidation of the British Rule was the uplift of the Hindus from moral degradation and a patient hearing to their grievances.

Rammohun Roy believed that, scientific and liberal English education of the Western type would uplift the people from moral degradation. The Fort William College established in 1800 by Lord Wellesley with the purpose "to fix sound and correct principles of religion and government in their minds at an early period of life was best security which could be proviced for the stability of British power in India."[109] The *reformer* apprehended the colonial objective and advised accordingly. When the Sanskrit College was about to be established, Rammohun wrote (the most unquoted portion of his letter to Lord Amherst) :

> "We now find that the government are establishing a Sanskrit School under Hindu pundits to impart such knowledge as is already current in India. This seminary can only be expected to load the minds of youth with grammatical niceties and metaphysical distinctions of little or no practicable use to the possessors or to the society."[110]

A deeper intimacy with the traditional Sanskrit learning would divert the entire efforts of the colonial government to the wrong track of traditionalism and division among the subjects. Improvement of the subjects from speculative philosophies, like Vedanta, Mimangsa and Nyay Shastras, was impossible.[111] These arguments seem to locate the *reformer's* sympathy for scientific and liberal education.

In reality, Rammohun Roy practised Lord Wellesley's directive. He was disgusted and grew suspicious of the radicalism and secular knowledge taught to the students of Hindu College. The Derozians had condemned the principles and practices of Hindu religion as vile and corrupt and unworthy of the regard of the rational beings.[112] In 1822, Rammohun Roy opened an Anglo-Indian School for imparting education in *English*. Religious and moral instructions formed part of the curriculum. William Adam commented in 1827 that "the doctrines of Christianity are not inculcated, but the duties of morality are carefully enjoined, and the facts belonging to the history of Christianity are taught to these pupils who are capable of understanding general history."[113] In 1827, the Vedanta College was established. The object was to explain the teachings of Vedanta through which his countrymen could be led out of their prevailing superstitions and idolatry into pure and elevated theism.[114] When Alexander Duff approached him for establishing missionary schools he expressed his approval and worked hard to make it a success.[115] To the *reformer*, education was to be based on religion and morality the objective being not simply providing students with information but rendering education itself practically useful to individuals and society as a whole. Speculative Vedantic philosophy, in itself, had little meaning for him. English education along these lines would bridge the communication gap between the rulers and the ruled.

In fact, he prepared the path for Macaulay's famous minute on education: "We must at present do our best to form a class who may be interpreters between us and the millions whom we govern—a class of persons Indian in blood and colour, but English in tastes, in opinions, in morals and in intellect."[116] The "Sumbad Bhuskar's" article explained the extent of the achievement in this direction:

> "The wealthy and influential classes of the people of this country ought at once to feel the truth of the remark that the king protects the people, whenever any danger threatens them, and that without the protecting care and vigilance of the former, the latter can save neither their lives, nor wealth, nor caste, nor honour. The truth of this observation has long ago been proclaimed in our moral Shastras..."[117]

From the argument it emerges that attachment to the shastras and caste, were retained though attachment to the rulers and a taste for foreign commodities also developed: a peculiar blending of feudal and bourgeois values. However, the influences of educational institutions were so narrowly confined in its spread effect that the 'benefits' which Rammohun Roy aspired for could not be attained. In the *mofussil* there reigned deep and dense ignorance.[118]

The *reformer* knew this and desired that educated persons of *character* and *capital* should be permitted to settle in India without any restriction.[119] This might mitigate the shortcomings of the former process. The colonisation of India by Europeans from respectable and intelligent class,[120] would improve the Indians from the age old bondage of ignorance, would raise them in wealth and thereby a mixed community in the pattern of Canada would be formed, who would "feel no disposition to cut off its connection with England."[121] Sir John Malcolm pointed out that "colonisation is one of the most likely means for the civilization of India," because the commerce of the country would be lucrative and the value of land would increase.[122] Rammohun Roy's argument was similar: a villager would approve colonisation because it would raise their wages.[123]

The desire of a section of the educated Indians for an European settlement became apparent when British enterprise and exports had begun to lead the world. She was looking forward for an extensive colonial market for her own industrial commodities and also sources of supply of raw materials. Lord Bentinck argued that colonisation would result in an extensive and intensive exploitation of Bengal's natural resources, while at the same time it would promote a *welfare consciousness* among the subjects.[124] Though Rammohun Roy, Dwarakanath Tagore, and their friends echoed this free-traders' argument, they had, however, a different motive. The Agency Houses, where the financial interests of these men were locked were then in a financial crisis; the settlement of Europeans with 'capital' may save the Agency Houses.[125] Rammohun Roy's participation in the Rickards sponsored first political association in India, the Commercial and Patriotic Association of 1820s, was marked by the same point of view.[126] However, the efforts failed because the demands were anachronistic compared to the changes in the production organisation in Britain: the Agency Houses fundamentally represented the interests of mercantile capitalism, though they carried over their functions in the early phases of dominance by industrial capitalism. Soon, the Managing Agency System operated to carry forward effectively the interests of industrial capitalism. Secondly, The limited colonisation by Europeans also failed to secure the objective which the Bengali 'Babus' expected it would achieve: elevation of the people from moral degradation.

Security of the alien rule and the propertied classes haunted Rammohun Roy. A free Press, he hoped, would reveal the grievances and aspirations of the people. Knowledge of their grievances would caution the government. In his *Appeal To the King In Council,* he wrote :

> "Free Press has never caused a revolution in any part of the world, because, while men can easily represent the grievances arising from the conduct of the local

> authorities to the supreme Government and thus get them redressed, the grounds of discontent that excite revolution are removed; whereas, where no freedom of the Press existed, and grievances consequently remained unrepresented and unredressed, innumerable revolutions have taken place in all parts of the globe..."[127]

In another memorial demanding the removal of obstacles to the freedom of Press, it was stated:

> "During the last wars which the British government were obliged to undertake against neighbouring Powers, it is well known, that the great body of Natives of wealth and respectability, as well as the landholders of consequence, offered up regular prayers to the objects of their worship for the success of the British arms from a deep conviction that under the sway of that nation, their improvement, both mental and social, would be promoted, and their lives, religion, and property be secured. Actuated by such feelings, even in those critical times, which are the best test of the loyalty of the subject, they voluntarily came forward with a large portion of their property to enable the British government to carry into effect the measures necessary for its own defence, considering the cause of the British as their own, and firmly believing that on its success, their own happiness and prosperity depended."[128]

Bentinck correctly realised, that these educated and wealthy men of Calcutta as a body 'seem incapable of political mischief, and the public press may be said to be as innocuous as out of it.'[129] When the freedom of Press was eventually secured in 1835, Mr. Leith, in a dinner in the Town Hall on 9th February, 1838, in honour of Sir Charles Metcalfe, proposed a toast to 'the memory of Rammohun Roy';[130] it was an honour which the colonial government bestowed upon him for his faithful services.

It has been argued that love of freedom was Rammohun Roy's strongest passion. He greeted the establishment of constitutional government in Spain, welcomed the progress of South America's struggle against Spanish Empire and rejoiced at the news of the French Revolution of 1830.[131] These incidents, however, do no make us proclaim him as a champion of freedom. First, he discriminated the British from the Spanish colonies or the British from the Spanish empire. A British colony was better off than a

Spanish colony. Moreover, in his article on Ireland, he could not wholeheartedly support the Irish rebels and advised the British government on the ways and means of establishing an empire and securing it. Secondly, his sense of freedom did not work in India. He said to V. Jacquemont that 'India requires many more years of English domination so that she might not have many things to lose while she is reclaiming her political independence.'[132] It is a humiliations on the part of Indians to eulogise a person who thought in terms of positive gain from her attachment with the British Empire. Rammohun Roy thought in terms of the class which had gained from the Empire and not in terms of the milling millions of India.

RELIGIOUS REFORMS OF RAMMOHUN ROY

Rammohun Roy's first religious tract, *Tuhfut-ul-Muwahiddin*, written in 1803-04, was a product of his early wanderings and influences of Islamic thought. In its introduction, he asserted the existence of a Supreme Being who was the source of creation and the governor of the universe. On this monotheistic premise, he launched a fierce attack on all irrationalities as expounded by the *Mujtahids* (religious expounders). They 'sow the seeds of prejudice and disunion in the hearts of each other to the deprivation of eternal blessing', and 'add hundreds of useless hardships and privations regarding eating and drinking, purity and impurity, auspiciousness and inauspiciousness, etc.', which are 'causes of injury and detrimental to social life and sources of trouble and bewilderment to the people.' These were shown to have sprung out of the self interest of the priest feeding on mass ignorance and slavishness to habit.[133] He emphasized that, 'to believe in the real existence of anything after obtaining proofs of such existence is possible to every individual man; but to put faith in the existence of such things as are remote from experience and repugnant to reason, is not in the power of a sensible means;[134] in other words, why should one believe in things which are inconsistent with the laws of perception ?[135]

Thus, the crux of *Tuhufts'* logic were : the existence of one and only Supreme Being; the negative and deceptive role of all religious intermediaries between god and man; and the irrationality of knowledge which is devoid of reason and inconsistent with the laws of perception. But, with advancement in age and social awareness, he retreated from his earlier rationalism both in theory and practice. Why this transformation ?

The kernel of Rammohun Roy's subsequent religious arguments was anchored on the traditional Vedanta philosophy as interpreted by Sankaracharya. The ancient philosopher viewed the world as divided into metaphysical categories, the highest from being speculation about and unity with eternal principles. Material reality did not exist. A great historian has correctly pointed out : 'The absence of logic, contempt for mundane reality, the inability to work at manual and menial tasks, emphasis upon learning basic formulas by rote with the secret meaning to be expounded by a high guru, and respect for tradition (no matter how silly) backed by fictitious ancient authority has a devastating effect upon Indian science.'[136] Just as Sankaracharya's elusive philosophy emerged out of the social crisis of organised opposition to Brahmanism by heterodox sects, popular cults and the Buddhist philosophy[137]; Rammohun Roy's change of faith and reliance on an abstruse philosophy owed to European influences and the social crisis of his own time.

Digby, under whom he had worked for long and assisted him in his official work, was instrumental in initiating him in the Vedanta doctrine and reformation. As a student of the Fort William College and conversant with Colebrooke's researches and the Vedanta doctrine, Digby was drawn to Indian reformation. Fellow students has left evidences of this fact. His central idea was to push Rammohun Roy into the current of reforms and conflicting agitations in Calcutta so that, the latter could take charge of a ship before it drifted towards "anti-foreignism". Rammohun Roy realised "the insufficiency of human *reason* for the production of the highest moral worth and the highest happiness."[138] Credit goes to Digby for chosing the right talent for such a magnificent task.[139] The *reformer* now evolved his "religious utilitarianism".

Sandford Arnot had observed Rammohun Roy 'became more strongly impressed with the importance of religion to the welfare of society, and the pernicious effect of skepticism... He often deplored the existence of a party which had sprung up in Calcutta... partly composed of East Indians, partly of the Hindu youth, who from education had learnt to reject their own faith without substituting any other. These he thought more debased than the most bigotted Hindu...."[140] The *reformer* strongly argued that changes should take place in their religion 'at least for the sake of their political advantage and social comfort.'[141] And further, the dogmatic belief in idolatry was injuring seriously the harmony of the society through 'dreadful acts of self-destruction and the immolation of the nearest relations.'[142] He admired Christian religion for "being conductive to moral principles and better adapted for the use of rational being".[143] K.C. Mitra had truly observed that 'Rammohun was a religious Benthamite and estimated different creeds existing in the world, not according to his notion of their truth or falsehood, but his notion of their utility...'[144] His entire religious philosophy was a shrewd manifestation of his desire to create an environment which would ensure security of the feudal class against the threat of peasant movements, to create an atmosphere of cohesiveness and awareness within the class about its own position, and secure the interests of the British bourgeoisie.

He considered 'idol-worship' to be inventions[145] of the poor mind and retreats from the theology of Vedanta.[146] He realised that the parochialism of the urbanized feudals could be eradicated by a thorough criticism of polytheism; but he failed to realise that in the existing social structure elevation of consciousness was impossible. Only a thorough dissolution of the pre-capitalist social structure could create the conditions for the growth of monotheism.

However, strict to his utilitarian principle, he recommended idol-worship for persons who are incapable of elevating their minds, or do not possess sufficient understanding: 'persons of feeble intellect', 'weak and ignorant persons', and 'those who are incapable of adoring the invisible supreme being.'[147] In other words, his acknowledgement of the necessity of idol-worship for the lower-class laymen was inevitable : *Bhakti* or adoration would secure and strengthen the personal ties on which feudal relations of production economically and ideologically survived.

Rammohun Roy's religious utilitarianism is more evident from his refusal to accept *mayabad* as final at least to the extent of social practice and moral code. He observed : ' Nor will youths be fitted to be better members of the society by the Vedanta doctrines which teach them believe, that all visible things have no real existence, that as father, brother etc. have no actual entity, they consequently deserve no affection and therefore the sooner we escape from them and leave the world, the better.'[148] The feudal moral of loyalty to all relations and servile obedience to persons of higher social status or immediate superiors moulded him to negate an anarchical behaviour latent in the Vedanta doctrine. His love for Christian morality[149] owed to this backward linkage. In comparison to Bentham, whose utilitarianism was a bourgeoisie solution to harmonise the antagonistic relations of labour and capital, Rammohun Roy's utilitarianism was derived from his feudal and higher caste linkage, and a sincere effort to negate the tensions within a colonial regime to the ultimate interests of the British Empire. The Bengali *reformer* understood the logic of Bentham when he applied his *model* in a colonial environment. The principles of *utility* and *ideological illusions* were astutely balanced.

When Rammohun Roy committed himself to the existence of an *incomprehensible* Supreme Being, his retreat from *Tuhfut* was complete. The kernel of all his songs composed for the Brahma Sabha negated the importance of *reason* as a logical category.[150] He quoted Vyasa to prove the existence of the Supreme Being 'by his effects and works, without attempting to define his essence.'[151] He stretched his irrationalism to the extent of saying: 'the Supreme Ruler bestows the consequences of... sins and holiness... by giving them other bodies either animate or inanimate,'[152] which amounted to the acceptance of the sacredness of caste and the Brahmanical nuisance of the theory of *karma* as the penultimate cause in determining caste stratification.

The ideological illusion which he created was given a concrete shape through the Brahma Samaj,[153] founded in 1830. The disciplines and practices of the Samaj revealed yet another retreat from *Tuhfut*. In 1803-04, he had criticised the role of all intermediaries between man and god as 'deceptors'. Also, in the *Abridgement of Vedanta,* this thesis was retained : the Brahmans are people 'whose prejudices are strong, and whose temporal advantage depends upon the present system.'[154] But, in the Brahma Samaj, two Telugu-Brahmins, considered to be most orthodox in their adherence to customs, were bestowed with the patent right to recite the Vedas in a side-room screened from the view of the congregation, where non-Brahmins would not be admitted.[155] On the opening day of the Samaj, the Brahmins who were present received gifts in money to a considerable extent after the prayers and singing of hymns were completed.[156] The utility and sacredness of the intermediaries were tacitly admitted.

The object of the Brahma Samaj was to elevate the people from the thraldom of superstition and idolatry, but it failed miserably. First, the activities of the Brahma Samaj were narrowly limited to the city of Calcutta. No attempt was made to set up branches in the rural areas. Secondly, even in the city, it was evident that Muslims and Christians would not come to offer their prayers. Thirdly, the orthodox upper caste Hindus, who were bound to polytheism, were not invited. The Sabha had restricted the audience of Vedic recital only to the Brahmans. The so-called 'orthodox' were thoroughly antagonistic to the proceedings of the Sabha.[157] In this respect, thus the *reformer* had failed to mobilize the 'neo-feudals' under one roof. Lastly, the lower-castes in Calcutta were not welcomed to listen to the abstract ideas.

Theoretically however, Rammohun Roy insisted that the Sabha's sole object was to raise the ideas of the people 'from groveling objects, which only appeal to the senses, to those which are of a mental nature.'[158] Had there been any need to maintain this theoretical posture ?

A British observer noted : 'The great majority of the community are attached to the popular ceremonies considering them as at least leading to the knowledge of God, or as laying in a stock of merit which will influence their condition in this or a future birth.'[159] Truly, polytheism was the popular religious practice,[160] because, in the existing social organisation there was no other way left to the people. The fundamental arguments of some of the popular religious sects of Bengal were : belief in one God, and the realisation of greatest happiness in the fulfilment of all desires in this material world. The Balaramis ridiculed idolatry; the Ramballavis denounced caste; the Saheb Dhanis worshipped no images, nor was caste a bar to them; and the Kartabhajas, as Gopal Krishna Pal reported, were 'a man-worshipping sect, and its object is to call forth and develop the latent divinity in man. This it seeks to accomplish, not by renouncing the world but by going through life's struggles manfully and heroically, sustained throughout with love for mankind and reverence for nature.'[161] Rammohun's desire of elevating human consciousness to that abstract level of unity with the Supreme Being was an illusory technique to divert the people from their principle of desire, fulfilment of which they craved for in this material world : a logic which nourished in itself the seeds of antagonism. To the *reformer*, the behaviour of Vaishnav sects and the mainstream of Vaisnav cult were immoral and corrupt.[162]

To sum up, Rammohun Roy's religious thinking should be seen in the perspective of his total outlook, and not as isolated abstract formulations. His theoretical arguments were politically motivated : to unite the 'neo-feudal' class, and develop the utilitarian principle of obedience and adoration among individuals and between classes in order to create a perfect social harmony. In practice however, he could not adhere to his own arguments and consequently failed to realise his objective.

SOCIAL REFORMS OF RAMMOHUN ROY

Rammohun Roy had 'laid the foundation of all the principal modern movements for the elevation of our people',[163] and was considered the pioneer and the brain behind the ultimate abolition of *Satidaha*.[164] These views demand closer scrutiny.

Scrafton wrote that in mid-18th century Bengal, the practice of *sati* was far from common and was only complied with by illustrious families.[165] Stavorinus noted its prevalence only among 'some castes.'[166] Possibly, some smaller castes, which were then emerging as influential castes in certain localities, were imitating the customs of the higher castes.

The Serampore missionaries were pioneers in the agitation against *satidaha*. William Carey had appealed to Lord Wellesley and worked in collaboration with Dr. Buchanan to stop the practice. Government interference—regulations 1812, 1813 and 1817—and the impact of missionary work had produced some results. The incidence of *satidaha* had been on decline since 1818;[167] a year which significantly coincided with Rammohun Roy's first assault on the practice of *satidaha*. His first book appeared in November 1818. The proceedings of the Nizamut Adalat dated 21 May, 1819, admitted that *satidahas* in small numbers were taking place in youth or even at an age.[168] G. Forbes, the First Judge of the Calcutta Court of Circuit, and C. Smith, the Second Judge of the Nizamut Adalat, pleaded in 1819 and 1821 respectively for the immediate abolition of *satidaha* and affirmed that such abolition would not generate troubles.[169] Harrington, the Chief Judge of the Nizamut Adalat, observed in his minute of 28th June, 1823 that the immediate abolition of *satidaha* would not generate political unrest.[170]

On December, 1829, by Regulation XVII, *satidaha* was declared 'illegal and punishable by the Criminal Courts.' The tide of opinion was so strongly against the practice that any Governor-General would have acted as Bentinck did.[171] The *Bengal Hurkaru* had rejected the pioneering role of Rammohun Roy in the ultimate abolition of *satidaha*.[172] Bentinck's minute on *sati* throws further light on the actual role of Rammohun Roy :

"It was his (Rammohun's) opinion that the practice might be suppressed quietly and unobservedly , by increasing the difficulties, and by the indirect agency of the police. He apprehended that any public enactment would give rise to general apprehension, that the reasoning would be, 'while the English were contending for power they duped it politic to allow universal toleration, and to respect our religion; but having obtained the supremacy, their first act is a violation of their professions, and the next will probably be, like the Mahommedan conquerors, to force upon us their own religion."[173]

In Jessore, the practice had completely declined between 1824 and 1828, which owed to the power of law exercised by the acting magistrate against which no public remonstrance was made.[174] According to Charles Metcalfe, there was really no fear of unrest.[175] In fact, the only opposition was, a petition from the orthodox Hindus on 19 December, 1829.[176]

Rammohun Roy's fear was imaginary, but his pious wish to abolish the practice cannot be doubted. However, the mind of the reformer has to be understood in the light of the above perspective. The practice of *satidaha* was associated with the degenerated social practices of a corrupt Brahminism which hardly touched the fringe of lower castes. Moreover, it has been correctly argued that both Rammohun and Vidyasagar came from Radi Kulina caste and their social reforms were directed towards safeguarding the interest of the caste and enhancing their social and economic position. The strict laws of endogamy, prohibition of widow remarriage and polygamy had left their caste polluted and childless. The caste was losing its purity and declining in population. It is significant to note that members of Rammohun Roy's *Atmiya Sabha* belonged to Radi Kulina or Bhagna Kulina caste.[177] Secondly, the practice of *satidaha* was already declining when the *reformer* took up the cause. It would have declined independent of his interference. But, its absolute abolition would have been impossible without legal enactment i.e. an exterior force. Considered pragmatically, the *reformer's* apathy towards legal enactment is condemnable.

Rammohun Roy was not a champion of women's liberation. He had glorified ascetic widowhood[178] and made no serious attempt to educate the women. In this respect, Radhakanta Deb was more advanced in outlook.

An important cause of India's social stagnation was caste and the multifarious social taboos associated with it. The *reformer* had realised the problem,[179] but undertook no intellectual or practical action against it. Some authors argued that he had opposed caste and brought out a translation of an ancient text *Vajra-suchi.*[180] Quite contrary, the argument of *Vajra-suchi* provided a rational vindication of caste discipline.[181] In his *Barhma-Pauttalik Sangbad* (1820), the observance of caste, diet and associated social norms by the believer in Brahma was defended. He wrote: "the Supreme Ruler bestows the consequences of.....sins and holiness.....by giving them other bodies either animate or inanimate."[183] This belief in the theory of *karma* is a traditional justification of caste. As such, he could not identify his interests with the Bengali Christians who were critical of caste.[184] Furthermore, in practice, Rammohun Roy wore his sacred Brahmin thread to the day of his death. His friend, Adam, wrote on 24 June 1827 : 'All the rules in the present state of Hindu society he finds it necessary to observe, relate to eating and drinking. He must not eat the food forbidden to Brahmins nor with persons of different religion from the Hindu or of different caste or tribe from his own.'[185]

Living in Calcutta and acquainted with the social practices of higher castes and moneocrats, Rammohun Roy never spoke a word against slavery extensively predominant in urban and rural Bengal.[186] He neither probed the causes, nor pleaded for adequate measures when the urban poor died in numbers owing to choked drainage, poor sanitary condition, lack of medical facilities, and poor work conditions in the city.[187]

The picture, no doubt, reveals a reformer strongly averse to any radical social reforms that would elevate the people from perennial backwardness.

CONCLUSION

In late 18th and early 19th century Bengal the objective of the British bourgeoisie was to establish its class hegemony in an alien society in collaboration with the 'neo-feudal' class, retaining to itself the position of dominance within the united front. The problem before this united front was the search for *effective means* to establish class hegemony. However, the processes of collaboration of the British bourgeoisie with the 'neo-feudal' class had created their own contradictions : within the 'neo-feudal' class, and between the 'neo-feudal' class and the alien bourgeoisie. The first contradiction became sometime antagonistic, while in the second case it was always non-antagonistic. It is against this total perspective that the proper estimation of Rammohun Roy's ideas and works should have rested.

The greatness of the *reformer* lies in that he was one of the individuals of that period who could enlighten the British bourgeoisie by providing them with certain definite channels through which the dominance could be established. His essential philosophy was the philosophy of all reformers : the doctrine of class harmony. In a colonial environment, the doctrine of class harmony within the framework of the hegemony of an alien British bourgeoisie gave impetus to subsequent distortions in Indian economy, society and ideology. Furthermore, the ideology of social harmony concealed in itself the violence through which the alien rulers had attained dominance in society. The belief that association with an advanced country would elevate the Indians from backwardness and enlighten them in western science, technology and philosophy, was illusive and elusive, because the Indian reformers knew from experiences in their life time that no positive steps in that direction have been taken. An eminent social scientist had correctly observed :

> "They lived in abysmal misery, yet they had no prospect of a better tomorrow. They existed under capitalism, yet there was no accumulation of capital. They lost their time-honoured means of livelihood, their arts and crafts, yet their was no modern industry to provide new ones in their place. They were thrust into extensive contact with the advanced science of the West, yet remained in a state of the darkest backwardness."[188]

Rammohun Roy was a conscious participant in the process of "anti-development"[189] of Indian society initiated by the British bourgeoisie in their interests. Incidentally the process is still continuing. The problems of Indian economy, society and ideology today are a product of continued dominance and exploitation of this country by foreign imperialism : its heritage goes back to the days of establishment of British Imperialism in India. The Indian Reformers "enlightened" under the umbrella of British Imperialism were taught to speak in the interests of their patron. The illusive and elusive track laid conjointly during the early 19th century was continued by Vidyasagar, Bankimchandra and Rabindranath. The last paid tribute to the Guru: "In this dark gloom of India's degeneration Rammohun rose up, a luminous star, in the firmanent of India's history, with prophetic purity of vision, and unconquerable heroism of soul. He shed radiance all over the land; he rescued us from the penury of self-oblivion...."[190] It would be a mistake and under-estimation to suppose that these intellectuals were not in a position to understand the process of violent distortion of Indian social and economic progress. In fact, they were not in a position to severe their links with their patrons. They neither possessed the requisite courage.

Historians have established Rammohun Roy as a 'progressive reformer'. What is the criterion of a 'progressive' person? A person is 'progressive' if his theory and social practice leads the society ahead. By this criterion, Rammohun Roy was certainly not progressive. His objectives, and the inner-contradictions from which he suffered and retreated, vindicate our standpoint. Persons who have 'eulogised' him belonged to classes prospering under the imperial umbrella, and ideologically tied to their masters. Combinedly, they have diffused the *illusions* needed to maintain the Raj. In a social structure which had not undergone any fundamental changes, the 'illusions' fostered by the Raj, and simultaneously carried forward by the enlightened intellectuals, survive till this day.

However, Rammohun Roy was the 'precursor' of modern movements' in a limited sense. His methods of agitation—through petitions and appeals before a selective and an affluent audience—were imitated by the intellectual politicians of India during the early phase of the national movement. Such a method of political agitation was basically directed towards the maintenance of the colonial order with minor adjustments of power to the satisfaction of the higher class agitators. The greatest contribution of Rammohun Roy lies in his basically political ideology of 'social harmony.' The political violence which stood by the *apparent* politics of social harmony of the then day is still the dominant *code of conduct* observed by the ruling classes to establish its hegemony in the society.

There were, nevertheless, in the Indian society other classes that had 'unconsciously' resisted the making of today's 'underdevelopment'. The 'heroes' from these classes were even two decades back *unknown*. It is the task of historians to learn from present experiences, trace the sources of underdevelopment and find out *areas of sympathy* that ran counter to the process of strengthening British Imperialism in India.*

REFERENCES

1. See, U.N. Ball, *Rammohun Roy,* Calcutta, 1933; Amal Home ed. *Rammohun Roy : The man and His work,* Calcutta, 1933, Lantt *Carpenter, Review of the Labours, opinions and character of Rajah Rammohun Roy : In a Discourse on Occasion of His Death, Bristol, 1833; P.K. Das, Raja Rammohun Roy and Brahmoism,* Calcutta, 1970 : C.A. Heimsath, *Indian Nationalism and Hindu Social Reform,* New Jersey, 1964, Chapter 1; S.M. Ganguli, *Bangalir Rashtra-chinta,* in Bengali, Calcutta, 1968, Chapter 1; B.N. Ganguli, *Concept of Equality,* Indian Institute of Advanced Study, Simla, 1975, p. 72; N. Macnicol, *The Making of Modern India,* O U P, 1924, p.p. 171-88; Tagore Research Institute compiled : *Rammohun Roy—Naba Yuger Neta,* in Bengali, Calcutta, 1974; and names of other authors we would come across in the process.
2. See, R.C. Majumdar, *On Rammohun Roy,* Calcutta, 1974; N.S. Bose, *The Indian Awakening and Bengal,* Calcutta, B.S. 1386, for a criticism of Dr. Majumdar's views. Dr. Majumdar had eulogsed Rammohun previously, pp. 37-38.
3. See, J. Campbell Oman, *The Brahmans, Theists and Muslims of India,* London, 1907, pp. 108-109. For a similar but sophisticated version, see Sumit Sarkar, *Rammohun Roy and Break with the Past,* and other articles in V.C. Joshi ed., *Rammohun Roy and the Process of Modernisation in Bengal,* New Delhi, 1970. For a slightly different view see, S.N. Mukherjee, *Social Implications of the Political Thought of Raja Rammohun Roy,* in R.S. Sharma ed. *Indian Society : Historical Probings in Memory of D.D. Kosambi,* New Delhi, 1974; 'Rammohun's model was a competitive market sociey'. p. 361.
4. Suprokash Roy, *Bharater Krishak Bidroha O Ganatantric Sangram,* Calcutta, 1966, vol. 1. pp. 183-220; and N. Dhar, *Vedanta and The Bengal Renaisance,* Calcutta, 1977, Chapter-1.
5. C. Hill, *The World Tuned Upside Down,* Penguin Books, 1976, p. 15.
6. N.K. Sinha, *The Economic History of Bengal,* Calcutta, 1968, Vol. 2, p. 79.
7. See, R. Guha. *The Rule of Property for Bengal,* Netherlands, 1963, for the growth of the idea of bestowing proprietory right on the zamindars.
8. Henry Pattullo, *An Essay upon the Cultivation of the Land and Improvement of the Revenues of Bengal,* London, 1772, p. 9.

* The writer desires to express his gratefulness to Ratan Das Gupta, Pulakesh Roy, Siddhartha Guha Roy and Ramendranath Dutta for advice and assistance received.

9. M. Martin, *The Progress and present State of Britsh India,* London, 1862, pp. 116-17. See, W.W. Hunter, *Annals of Rural Bengal* Reprint, Calcutta n.d., pp. 56-58, for an account of the ruin of the old landed families. Also, Ratnalekha Ray, *Change in Bengal Agraraian Society, 1760-1850,* Manohar, 1979; and Siraj-ul-Islam, *The Permanent Settlement and Its Results, 1793-1819.* Dacca. Dr. Islam states that 68.2% of the land underwent transfer.
10. C.H. Philips ed. *The Correspondence of Lord William Cavendish Bentinck.* Oxford, 1977, Vol. 1; Letter No. 157, 8th November 1829, p. 339
11. B.B. Chaudhuri, '*Agrarian Relations in Bengal, 1859-1885*' in N.K. Sinha ed., *History of Bengal* Calcutta University, 1967, pp. 237, 240.
12. *Ibid.*, pp. 277-78. Also, D. Warriner, *Land Reform In Principle and Practice,* Oxford, Clarendon, 1969, p. 158.
13. Quoted from S. Gopal. *The Permanent Settlement In Bengal and Its Results,* London, 1949, p. 40.
14. Hollinbery, *The Zemindary Settlement of Bengal,* Vol. 1. Calcutta, 1879, Appendix IV, p. 55.
15. *Friend of India,* April, 1852.
16. Hollinberry, *op. cit.,* Appendix XII and XIII; also N.K. Sinha, *op. cit.,* Vol. 2.
17. *Report of the Land Revenue Commission, Bengal* (B.G. Press, 1940), Vol. 1., p. 37.
18. Letter No. 104, 30th May1829; C.H. Philips ed. *op. cit.,*Vol. 1.
19. H.R. Ghosal, *'Industrial Productions In Bengal in the early Nineteenth Century',* in B.N. Ganguli ed. *Readings in Indian Economic History* Delhi, 1961, p. 118.
20. A. Sen, *'Iswarchandra Vidyasagar and His Elusive Milestone'* (Occasional Paper, C.S.S.S.C., No. 1), p. 75.
21. See, J. Taylor, *A Sketch of the Topography & Statistics of Dacca,* Calcutta, 1840, pp. 363-66; also. D. & B. Bhattacharya ed. *Census of India 1961 : Report on the Population Estimates of India, 1820-1830,* Vol. 4, p. 326. Also, V. I. Pavlov, *Historical Premises for India's Transition to Capitalism,* Moscow, 1978, pp. 340-41.
22. H.H. Wilson, *History of British India,* London, Book 1, Chapter 8.
23. *Correspondence of Bentinck,* Letter No. 104 C.H. Philisps ed. *op. cit.*
24. Parliamentery Papers, House of Commons, Vol. 10, pt. II, 1831-32, p. 523; Letter from Commercolly, 26 Feb. 1789, B.T.C., 19 May 1789; Board of Trade (Opium) proceeding, 30th July, 1811 and 4th Nov. 1817; also, F. Buchanan, *Patna-Gaya Journal,* Patna, 1925, Vol. 2., p. 524.
25. J. Crawford, *An Inquiry Into Some of the Principal Monopolies of the East India Company,* London, n. d., P. 9; also, Henry St. George Tucker. *A Review of The Financial Situation of the East India, Co. In 1824,* London, 1825, pp. 51-52.

26. Board of Customs, Salt and Opium (Salt). Proceeding No. 17, 4th May 1819; also No. 1, 25th September 1821.
27. See, Rammohun's reply No. 6, March 19, 1832, in S.C. Sarkar ed. *Rammohun Roy on Indian Economy*, Calcutta, 1965, p. 82.
28. See, N.K. Sinha ed. *Midnapore Salt Papers*, Calcutta, 1954, Introduction.
29. Dalhousie's Minute dt. 11 September 1852 and F. Halliday's evidence, qroted from R.C. Dutt, *The Economic History of India*, New Delhi, Vol. 2, pp. 104 & 110.
30. B. Chowdhury, *Growth of Commercial Agriculture in Bengal, 1757-1900*, Calcutta,1964, Vol. 1, p. 85
31. N.K. Sinha, *The Economic History of Bengal*, Calcutta, 1962, Vol. 2, p. 224.
32. J. Rosselli, *Lord William Bentinck : The Making of a Liberal Imperialist, 1774-1839*, Sussex University Press, 1974, p. 183.
33. J. Rosselli. *op. cit.*, p. 210.
34. C.E. Trevelyan, *The Education of the People of India*, London, 1838, pp. 192-95.
35. For missionary activities see, K.P. Sengupta, *Christian Missonaries in Bengal 1793-1833*, Calcutta, 1971; and K. Ingham, *Reforms in India; 1793-1833*, Cambridge University Press, 1956.
36. The traditional allocation of work and duties including the police powers of the zamindars were undermined. The neo-feudals, thus, became more alienated unproductive class depending exclusively on rents. See, A. Aspinall, *Cornwalis in Bengal*, Manchester, 1931, pp. 104-13, 174.
37. Though M. Martin had observed: "I do not agree that India is an agricultural country; India is as much a manufacturing country as an agricultural, and he who would seek to reduce her to the position of an agricultural country seeks to lower her in the scale of civilization"—See, R.C. Dutt, *Economic of History of India*, New Delhi, 1970, Vol. 2, p. 81.—and comparative assessment of economic development in England and India before 1750 had been treated favourably by V. Anstey, *Economic Development of India*, London, 1949; and R.P. Saraf, *The Indian Society*, Madras, 1974; but our statement has been made from no such comparative angles. Our emphasis is on the difference between what Bengal actually was and what actually the imperialist government tried to Advertise.
38. For some trends of this ulcerous acculteration see. Benoy Ghosh, '*Social Change*' in *Renascent Bengal, 1817-1857*, Asiatic Society, 1972, pp. 16-17.
39. S.N. Mukherjee in *Caste, Class and Politics In Calcutta 1815-38* in Leach and Mukerjee ed. *Elites In South Aisa*, Cembridge University Press, 1970, —has erroneously argued that the antagonism among the 'dals' were purely struggle for struggles

sake because each 'dal' were composed of many castes and their politics did not reflect any ideological commitment apart from their alienation from mass politics. For a compartive approach without pointing out the dominant trend, See A. Cobban, *A History of Modern France,* Vol. 1, Pelican Original, 1968, Section III. The important approach is, however, to emphasize the "dominant trend". Sec, A. Soboul, *The French Revolution,* London 1971, 2 Vols.

40. B.N. Banerjee, *Raja Kadhakanta Deb's Services to the country, Indian Historical Records Commission,* Vol. 9, 1926.
41. R. Heber, *Narrative of a Journey through the Upper Provinces of India from Calcutta to Bombay, 1824-25,* London 1828, Vol. 1, p. 92. Also see, R.C. Mitra, *Education,* p. 453, in N.K. Sinha ed., *The History of Bengal, 1757-1905,* University of Calcutta, 1967; and K.K. Dutta, *Education and Social Amelioration of Women in Pre-Mutiny India,* Patna, 1936.
42. K.C. Mitra, *Memoirs of Dwarakanath Tagore,* 1870, p. 36. Also, *Samachar Darpan* 10 December, 1831 and 31 March, 1838.
43. Radhakanta Deb did not subscribe to such a traditional view. See, B.N. Banerjee, *Raja Radhakanta Deb op. cit.*
44. J.C. Bagal, *Derozio,* in Bengali, Calcutta, 1976; Benoy Ghosh, *Bidrohi Derozio,* in Bengali, Calcutta, 1961; and E.W. Madge, *Henry Derozio : The Eurasian Poet and Reformer,* ed. by S. Roy Choudury, Calcutta, 1967, are good accounts on Derozio and his thought.
45. *The Englishman,* 1st June 1836; and *India Gazette,* 5th October, 1831.
46. S. Sastri, *Ramtanu Lahiri O Tatkalin Banga Samaj,* in Bengali, Calcutta, 1957, p. 102.
47. See, S.C. Sarkar, *Bengal Renaissance and other Essays,* New Delhi, 1970, Chapter III; Sumit Sarkar. The Complexities of Young Bengal's in *Nineteenth Century Studies,* No. 4, Oct., 1973.
48. *Bengal Chronicle,* 27 May 1827; *Calcutta Gazette,* 4 June and 28 May 1827; also Radharaman Mitra, *Kalikata Darpan,* Calcutta, 1980, p.; and N.S. Bose ed., *Calcutta–People and Empire,* Calcutta, p. 165.
49. *Samachar Darpan,* 21 August 1819, 2nd June 1827; *Samachar Chandrika,* 12th May, 1830; See A.C. Dasgupta ed., *The Days of John Company, Selections from Calcutta Gazette, 1824-1832,* Calcutta, 1959, p. 214, Henceforth, *John Company.*
50. See, Benoy Ghose, *Vidyasagar O Bangali Samaj,* in Bengali, Calcutta, 1973, p. 443.
51. *Calcutta Gazette,* 4 November, 1824, *John Company,* p. 35.
52. See, D.B. Mitra, *The Cotton Weavers of Bengal,* Calcutta, 1978, pp. 140-44; Also, H.R. Ghosal, *Economic Transition in the Bengal Presidency.*

53. Suprokash Roy, *Bharater Krishak Bidroha O Ganatantric Sangram,* in Bengali, Vol. 1.; also, *Calcutta Gazette,* 6th March, 1826, *John Company,* p. 123.
54. H. Sanyal, 'Social Mobility in Bengal : Its Sources and Constrants,' *Indian Historical Review,* Vol. 2, No. 1, July 1975. Also, J. Bhattacharya, *Hindu Castes and Sects.* Calcutta.
55. *Calcutta Gazette,* 1st March, 1830, *John Company,* p. 488.
56. See, Section on 'Religion'.
57. Cf, W.K. Ferguson, *Europe in Transition, 1300-1500,* Boston, 1962, Chapter 1. For a theoritical and empirical analysis, See, K. Marx and F. Engels, *The German Ideology,* Moscow, 1976, Vol. 1, passim; K. Marx, *Toward the Critique of Hegel's Philosophy of Righ,* in L.S. Feuer ed., *Marx-Engels Basic Writings on Politics and Philosophy,* Fontana Library, 1969, pp. 303-307 and C. Hill, *Change and Continuity in 17th Century England,* London, 1974, Chapters 3 and 4.
58. For the entire section see, Bhavani Charan Bandyopadhyay, *Kalikata Kamalalaya,* in Bengali, Calcutta, B.S. 1342 reprint; Salauddin Ahmed, *Social Ideas and Social Changes in Bengali 1818-1835,* Leiden, 1965; Kopf, *British Orientalism and the Bengal Renaissance,*California, 1969; and K.K. Datta, *Survey of India's Social Life and Economic Conditions In Eighteenth Century, 1707-1813,* Calcutta, 1961.
59. N.N. Basu, *Banger Jatiya Itihas, Brahman Kanda,* Calcutta, 1331, B.S., pp. 114-134.
60. B.N. Banerjee, 'Rammohun Roy and an English Official', *Modern Review,* June 1929.
61. B. De, *A Biographical Perspective on the Political and Economic Ideas of Rammohun Roy,* in V.C. Joshi ed., *Rammohun Roy, op. cit.,* pp. 140-41.
62. B.N. Banerjee, 'Rammohun Roy : The First Phase', *Calcutta Review,* 1933, Vol. 49.
63. Board of Revenue Proceedings Letter from S. Davis, Collector of Burdwan, to the Board dtd. 14 August 1794. Proceeding 19 August, 1794, No. 4.
64. Letter dtd. 22 March, 1796, *N. Byabharata* of 1330 B.S. *Ashwin,* quoted from B.N. Banerji, *Calcutta Review, op. cit.*
65. Rammohun Roy, *Autobiographical Letter,* quoted in full in M. Carpentar, *The Last Days in England of the Rajah Rammohun Roy,* Calcutta, 1976, pp. 14-16.
66. R. Chanda and J.K. Majumdar ed., *Selections from Official Letters and Documents Relating to the Life of Raja Rammohun Roy,* Calcutta, 1938, Vol. 1, letter dtd. 11 May 1819, No. 115, pp. 190-191. Henceforth, *Selections.*
67. J.C. Ghose ed., *The English Works of Raja Rammohun Roy,* Calcutta, 1901, Vol. 2. pp. 18-19.

68. See, B. Chowdhury, 'Land Market in Eastern India, 1793-1940', *Indian Economic and Social History Review,* 1975, Vol. 12, Nos. 1 & 2.
69. *Selections,* p. XXXIX.
70. *Ibid.,* No. 103, p. 98.
71. Cf. F. Max Muller, *Rammohun to Ramkrishna,* Calcutta, 1952; he had argued that Rammohun Roy was great, because he was *unselfish,* pp. 17-18. This is erroneous. Even in his money transctions with his brother who had fallen in debt and was gaoled, Rammohun treated the matter as part of a day's businessan ordinary moneylending transaction. He gave Rs. 1000/- for his brother's release on condition that it was to be returned with interest. See, I, Singh, *Rammohun Roy,* Bombay, 1958, Vol. 1, pp. 107-108.
72. See, *Selections,* p. 1 xxxix.
73. Rammohun Roy, *Final Appeal to the Christian Public,* in J.C. Ghosh ed., *English Works,* Vol. 3, p. 105.
74. V.I. Lenin, *Conspectus of Hegel's 'The Science of Logic'. Collected Works,* Vol. 38. Also see, Section I. Moscow.
75. There were altogether 25 peasant uprising between 1760 and 1835. See, Suprokash Roy, *Bharater Krishak Bidroha O Ganatantric Sangram.*
76. Rammohun's argument borrowed from Suprokash Roy, *Ibid.,* p. 205.
77. N.N. Chatterjee, *Mahatma Raja Rammohun Roy's Jibancharita,* in Bengali, Calcutta, B.S. 1318, pp. 47-48; I. Singh, *Rammohun Roy,* Vol. 1, p. 172; and N. Dhar, *Vedanta and the Bengal Renaissance,* p. 65.
78. W. Digby, *Prosperous British India,* New Delhi, reprint 1969, p. 57 (see, evidences); and *Reports and Documents connected with the Proceedings of the E.I. Company in regard to the Culture and Manufacture of Cotton, Raw Silk and Indigo in India,* London, 1863, pp. 9-10.
79. L.C. Mitra, *History of Indigo Disturbance In Bengal with a Full Report of the Nil Durpan Case,* Calcutta, 1903, p. 18; and R. Reynolds, *White Sahibs in India,* London, 1946, p. 108.
80. *Indigo Commission Report,* Appendix No. 16.
81. P. Sengupta, *Nil Bidroha O Bangali Samaj,* in Bengali, Calcutta, 1978, pp. 48-49; and B.N. Banerji ed., *Sambad Patre Sekaler Katha,* in Bengali, 18 May, 1822, Calcutta, Vol. 1. p. 155
82. C.H. Phillips ed., *Correspondence of Bentinck,* Vol. 2, Letter No. 429, 10 April, 1832, *para* 5.
83. *Ibid, paras* 14 and 16.
84. *Indigo Commission Report,* Appendix No. 14.
85. L.C. Mitra, *History of Indigo Disturbance,* p. 20.
86. C. Palit, *Tension in Bengal Rural Society,* Calcutta, 1975.

87. *Asiatic Journal,* March, 1829.
88. *Asiatic Journal,* New Series, May-August, 1830, Vol. 2.
89. J.K. Majumdar ed., *Indian Speeches and Documents on British Rule, 1821-1918.* Calcutta, 1937, p. 42.
90. See, Colin Fisher's article, 'Planters and Peasants : the ecological context of the Agrarian unrest on the Indigo plantations of North Bihar's in C. Dewey and A.G. Hopkins ed., *The Imperial Impact: Studies in the Economic History of Africa and India,* London, 1978.
91. For a detailed discussion of this argument see, Amit Bhaduri, *The Economic Structure of Agricultural Backwardness,* manuscript : Norway, 1972, *Passim;* or by the same author, *Towards a Theory of Pre-Capitalist Exchange in* A. Mitra ed., *Economic Theory and Planning : Essays in Honour of A.K. Das Gupta,* Calcutta, 1974, p. 139.
92. J.K. Majumdar ed., *Indian Speeches and Documents on British Rule,* pp. 46-47.
93. Cf. Similar views expressed also by Bankimchandra Chattopadhyay in his novels, *Ananda Math* and *Debi Chaudhuranee,* in *Bankim Rachana Samagraha,* Calcutta, 1974, Vol. 2.
94. *The Calcutta Municipal Gazette,* 22 December 1928.
95. Quoted from, *The Last Days in England of the Rajah Rammohun Roy, op. cit.*
96. 'On the Prosperity of Bengal in 1829', in J.K. Majumdar ed., *Indian Speeches and Documents on British Rule,* pp. 36-41.
97. *Ibid.*
98. See, F. Engels, *The Peasant War In Gemany,* Moscow, 1974, Appendix IV.
99. Rammohun held highest opinion on English liberalism and the British system of Parliamentary control. But, prior to the Reform Bill of 1832, the Parliament was controlled by a conservative aristocracy through the restricted and the rotten borough system of representation. Against the strong tide of working class movement and middle-class resistance, classical bourgeois liberalism pleaded for *an* artificial harmony between the antagonistic classes. See, Guido de Ruggiero, *The History of European Liberalism;* translated by R.G. Collingwood, London, 1927, Part I; also, R. Cobden, *Speeches,* London, 1870, Vol. 1. pp. 362-63 and J.S. Schapiro, *Liberalism—Its Meaning and History,* New York, 1958, pp. 32-43.
100. S.C. Sarkar ed., *Rammohun Roy on Indian Economy,* Calcutta, 1965, Chapters 4 & 5.
101. 20 June 1832, in J.K. Majumdar ed., *Rajah Rammohun Roy and Progressive Movements in India—A Selection from Records 1775-1845,* Calcutta, 1941, pp. 484-85.
102. S.C. Sarkar, ed., *Rammohun Roy on Indian Economy, Ibid.*

103. *Ibid.*
104. See, Section on *Political Economy.*
105. S.C. Sarkar, ed, *Rammohun Roy on Indian Economy,* p. 12.
106. *Ibid,* Chapter 4.
107. B.N. Ganguli, 'Rammohun Roy on India's Contemporary Economic Problems', in S.L. Sinha ed., *Economic and Social Development—Essays In Honour of Dr. C.D. Dehmukh,* Bombay, 1972, p. 295.
108. See, *Mirat,* 11 October, 1832, quoted from Abdul Wadud, *Creative Bengal,* Calcutta, 1950, p. 23. The argument was : "Bind yourself with ties of love with your subjects and thus be assured of victory against your foes; For to the just king, has subjects are soldiers." Also, "Do not say that these rapacious ministers are the wellwishers of his Majesty; For in proportion as they augment in revenue of the State, they diminish his popularity; O Statesmen, apply the revenue of the King towards the comfort of the people; Then during their lives they will be loyal to him."—See, Ramananda Chatterjee, *Rammohun Roy and Modern India,* Calcutta, 1972, p. 18.
109. Minute dtd. 10 July, 1800, quoted from from N. Dhar, *Vedanta and The Bengal Renaissance,* pp. 40-43.
110. *The English Works of Rammohun,* Centenary ed. Sadharan Brahmo Samaj, Calcutta, 1934, p. 101.
111. *Ibid.,* p. 102.
112. S. Sastri, *Ramtanu Lahiri O Tatkalin Banga Samaj,* pp. 101-102. Rammohun's fear of irreligious thinking was so profound that, when told a person was once a polytheist, had become a deist and then an atheist; he commented that, at last he would become a beast. *Ibid.,* p. 80.
113. D.K. Biswas and P.C. Ganuli ed., S.D. Collet's, *The Life and Letters of Rajah Rammohun Roy,* Calcutta, 1962, p. 184.
114. *Ibid.,* p. 190; also *History of the Brahmo Samaj,* Calcutta, 1974, p. 27.
115. George Smith, *Life of Alexander Duff,* London, 1879; and William Paton, *Alexander Duff : Pioneer of Missionary Education,* London, 1923, Chapters 4 & 5.
116. *Correspondence of Bentinck,* Vol. 2 : Letter No. 793, dtd. 2nd February, 1835.
117. *Sumbad Bhuskar,* 26 May, 1857.
118. K.C. Mitra, *On the Progress of Education In Bengal,* Calcutta nd. p. 16.
119. Quoted from U.N. Ball, *Rammohun Roy,* Calcutta, 1933, p. 225.
120. *India Gazette,* Fiat Justitia's Letter, 27th Jne, 1832.
121. See, B.N. Ganguli's article, *op. cit.* in S.L. Sinha ed., *Essays In Honour of Dr. C.D. Desmukh,* pp. 306-307.

122. J.K. Majumdar ed., *Raja Rammohun Roy and Progressive Movements in India,* pp. 434-36. Also, for the consequence of 'free commerce' section on *Political Economy.*
123. *Samachar Darpan,* 4th June, 1831; and *Calcutta Monthly Journal,* June, 1831.
124. *Correspondence of Bentinck,* Vol. 1, Letter No. 104.
125. B. De's article in V.C. Joshi ed., *Rammohun Roy and the Process of Modernisation in Begal,* p. 143.
126. Ashok Sen's article in V.C. Joshi ed., *Ibid.,* p. 130.
127. J.C. Ghosh ed., *English Works of Rammohun,* Vol. 2, p. 305.
128. *Ibid.,* p. 280.
129. *Correspondence of Bentinck,* Vol. 1, Letter No. 73 : Minute on Press.
130. B.B. Majumdar, *History of Indian Social and Political Ideas : From Rammohun to Dayananda,* Calcutta, 1967, p. 23.
131. R. Chatterjee, *Rammohun Roy and Modern India,* Calcutta, pp. 16-19.
132. *Modern Review,* June 1926.
133. All quotations are from *Tuhfut.* See, S.C. Sarkar, *Bengal Renaissance and other Essays,* Delhi, 1970, pp. 77-97; Collect, *Life and Letters of Rammohun,* pp. 19-20; and Sumit Sarkar, "Rammohun Roy and the Break with the Past," in V.C. Joshi ed., *Rammohun Roy and Process of Modernisation in Bengal,* p. 50. Rammohun Roy wrote : "Many learned Brahmans are perfectly aware of the absurdity of idolatry, and are well informed of the nature of the purer mode of divine worship. But as in the rites, ceremonies, and festivals of idolatry, they find the source of their comforts and fortune, they.... advance and encourage it to the utmost of their power, by keeping the knowledge of their scriptures concealed from the rest of the people"—see, *Preface to the Ishopanishad, in* R. Roy, *Translation of Several Princpal Books, Passages, and Texts of the Vedas and of Some Controversial Works on Brahmanical Theology,* Calcutta, 1904.
134. *Tuhfut,* see Collect, *Ibid.,* p. 20.
135. Cf. A Similar notion could be found among the Lokayatas. See, D. Chattopadhyay, *Lokayata,* New Delhi, 1978.
136. D.D. Kosambi, *The Culture and Civilisation of Ancient India in Historical Outline.* New Delhi, 1972; p. 174-75.
137. R. Thapar, *A History of India,* Pelican Original, Vol. 1., p. 185; and S.C. Mookerjee, *The Decline and Fall of the Hindus :* Sankara forcefully persecuted the Buddhists; Calcutta, 1914, pp. 75-77.
138. N. Dhar, *Vedanta and the Bengal Renaissance,* p. 43.
139. I. Singh, *Rammohun Roy,* Vol. 1.; and D. Kopf, *British Orientalism and The Bengal Renaissance,* p. 197.
140. S.D. Collet, *Life and Letters of Rammohun Roy,* p. 371.

141. *Ibid.*, Letter dtd. 18th January, 1828, p. 213.
142. *Introduction to the Ishopanishad,* in J.C. Ghose ed., *English Works of Rammohun,* Vol. 1. pp. 86-87.
143. S.D. Collect, *Life and Letters of Rammohun Roy,* Letter to Digby, pp. 71-72.
144. *Calcutta Review*, Vol. CV, 1845, p. 168.
145. *Preface to the Ishopanishad, English Works,* Vol. 1.
146. *Arbidgement of Vedanta,* in K. Nag and D. Burman ed., *The English Works of Raja Rammohun Roy,* Pt. II. p. 60.
147. *The Brahmanical Magazine*, II & IV. see also, *Preface to the Ishopanishad.*
148. *Rammohun Rachanavali,* in Bengali; Haraf Publication, Calcutta, 1973.
149. The basic principles of Christan morality were : love thy neighbours, obedience to superiors, and abhorence of violence.
150. See, N. Guha ed., *Rammohun Roy : The Complete Songs,* Nos. 8, 12, 14 & 19; Calcutta, 1973.
151. *Abridgement of Vedanta.*
152. *Kavitakarer Sahit Vichar, and Brahmanical Magazine No. II of 1821;* see, *Rammohun Rachanavali.*
153. For details on Brahma Samaj see, N.C. Ganguli, 'Foundations of the Brahmo Samaj' in *Modern Review,* September, 1928, Vol. 44, No. 3; G.S. Leonard, *A History of the Brahmo Samaj from its Rise to 1878 A.D.*, Calcutta, 1879; J.N. Farquher, *Modern Religious Movement in India,* New York, 1915; Sivanath Sastri, *History of the Brahmo Samaj,* Calcutta, 1974.
154. See, *Introduction to Abridgement of Vedanta.*
155. S. Sastri, *History of the Brahmo Samaj,* Calcutta, 1974, p. 25.
156. M. Martin, *History of the British Colonies,* quoted from Collect, *Life and Letters of Rammohun,* Chapter VII.
157. Iqbal Singh, *Rammohun Roy,* p. 146.
158. J.K. Majumdar, *Rammohun Roy and Progressive Movements,* No. 43, p. 90.
159. W. Ward, *A View of the History, Literature, and Religion of the Hindus.* London, 1817, Vol. 1, p. xii.
160. A.C. Boquet, *Hinduism,* London, 1948, p. 135.
161. J.H.E. Garrett, Nadia Distirct Gazetteer, Calcutta, 1910, pp. 48-50; D. Sen, *Chaitanya and His Age,* Calcutta, 1922, pp. 346-49, P.N. Bose, *A History of Hindu Civilisation Under British Rule,* New Delhi, 1975, Vol. 1, p. 179; A.K. Dutta, *Upasaka Sampradaya,* in Bengali, Calcutta, 1911, Vol. 1; and S.B. Dasgupta, *Obscure Religious Sects,* Calcutta, 1976.
162. N. Macnicol, *The Living Religions of the Indian People;* revised edition by M.H. Harrison, New Delhi, 1964, pp. 90-91.
163. Ramananda Chatterjee, *Rammohun Roy and Modern India.*

164. See, F.K. Martin's Letter, dtd. 26 November, 1829, to the Editor of *Bengal Hurkaru and Chronicle.*
165. Scrafton, *Reflections on the Government of Indostan,* London, 1763, p. 11.
166. J.S. Stavorinus, *Voyages to the East Indies,* London, 1798, Vol. 1, p. 441.
167. See, A. Mukherjee, *Reform and Regeneration in Bengal, 1774-1823,* Calcutta, 1968, Chapter IV; K. Ingham, *Reformers in India 1793-1833,* Cambridge University Press, 1955, pp. 46-54; E. Thompson, *Suttee.* London 1928, p. 7 : credits Bentinck for abolition. Also, Gorachand Mitra, *Satidaha,* in Bengali, Calcutta, B.S 1384–he criticizes R.C. Majumdar's views, pp. 205-210; and S.K. Mitra, *Hoogli Jelar Itihas O Bangasamaj,* in Bengali, Calcutta, 1962, Vol. 1, p. 205.
168. *Parliamentary Papers, House of Commons,* 1821, Vol. 18, p. 222.
169. *Ibid.*, Vol. 18, p. 224; also 1823, Vol. 17, p. 63.
170. *Ibid,* 1825, Vol. 24, pp. 8-18.
171. F.J. Shore, *Notes on Indian Affairs,* London, 1837, Vol. 2, p. 217.
172. *Bengal Hurkaru,* 28 November, 1829.
173. *Correspondence of Bentinck,* Vol. 1, Letter No. 157, and *The Asiatic Journal and Monthly Register*, New Series, Vol. 12, September-December, 1833, pp. 203-204.
174. *Correspondence of Bentinck,* ibid., p. 340.
175. *Correspondence of Bentinck,* Vol. 1, Letter No. 159, 14 November, 1829.
176. *Ibid.*, Letter No. 168, 19 December, 1829.
177. B. Bandyopadhyay ed., Sambad Patre Sekaler Katha : Samachar Darpan, 23rd January, 1820, Vol. 1, pp. 300-02; *Samachar Darpan,* 12th April, 1834, Vol. 2, p. 492, B. Ghose, *Vidyasagar O Bangali Samaj;* and S.N. Mukherjee, *The Social Implication of the Political Thought of Raja Rammohun Roy,* in R.S. Sharma ed., *op. cit.*
178. R. Roy, *Pathya Pradan, Granthavali,* Bangiya Sahitya Parishad ed. Calcutta, 1359, B.S. Vol. 6, p. 140.
179. Letter dt. 18th January, 1828, Ramananda Chatterjee, *Rammohun Roy and Modern India.*
180. Collect, *Life and Letters of Rammohun,* p. 213 : and Sumit Sarkar, *Rammohun and Break With the Past,* in V.C. Joshi ed., *R.Roy and Process of Modernisaton in Bengal,* p. 53.
181. For the text, B.N. Banerji and Sajanikanta Das ed. *Rammohun Granthavali,* 4, p. 48.
182. *Ibid.*, Vol. 6, pp. 138-64.
183. *Brahmanical Magaznine* No. II (1821) and *Kavitakarter Sahit Vichar* (1820).
184. Rev. K.M. Banerjee, *Essay on Hindu Caste,* Calcutta, 1851, Chapters 2 to 5.

185. J. Morrison, *New Ideas in India During the Nineteenth Century,* London, 1906, p. 126; J.D.M. Dearrett, *Religion, Law and the State In India,* London 1968, p. 59; and R.C. Majumdar, *On Rammohun Roy,* Calcutta, 1972, pp. 40-41.
186. D.R. Banerji, *Slavery in Britis India,* Bombay, 1933, p. 9.
187. A.K. Das Gupta ed., *Selections from the Calcutta Gazette*; the athor is also indebted to Ratan Das Gupta for adding this point.
188. P.A. Baran, *The Political Economy of Growth,* New Delhi, 1958, p. 171.
189. The phrase has been borrowed from C.R. Hensman *Rich Against Poor,* Pelican Books, 1975.
190. *R. Tagore, "Inaugurator of the Modern Age in India"*, in A. Home ed., *Rammohun Roy : The Man and His Work,* Calcutta, 1933, pp. 3-4.

—SURANJAN CHATTERJEE

CHAPTER - IV

MACAULAY'S EDUCATIONAL MINUTES

The Indian career of Lord Macaulay extends from 1834 to 1837. During these three years he was the means of reforming the eudcation of India, and as we now see, of simplifying the Law of India also. Few men have been by themselves so instrumental in impressing their stamp on the history of a nation's progress. By his educational reforms the whole system of instruction was directed into the channels which more or less it still retains. By his Penal Code he will direct men. He has more than any other man influenced the School life of the thousands who now crowd our English Schools. They probably know it not, but it is right that they should know and honour the man to whose vigorous exertion they owe their present advantages. His other great work that of reforming the Law was for a quarter of a century under consideration from time to time and one important section that of the Penal Code has, within the last three months, become the law of the land. Seldom does it fall to the lot of one man to be at once the chief Educator and the chief Lawgiver of a vast nation. Such an extraordinary character deserves more than ordinary consideration from Hindus.

Macaulay was born in 1800, and therefore we may tell his age by the years of the century He was 34 years old when he came to India. His father Zachary Macaulay was for some time the Governor of Sierra Leone, and afterwards the friend and fellow labourer of Wilberforce and Clarkson in effecting the abolition of slavery. Macaulay was educated at home, and when he describes the advantages derived from female instruction, he speaks from personal experience. He entered Trinity College, Cambridge, at the age of eighteen, and after carrying off the highest classical prize took his degree in 1822. He subsequently won a fellowship at Trinity. The ability he displayed at the Union dabating Society at Cambridge attracted the attention of all his contemporaries and brought him to the notice of public men........./214/

Macaulay's first speech on record was made in 1824, at an Anti-Slavery Meeting. It was a noble composition, but of course gave offence to the West India Planters. In 1825, Macaulay contributed to the Edinburgh Review his famous Essay on Milton. It was the first of that brilliant series with which during twenty years he enriched that Review. Soon afterwards in his essay on history he drew a comparison between the Romans in the time of Diocletian and the Chinese. If Hindus were substituted for Chinese the parallel would still be true, Macaulay says, 'It would be easy to indicate many points of resemblance between the subjects of Diocletian and the people of the celestial empire where, during many centuries, nothing has been learned or unlearned; where Government, where education, where the whole system of life is a ceremony; where knowledge forgets to increase and multiply, and like the talent buried in the earth, or the pound wrapped up in the napkin, experience neither waste nor augmentation. The torpor was broken by two great revolutions, the one moral, the other political : one from within, the other from without.'

This state of national torpor was the abhorrence of the Essayist, and when the Essayist rose to be member of the Supreme Council of India, and President of the Committee of Public Instruction, that abhorrence became a principle of action and waged uncompromising war with the time-consecrated abuses of toles and Madrussas. Nothing but deeply-seated convictions, unflinching resolution, and vigorous exercise of amazing powers of language and argument could vanquish the serried line of veterans ranked in defence of error.

Macaulay's Minute of the 2nd February, 1835, was the final and decisive blow that settled the contest. On the 7th of the next month Lord Bentick passed the famous resolution which turned the course of the stream of public education. Sidney Smith wrote to a friend in 1838, "Get and read Macaulay's papers upon Indian Courts and Indian Education. They are admirable for their talent and their honesty, we see why he was hated in India, and how honourable to him that hatred was." /216/

The first attempt for the enlightenment of the natives of India in the science and literature of Europe was the establishment in 1816 of the Hindu College. This celebrated institution owes its origin to the exertions of Sir Edward Hyde East, David Hare, and Raja Rammohun Roy. When the native community of Calcutta were roused to consider the plan for the establishment of a *Maha*

Bidyalaya (i.e. great seat of learning) as the Hindu College was originally termed, it was found that many of the orthodox Hindus held aloof from the plan, and refused to cooperate in any movement with Raja Rammohun Roy. Rammohun Roy accordingly, with a magnanimity worthy of his noble character, retired from the management of the proposed institution. Self-denial such as this is almost unknown in Calcutta, for he was the earliest advocate of the establishment of the Collage, and was eminently fitted by the gifts of nature, by his high position, wise discretion, deep learning, and earnest patriotism, to develope and carry out his own project. He was willing nevertheless to be laid aside, if by suffering rather than by acting he could benefit his country.

The Hindu College was for many years under native management. In 1823, the funds were so low that application was made to Government for aid; which was liberally conceded. The capital of the College moreover was reduced to Rupees 21,000 by the failure in 1827 of Baretto's house in which it was deposited. The income accordingly fell to less than Rs. 100 a month. Government supplemented the rest with ever increasing liberality, but till 1841, when its contribution was Rs. 30,000 a year, took but little share in the management. The Hindu College therefore is seldom mentioned in the controversies which raged in the Committee of Public Instruction concerning the management of Government schools.

This Committee was established in1823 by the Governor-General in Council, and in the instructions addressed to its members, the object of their appointment is stated to be the "considering and from time to time submitting to Government the suggestion of such measures as it may appear expedient to adopt with a view to the better instruction of the people, to the introduction of useful knowledge, including the sciences and arts of Europe, and to the improvement of their moral character."

The institutions placed under its charge were the Arabic College at Calcutta, and the Sanskrit College at Benares. The Calcutta College was established in 1781 by Warren Hastings, who at his own expense supplied a school house. Government gave lands yielding about Rs. 30,000 a year, and designed the/217/ college for instruction in the principles and practice of Mahomedan law. The Benares College was projected by Mr. Jonathan Duncan, the Resident at that city, in 1791, with a view to "endear our Government to the native Hindus, by our exceeding in our attention to them and their systems the care ever shown by their own native princes." Lord Cornwallis in 1791 assigned for the support of the College Rupees 14,000 a year, afterwards increased to Rupees 20,000.

On their foundation the College at Calcutta and Benares were placed under native management, and abuses of the grossest kind soon became universal. Mr. Lushington says in his work on the Charities of Calcutta that "The Madrussa was almost useless for the purposes of education;" and that "its ample resources were dissipated among the superior and subordinate drones of the establishment." In 1820, Dr. Lumsden was appointed Secretary and, under his charge, abuses were checked and many reforms in discipline and study were introduced.

After the departure of Mr. Duncan, the early years of the Benares College were remarkable only for an utter absence of instruction and order. Gigantic misappropriations of funds were made by the first Rector, styled by the wonderful name of Sero Shastri Gooroo Tarkalankar Cashinath Pundit Juder Bedea Behadur, Mr. Brooke, the Governor-General's Agent suggested improvements which were with some amendments carried out by Mr. W.W. Bird in 1812. In 1820, Captain Fell was appointed Secretary and Superintendent, and under him the College attained the reputation for Sanskrit learning that it has since maintained.

With these two institutions the General Committee of Public Instruction commenced its labours. The Sanskrit College at Calcutta was opened by it in 1824; the Delhi College was opened in 1825, for instruction in Arabic, Persian and Sanskrit. The Allahabad School was opened in 1834, and encouragement was given to private Schools at Bhagulpore, Sagar, Midnapore. & c.

In 1834, the operations of the Committee were brought to a stand by an irreconcileable difference of opinion as to the principles on which Government support to education should be administered. Half of the Committee called the "Orientalists" were for the continuation of the old system of stipends tenable for twelve or fifteen years to students of Arabic and Sanskrit, and for liberal expenditure on the publication of works in those languages. The other half called the "Anglicists" desired to reduce the expenditure on stipends held by "lazy and stupid school boys of 30 and 35 years of age,"/218/ and to cut down the sums lavished on Sanskrit and Arabic printing. At this juncture, Government requested the Committee to prepare a scheme of instruction for a College at

Agra. The Committee were utterly unable to agree on any plan. Five members were in favour in Arabic, Persian and Sanskrit learning, and five in favour of English and the Vernacular, with just so much of the Oriental learned languages as would be necessary to satisfy local prejudices.

The Orientalist party consisted of the Hon'ble H. Shakespear, Messrs. H. Thoby Prinsep, James Prinsep, W.H. Macnaghten, and T.C.C. Sutherland, the Secretary of the Committee. The Anglicists were Messrs. Bird, Saunders, Bushby, Trevelyan, and J.R. Colvin.

Of this Committee, Sir W.H. Maonaghten became Envoy in Afghanistan and was assassinated there, and the Hon'ble J.R. Colvin died during the mutinies at Agra. James Prinsep is immortalized by his Sanskrit discoveries, and Sir Charles Travelyan still remains alive, beloved and honoured. He deserved, though he did not obtain, for his zealous educational labours in Bengal, the love he has won for his Government at Madras.

Over this Committee, Macaulay on his arrival in India was appointed President, but he declined to take on active part in its proceedings, till the decision of the Supreme Government should be given on the question at issue. The letters of the two parties in the Committee setting forth at great length their opinions, and bearing date the 21st and 22nd January, 1835, came before Macaulay in his capacity of Legislative Member of the Supreme Council, and on them he wrote his minute of the 2nd February, which was followed on the 7th March by Lord Bentinck's decision of the case in favour of the English language. Soon after this decision many new Members were added to the Committee, among whom may be mentioned Sir Edward Ryan, Mr. Ross D. Mangles, Mr. C.H. Cameron, Colonel James Young, Baboo, now Raja Radha Kant Deb,Baboo Rossomoy Dutt, Mr. C.W. Smith, Captain, now General Sir J.R.H. Birch, and Dr. Grant, Sir Benjamin Malkin was added at a later time.

The business of the Committee was chiefly conducted by minute books. The minutes of Sir Charles Trevelyan are very elabroate. He was indefatigable in the cause of education, and had something to say on every subject. Macaulay's minutes are neither so numerous nor so long as Trevelyan's. Threefourths of his opinions on the proposals submitted by Mr. Sutherland, the Secretary, are conveyed in the concise expressions "I approve," "I do not object," "I would decline the offer,"&c. /219/

Should some of the opinions of Macaulay concerning expenditure appear unnecessarily harsh and niggardly, it must be remembered that the sum available for English education was but the pittance that could be saved by reductions in the oriental assignments, and that it was right for him to spend with strict frugality, what was gained at the cost of many painful struggles.

It is often said that if a person cannot write fived lines of English without blots and corrections, he must be a very poor scholar indeed. Now, there is no doubt that neatness and accuracy are highly desirable, and that the clear and beautiful writing and the finished style of Lord Dalhousie and of Lord Canning indicate a wonderful power in the use of language. Yet it is a great mistake to imagine that the absence of a habit of writing without corrections is a sure mark of inferiority. Scarcely five consecutive lines in any of Macaulay's minutes will be found unmarked by blots or corrections. He himself in a minute, dated 3rd November, 1835, says, "After blotting a good deal of paper I can recommend nothing but a reference to the Governor-General in Council." No member of the Committee of Public Instruction in 1835, wrote so large and uneven a hand as he, and my copyist was always able instantly to single out his writing by the multiplicity of corrections and blots which mark the page. These corrections are now exceedingly valuable, more valuable than the minutes to which they belong. They are themselves a study, and well deserve a diligent examination. When the first master of the English language corrects his own composition, which appeared faultless before, the correction must be based on the highest rules of criticism.

The great minute of the 2nd February, combines in a small compass the opinions which are expressed in nearly the same words through a score or two of detached remarks in the records. This minute was published in England in 1838, but is difficult to obtain India. I could not find it in any one of the four great Libraries of Calcutta, in the Public Library, nor in the Libraries of St. Pauls Cathedral, of the Asiatic Society, and of the Presidency College. Mr. Arbuthnot, the Director of Public Instruction in Madras, has conferred an obligation on all interested in the preservation of valuable papers by including it in one of his Reports. To rescue it from the oblivion into which it has fallen in Bengal, I add it to these unpublished minutes.

Macaulay's unpublished educational minutes are scattered among some twenty volumes of the records of the General

Committee. Four of these volumes are now lost. Some of the/220/ books were circulated among the fourteen or fifteen members of the Committee, others were sent only to Subcommittees, containing five or six members. There were Subcommittees on finance, on books, on the selection of schoolmasters, on the Medical College, and on the Hooghly College. Of the books which went the round of the whole Committee, two were reserved for particular subjects, one marked G. was for the selection and printing of books, and another marked I. for Medical College questions. The other books were kept in constant circulation, and as they came back to the Secretary, were started a fresh with precis of new topics for discussion. The same matter is consequently discussed at its different stages in different books. The General Committee seldom met. All business was transacted by the books. Several of the Members urged their opinions with greater warmth and earnestness than is now customary in official correspondence. Lord Auckland in his elaborate educational minute of the 24th November, 1839, remarks concerning their discussions, "Unhappily I have found violent differences existing upon the subject of education, and it was for a time (now I trust past or fast passing away,) a watchword for violent dissension and in some measure of personal feelings. I judged it best, under these circumstances, to abstain from what might have led me into unprofitable controversy, and to allow time and experience to act with their usual healing and enlightening influence upon general opinion."

—HENRY WOODROW

CHAPTER - V

SWAMI DAYANAND SARASWATI HIS LIFE AND WORKS

A nation grows into what it shall be by the force of that which it was in the past and is in the present, and in this growth there come periods of conscious and subconscious stock-taking when the national soul selects, modifies, rejects, keeps out of all that it had or is acquiring whatever it needs as substance and capital for its growth and action in the future: in such a period of stock-taking we are still and Dayanand was one of its great and formative spirits.

Sri Aurobindo
Bankim-Tilak-Dayanand,
pp. 36-37

Swami Dayanand Saraswati was a typical fearless social and religious reformer in the 19th century. Through his life and career he preached Indians to imbibe courage, fortitude, moral soundness, power, strength of body and mind and such other virtues as would make them independent and possessors of sovereign imperial sway. He claimed India for Indians.

Dayanand stands out by himself, with peculiar and salutary distinctness, one unique in his type and he is unique in his work. He was mystic and Yogi and could remain in *Samadhi* for 18 hours at a stretch. He would live on milk alone for days together. He remained hungry sometimes as it was not his custom to beg for food. He faced hardships and was stoned and poisoned many times. Like a true saint he forgave them. Nobel-laureate Romain Rolland, Sri Aurobindo and Sir Syed Ahmed Khan paid him rich tributes for his character, wisdom, strong will and courage.

Dayanand's message was 'Back to the Vedas' and to lay the foundations of society on them. His interpretation of the Vedas was not only scientific and rational but also this was surely a master glance of practical intuition on his part, for, in a real sense, the Vedas were the original source of religion, culture and civilization of India; they were the real foundations of Indian thought, philosophy and knowledge.

Born of a Brahmana family at Tankara in the State of Morvi, South Gujarat, Dayanand turned out to be a rebel and militant child of his family and the age in which he was born. His father Krashanji Laji Trivedi tried his best to prepare the child in the Shaiva traditional way. In the process Dayanand learnt certain lessons in Sanskrit grammar and some Vedic text by heart. He accompanied his father on his religious missions. He is said to have completed his formal education in 1838. His father had a banking house, a hereditary office, and he wanted Dayanand to help him in his business.

Like all other great men of the world Dayanand also passed through periods of conflict, suffering and an urge to seek the truth.

The conflict came when his faith in the traditional religious practices was shaken at the sight of a mouse dancing on the idol of Lord Shiva for whom he was made to fast. He felt that it was impossible to reconcile to the idea of an omnipotent, living god, with the idol which allowed the mouse to run over his body and polluted his image without the slightest protest from him. All his father's arguments and persuasion could not end his conflict.

Soon after, notwithstanding the best possible care, his younger sister expired. It was his first bereavement, and the shock he received was very great. He said, 'Friends and relatives were sobbing and lamenting around me but I stood like one pertified, plunged in revery.'[1] He realised that no one could escape death and he too could be snatched away any time. He asked himself: "What should I do to alleviate this human misery? Where shall I find the assurance for and means of attaining salvation? I came to a decision then and there that I would strive to find an answer to these questions, cost whatever it might, so that I could save myself from the untold miseries of the dying moments."[2]

His uncle who loved him dearly also passed away shoortly afterwards. "His death left me in a state of utter dejection and with a still profounder conviction I settled in my mind that there was nothing stable, nothing worth living for in this world."[3]

Apprehending marital wedlock, he left home in 1846 in search of truth/*Moksha*. For more than 15 years he wandered through one part of the country to the other—on the banks of the rivers, thick jungles, in the hermits of various *yogis, sadhus, sanyasis;* on the peaks of the hills to learn the science of *yoga* and through *yoga*, the *Moksha* which was his ambitions of life at that time. Ultimately he found a guru in Swami Virjananda at Mathura with whom he stayed for 3 years (1861-63). Swami Virjananda was a great grammarian. Dayanand had so far devoted himself to vedanta, *yoga* and some grammar. Perhaps it is quite possible that after his wanderings in the country and meetings with *sadhus, yogis, sanyasis* of various sects, he might have discovered that the deepest secret of religion and *moksha* lay hidden in the Hindu scriptures and as they are in Sanskrit, they could be opened only with the key of grammar. It was for this reason that he came to Virjananda, who was recognised as an established authority on grammar.[4]

During his stay with Swami Virjananda, besides mastering the *Ashtadhyayi, Mahabhashya, Nirukta, Nighantu,* which provided him with the key to unlock the treasury of the Vedas, Dayanand learnt to control his body and mind through yogic powers.

Having finished his studies, Dayanand made customary offerings of cloves, so dear to Swami Virjananda, as *dakshina* to his teacher, saying that he was a poor man and could not offer anything except that. Virjananda's reaction to it was indeed wonderful. He observed: "I demand from you something else as a dakshina. Take a vow before me that so long as you live you will work incessantly to spread true knowledge of the *Vedas* and the *Arsha-granthas* and condemn works which teach false doctrines and tenets; and that you will even give your life if necessary in re-establishing the Vedic religion. Dayanand bowed and vowed "*Tathastu*—so it be."[5]

"This is my *dakshina.*" True to his word Dayanand fulfilled his vow to the last breath of his life.

After taking leave of his *gure,* Dayanand came to Agra in April 1863 and stayed here for two years passing most of his time in practising yoga and studying the *Vedas* and *shastras* thus preparing himself for the mission for which he had pledged himself before his *guru* Swami Virjananda.

Dayanand visited almost every part of India from Cape Comorin to the Himalayas and from Calcutta to Bombay. He was a man with a poweful intellect and social conscience. He challenged traditional beliefs and rituals. His personality and teachings affected the lives of millions of people.[6] He denounced evils and vulgarities spread by the vested interests in the name of religion. Vedas in hand he challenged the Hindu orthodoxy to prove if they could justify on their basis polytheism, pantheonism, idol worship, casteism, untouchability, infant marriage, forced widowhood, *sati*, infanticide and numerous other superstitions degenerating Hinduism. The whole front line and the reserve of orthodoxy came forward to silence him, but Dayanand brought them to their knees.[7]

After socio-religious work of reform in the Hindu society, Dayanand's next concern was to arouse national consciousness among his people. He was, undoubtedly, one of the major figures of India's national resurgence. Some of the writers strongly feel that the events of 1905 in Bengal was a direct impact of Dayanand's teachings.[8]

Throughout his life Dayanand endeavoured to purge the humanity of the prevalent social and religious evils. He was a visionary who looked far ahead of his times and visualized a society based on social justice, equality of opportunity and political freedom. He was of the view that character of the nation was the real foundation on which the superstructure of political uplift could be built.

He aimed at regeneration of the Indians and though Indians the whole humanity. He tried to expound Truth and to bring the followers of all religions together on one platform. He worked hard to make them free from malice. He generated the feelings of love and worked for their welfare and peaceful world existence.

Although charges are made against him that his attack on other religions had done more harm than good to the Indian society, but researchers in the field have absolved Dayanand of these charges because he never rejected that was good in other religions and never spared Hinduism of its social evils. Dayanand felt that there were learned men in all religions and if they could give up prejudices, accept all these broad principles on which all religions were unanimous, reject differences and behave affectionately towards each other, much good would be done to the world, the miseries of the people would decrease and usher an era of happiness.[9]

Dayanand is often blamed that he criticized the different religions and the different sects of Hindu society. However, his main aim was to criticize not only those elements in different religions which led the masses to fight each other. He had no malice or hatred towards any religion; he simply criticized what he thought as untrue (in that religion), and wanted to bring different faiths under the banner of one universal religion. He was of the view that "all these things which are common to all religions obviously condemn false things, for they create differences in different faiths. It is my object to put clearly before public all the secrets and open things of all religions, so that all and sundry may be able to exchange their views and reach some unanimity."[10]

Dayanand strove hard to preach universal truth to bring all men under one religion so that they may, by ceasing to hate each other and firmly loving each other, live in peace and work for their common welfare.[11]

He could not be contented with mere theoretical propositions in this respect and embarked on practical ventures. He invited a conference of the representatives of almost all the religions in India on the occasion of the Delhi *Durbar,* 1877, in which Keshab Chandra Sen, Sir Sayyed Ahmad Khan, Munshi Alakhandhari and others participated. Though the conference led at that time to no practical results, yet it served a big purpose; it paved the way for the later religious parliaments and conferences working for peace and happiness of mankind.[12]

It is a strange coincidence that Dayanand was poisoned by a Hindu but was treated by a Muslim doctor, Alimardan Khan. He passed away on October 30, 1883 and cremated at Malusar Cremation Grounds, Ajmer.

> *"In the matter of Vedic interpretation, I am convinced that whatever may be the final complete interpretation, Dayanand will be honoured as the first discoverer of the right clues. Amidst the chaos and obscurity of old ignorance and age-long misunderstanding his was the eye of direct vision that pierced to the truth and fastened on that which was essential. He has found the keys of the doors that time had closed and rent asunder the seals of imprisoned fountains."*

Sri Aurobindo
Bankim-Tilak-Dayanand,
pp. 44.

Dayanand was a widely travelled and well read person. During his life-time he had held many discourses and held many *shastrathas* with the followers of other faiths such as Christians, Muslims, orthodox Hindus and many others; he wrote many books, pamphlets and tracts on religious rituals. His work included around 26 books, besides a number of minor unpublished works, a number of published lectures and reports, and his personal correspondence.

In 1863 he published his first work *Sandhya* (I) after completing his studies with Swami Virjananda. *Bhagavata-Khandanam* (2) was published in 1864 and distributed at the *Kumbha Mela*, Hardwar. It rejected the Bhagavata as *Unarsha* work. *Advaita-mat-Khandanam* (3) denounced the doctrine of non-duality of Shankaracharya's *Advaita*. It was followed by *Satyarth Prakash* (4) which was originally written in Hindi. It has been translated into many Indian and foreign languages. It is divided into two parts, its first part gives rules for a positive life, while the second part analyses the falsities in various religions.

Describing the five *yajnas* to be performed daily, Dayanand published *Panchamahayajna vidhi.* (5)

Veda-Viruddha-mat-Khandnam (6) was originally written in Sanskrit. Shyamji Krishna Varma translated it in Gujarati and Bhimsen into Hindi. This work denounces idol-worship, belief in *avatars,* etc. It refutes the tenets of the Vallabhachari and other Vaishnava sects.

Vedanti-dhwanta-nivarana (7) is available in English also. It gives the meanings and expositions of the four principal aphorisms on which the neo-Vedantists rely to prove the oneness of God and Soul. This study refutes their contention and cites *Brahmans, Upanishads.*

Shikshapatri-dhwanta-nivarana (8) came as a reaction to *Shikshapatri* written by the founder of the Swami Narayan sect, *Aryabhivinaya* (9) gives *mantras* from all the four Vedas. It is a book of prayer and is translated in English.

Sanskaravidhi (10) was compiled to help people to perform properly the sixteen rites from conception to death.

Rigvedadi-bhashya-bhumika (11) discusses the origin and subject matter of the Vedas. It was written in Sanskrit and Hindi and is also translated in English.

Bhranti-nivarana (12) is a sample of *Rigveda* commentary.

Aryaddeshya Ratnamala (13) contains definitions and expositions of 100 such terms as one generally comes across in reading Hindu philosophy and Dayanand's works.

Vedabhashya (14) is a monumental work. This helps in understanding the method of Vedic interpretation adopted by Dayanand.

Autobiography (15) was written in Hindi and was published in an English translation in the *Theosophist* issues of October and December 1879 and November 1880. Dr. K.C. Yadav has in 1976 brought about a scholarly and scientific version of it, published by Manohar Book Service, New Delhi.

Ashtadhyayi-Bhashya (16) is a commentary on the famous grammarian Panini's *Ashtadhyayi*.

Gotama-Ahalya ki Katha (17) is a re-interpretation of the legend of Gotama—Ahalya, quite different from the versions available in the *Puranas*.

Sanskrit vakya Prabodh (18) is an aid to learn and talk in Sanskrit. *Vyavaharbhanu* (19) deals with various popular and everyday topics. These teachings are supported by interesting anecdotes and incidents.

Bhramochchhedan (20) is a reply to Raja Shivprasad *Sitar-e-Hind* of Benares's objections to Swamiji's *Rigvedadi-bhashya-bhumika*.

Anubhramochchedan (21) was published as a rebuttal, when Raja Shivaprasad published an answer to Swamiji's *Bhramochchhedan*.

Vedanga Prakash (22) published in 14 parts shows the different ways in which the grammar of the Vedic Sanskrit and that of classical Sanskrit deal with various grammatical matters.

Gokarunanidihi (23) pleads for the protection of cows in particular and other animals in general. It is available in English also.

Some of his important discourses and lectures published are *Shastrarha* (24), *Shastrartha Hugli* (25) published in Bengali; later a Hindi version was published under the title of *Pratima-Pujan-Vichar. Poona-Pravachana* (26) was first published in Marathi, later it was translated into Gujarati. Its Hindi version is known as *Upadesh Manjari*. *Shastrartha-Bareilly* (27) was first published under the title *Satya-satya-viveka* in Urdu. *Shastrartha-Ajmer* (28) was published both in Hindi and Urdu in *Aryadarpan* of Ajmer. *Shastrartha-Masuda* (29) was published in *Desh-Hitaishi* of Ajmer. *Shastrartha-Udaipur* was published by Pandit Lekhram in his biography of Dayanand.

There are also a number of letters and notices in printed form. Prominent among these are *Rishi Dayananda Ka Patravyavahar* (30), *Rishi Dayanand Saraswati ke Patra aur Vijnapan* (31), *Rishi Dayanand Saraswati Ke Patra aur Vijnapanan ke Parishisht* (32), *Rishi Dayanand ke Patra aur Vijnapan* (33), Vol. I, and *Rishi Dayanand ke Patra aur Vijnapan* (34), Vol. II.

From the study of the life and works of Swami Dayanand Saraswati, it is found that his manner of working was very different. Here was one who did not infuse himself informally into the indeterminate soul of things, but stamped his figure indelibly as in bronze on men and things. Here was one whose formal works are the very children of his spiritual body, children, fair and robust and full of vitality, the image of their creator. Here was one who knew definitely and clearly the work he was sent to do, chose his materials, determined his conditions with a sovereign clairvoyance of the spirit and executed his conception with the puissant mastery of the born worker.

Dayanand seized on all that entered into him, held it in himself, masterfully shaped it there into the form that he saw right and threw it out again into the forms that he saw to be right. That which strikes us in him as militant and aggressive, was a part of his strength of self-definition. He was not only plastic to the great hand of Nature, but asserted his own right and power to use Life and Nature as plastic material....

On the basis of his deep study of the *Vedas, Upanishadas* he ridiculed the incompatible tradition that Vedas were merely the Mythological and ritual books; he proved that these were the authoritative revelation and inspired Book of Knowledge, the source of all sanctions and standard of all truth.

Dayanand brought back an old Aryan element into the Indian national character.[13]

REFERENCES

1. K.C. Yadav, *Autobiography of Dayanand Saraswati,* New Delhi, 1976, p.17.
2. *Ibid.*
3. *Ibid.*
4. Ganga Ram Garg, *World Perspectives on Swami Dayanand Saraswati,* New Delhi, 1984, p. 13.
5. K.C. Yadav, *op. cit.,* f.n. 100.

6. Tribute paid by Smt. Indira Gandhi, the then Prime Minister of India, on the occasion of the Nirvana Centenary Celebrations of Swami Dayanand Saraswati, Ibid. p. ix.
7. K.C. Yadav, *op. cit.*, p. 3.
8. A.D. Rein Court, *The Soul of India,* London, 1961, p. 236. Quoted in K.C. Yadav, *op. cit,* p. 6, f. n. 20.
9. *Satyartha PraKash,*Introduction, pp. I-X.
10. *Ibid.*
11. Haridas Bhattacharya (ed.), *The Cultural Heritage of India,* Vol. IV, Calcutta, 1956, p. 635.
12. *Ibid.*
13. Sri Aurobindo, *Bankim-Tilak-Dayanand,* pp. 32-44.

—RAJ KUMAR

CHAPTER - VI

THE MYSORE-MARATHA RELATIONS

A serious controversy arose in 1785 over the right of Tipu to enhance the annual tribute from one of his Zamindars, the Desai of Nargund, which finally led to the Mysore-Maratha War of 1784-87. Narguan is a small principality in the north of Mysore, and it was conquered in 1778 by Haidar who compelled its chief, Venkata Rao Bhave, a Brahmin Desai, to pay an annual tribute and acknowledge the supremacy of Mysore.[1] Nana Phadnis conferred the right of Haidar over the principality by the arrangements of 1780, whereby a powerful confederacy of Indian powers had been formed against the British. This Confederacy, however, did not last long, and the British machinations successfully dissolved it in 1782 by theTreaty of Salbai. After the Mysore War Tipu turned his attention to the settlement of his affairs in the different parts of his territories, and observed that Nargund deserved his attention more than any other part.

During the Mysore War with the British, Tipu had noticed that the Desai of Nargund had indulged frequently in subversive activities aganist Mysore. He had not reconciled himself to a subordinate position of a tibutary to Mysore, and ever since the conquest of his principality, he had not ceased to look upon the Peshwa as his Overlord. He had secretly carried on hostile correspondence with influential persons at Poona to seek their support against Mysore. His minister, Kolapant Pethe, had instigated the Maratha chiefs to invade Nargund and recover all the lands south of the Krishna.[2] He addressed a letter to Chintana Rao Patwardhan to seize the opportunity of Haidar's death for the invasion of Mysore.[3] When the Marathas did not respond favourably to his instigations, he turned to the English, knowing well their enmity towards Mysore. He opened correspondence with them and pretending himself to be an independent chief, he offered them his cooperation against his own master. He applied to the

Bombay Government through an Englishman under his service, named Yoon, for the assistance of some British troops for invading Mysore from the north.[4] Had this application been made a little earlier when the English were still at war with Tipu, it would have led to a very embarrassing situation for Tipu, but it was made at a time when the English were negotiating at Madras for a separate peace with Tipu, and hence no notice was taken by Bombay of Desai's overtures.

Besides these subversive activities, the Desai had offended Tipu in other respects as well. He had excited the peaceful subjects of Mysore to rise in revolt. He had induced the neighbouring Poligars of Punganooru Madanapalli and other places to rise their contumacious heads. He, attacked the fort of Sedum in the district of Garramaconda and had "opened the doors of fraud and treachery on the peasants of the Country".[5] Despite the pressing demands, he had evaded the payment of the usual tribute to Mysore, and was two years in arrears. He had hoped that Tipu would not compel him to pay the tribute, because he belonged to a powerful group of the Marathas, namely the Patwardhan, who would assist him in case he chose to break his connections with Tipu.[6] He kept Poona Court continuously informed of all the developments in Nargund and tried to embitter the Mysore-Maratha relations.

Owing to these hostile activities, Tipu felt justified that he should threaten the Zamindar in order to keep him loyal to Mysore. Therefore as a punishment he thought of a device which would hit the Desai in two respects, one by the enhancement of the annual tribute, and the other by the peremptory demand for the payment of the arrears of two years. The activities of the Desai had gone on unchecked for these years, because Tipu was engaged in a war against the English. After the conclusion of the Treaty of Mangalore, he decided to take action against him. When Tipu demanded the arrears, the Desai refused to pay them. On the other hand he immediately sought the help of the Poona Government and complained that Tipu had arbitrarily enhanced the tribute on him. Tipu knew that Nana could not stand aloof in view of the Desai's relations with the Patawardhans. Therefore, he despatched two envoys, Muhammad Ghiyas Khan and Noor Mohamed Khan, to the Poona Court to explain the true state of affairs and to prevent Nana from taking sides with the Desai. Tipu's intention was to give the Poona Government a chance to bring the Desai to reason. If he still persisted in his attitude, there was no alternative but to chastise him. The Sultan felt, "If a petty Zamindar and a subject of our Government like this may not be punished, how shall our authority be maintained?"[8] The justice of his case was admitted even by Rao Rasta, a Maratha Sardar, at the Poona Court.

But the Poona Government without enquiring fully into the facts of the case declared that the demand made by Tipu was much more than the usual tribute realized in the past Nana expressed the view that Tipu had absolutely no right to make any arbitrary and exorbitant demand. Added to this he quoted the convention that guided the exaction of tributes from the Brahmin tributaries—"that Jagirdhars on the transfer of districts were liable to no additional payments and that the *rights of Sawasthanas* who had been guilty of no treason against the State to which they owed allegiance had been invariably respected".[9] Here Nana ignored the fact that the Zamindar had been actually guilty, according to Tipu, of high treason for he was virtually exhausting all means to subvert Tipu's power. Therefore, far from solving the problem Nana's interference complicated the issue. Tipu would not submit to a declaration which would diminish this authority in the eyes of the Desai. He replied that his authority would be at an end if a foreign power intervened in his internal affaris, and that he had every right to levy whatever he chose from his subjects. Besides, even according to the general principle enunciated by Nana with respect to the Brahmin Zamindars, the Desai deserved chastisement as he was actually guilty of treason against the State, and that his past record was one of continuous disloyalty towards Tipu. Therefore, Tipu said that he was not bound to respect the "rights of Sawasthanees". Despite these excesses Tipu was willing to excuse the Desai if the latter were to make "due compensations for the injury sustained by our dominions and payment of the arrears due by him for several years past".[10] These terms were not acceptable to Nana, and the refusal precipitated the situation to a showdown.

Having failed in peaceful persuasions to bring round the Desai, Tipu wished to try force. He sent his comander Syed Ghaffar to enquire into the conduct of the Chief, and it was reported that the Desai was instigated by Parasaram Bhao into contumacious design. Tipu was informed that a serious rebellion was brewing, and that speedy action was imperative. Therefore, Tipu detached two separate bodies of troops to threaten the Desai who still offered a chance to submit.[11] But the Desai chose to resist expecting help from the Marathas. He fought bravely for a time. The fort was besieged by the Mysore troops, and the Desai was daily expecting help from the Marathas. When Parasaram Bhao came to know of the attack he urged Nana immediately to send relief.[12]

Though Nana was willing to assist the Nargund Chief, he was prevented from precipitate action by the distraced state of the Maratha affairs. He sent orders to the Maratha commanders not to precipitate hostilities, as the preparations for war were not fully completed. The presence also of Tipu's *vakils* in the Poona court had the effect of refraining Nana from any hasty action. Nana seemed conciliatory and hoped to settle the dispute peacefully. The *Vakils* convinced him of the equally pacific intentions of their master.[13] But contrary to the orders of Nana, a party of the Maratha troops made a premature attack on Tipu's army and it was repulsed with great loss.[14] Nana was put to an embarrassing situation, and he decided to retrieve the Maratha prestige by the immediate despatch of Parasaram Bhao and Ganesh Pant Behro with a considerable force to the relief of Nargund. Nevertheless, he took the precaution of instructing Bhao to avoid hostilities of Tipu's commanders had raised the siege. Nana contacted Tipu also, expressed his concern over the affair and desired accommodation. Tipu was equally well-disposed the solve the dispute peacefully, and would go a step further by offering to pay two years of tribute to Poona Government if his sovereignty over Nargund was recognized by Nana.[15] His *vakils* at the Maratha court were actually in possession of this cash to remit in case a settlement was feasible.[16] Tipu was willing to raise the siege if the Desai agreed to pay the arrears and some compensations for the ravages. The siege was actually raised, and the commander of Tipu's forces, Burhanuddeen, withdrew from Nargund. The cause for the relinquishment of the siege was not so much the scarcity of water, which has been made out to be the main cause by Grant Duff, but the anxiety of Tipu to settle the dispute peacefully. Rao Raste, the Maratha Chief who was well-disposed to Tipu at the Poona Court, was instrumental in persuading Tipu to take these measures.[17] Such a step would have brought about a negotiated settlement in which Raste would have played a major part, but Nana was not willing to allow any enhancement of Raste's prestige. Moreover, Nana was advised that Tipu had raised the siege not out of any desire for peaceful settlement of the dispute, but on the approach of a powerful body of Maratha troops, and that Burhanuddeen was not capable of prosecuting the siege. Nana, however, informed Bhao that as the siege was actually raised, nothing should be done to provoke Tipu's troops to further hostilities and ordered him to evacuate the Desai and his minister to some place of safety, but they refused to be evacuated.[18] Contrary to the orders of Nana, Bhao and Ganesh Pant fell on Tipu's troops, but were once again repulsed.[19] Nana was highly displeased with this action and reprimanded the Maratha commanders. But to cover the loss of face he sent Tokoji Holker with a big force and busied himself in preparing for a major campaign.[20]

Thus a situation was brought about where an armed clash became inevitable. If both sides had acted with restraint and moderation, the clash could have been averted. Tipu's *vakils* had long been at Poona Court professing pacific intentions of their master. They had been specially deputed to settle the Nargund dispute. They possessed ready cash to be remitted as a proof of Tipu's sincerity of friendly relations. The *Vakils* were willing to pay two years of tribute to the Peshwa if Tipu's claim to the fort of Nargund was accepted. It appeared quite reasonable to Nana and as a temporary measure he consented to the proposal. He allowed a period of 27 days for the *vakils* to obtain the approval of their master for the payment of the amount.[21] It looked as if a peaceful solution was at last worked out.

But it was more a delusion than a reality. The differences were too deep to be resolved by mere professions of peaceful intentions on the part of both parties. The negotiations failed because Tipu realized that the Marathas were committed to hostilities sooner or later. They had not reconciled themselves to the loss of their possessions in the north of Mysore which Haidar had acquired at a time when the Marathas had fallen into a spell of internal disputes. A number of other factors had further estranged the relations between Mysore and the Marathas. When a general Confederacy of Indian powers had been organized in 1780, in the Formation of which the Marathas had taken active part, but in the execution of which the Mysoreans had played the most dominant part, the Marathas were the first to conclude a separate peace with the English, thus stabbing the Confederates in the back. Mysore was left all alone to bear the full brunt of the English attack. Added to insult, the Marathas had agreed to join hands with the English in compelling Mysore to come to terms with the English. In the event of refusal on the part of Mysore, the Marathas had agreed to send a force to northern parts of Mysore and join the British in other sectors in compelling Tipu to sue for peace. But there was one exception when Nana would restrain from joining the English. If the Mysoreans were to evacuate the territories in the north of Tungabhadra and surrender these to the Marathas, Nana had told them that he would not only continue the English war with renewed vigour, but also would compel Sindhia to revoke his treaty with the English and secure his cooperation for the alliance.[22] Here the intentions of the Marathas are quite clear that the recovery of their lost possessions was more important to them than fighting the British who had wrought such havoc in the country. An offensive alliance between the Marathas and the English was actually concluded on 28 October 1783 through the mediation of Sindhia, and Tipu knew very well that he had to face sooner or later a combined attack of the British and the Marathas. With this intention he concluded a separate peace with the English at Mangalore. This was a serious diplomatic blow to the Marathas, for they had been recognized as the principals in the war, and it was only through them that a general peace should have been concluded. When a separate peace was concluded ignoring their presence, Tipu tried to over-reach them, and thus excited their jealousy all the more. Tipu was claiming to be equal, although the Southern powers including the English had expected that after Haidar's death, Tipu would be so weak as to allow all other powers to realise their respective aims. But he belied their expectations and concluded the Treaty of Mangalore which was a diplomatic victory for him and which had disappointed the Marathas in their aim to recover the northern parts. Tipu had emerged with enhanced prestige after the Mysore war which excited the jealousy of his neighbours.

Tipu on the other hand should have acted with great caution after his successful conclusion of the war with the English, if his prime object was to eliminate the British from the contest for power in India. But he was also led to pursue narrow and selfish aim of asserting his right over a petty zamindar. Whatever legal and political justifications there might have been to punish a recalcitrant zamindar, there was no need to reduce a principality by incurring the displeasure of a powerful neighbour whose co-operation was essential to check the British expansion in India. But the Indian powers lost sight of national interests in the pursuit of their policy of self-aggrandisement. The case of Nargund is a typical example of how the Indians were unwilling to subordinate their petty quarrels even in the face of grave danger from an external power. Tipu decided to withhold the payment of money to Nana thinking that his money would be utilised for war preparations against him, but the payment of this amount alone would have prevented the Marathas from breaking off negotiations. Tipu was now anxious to capture Nargund before the commencement of the monsoons, and before the approach of the Confederate army, which was being hurriedly rushed to the scene. For a long time the Marathas and the Nizam were negotiating for an alliance which had a fair chance of successful conclusion at that time. From Tipu's stand point it would be an enormous loss of prestige if he was unable to assert his right over a petty zamindar. As the confederates had not put their armies in the field Nana appeared to be conciliatory, but in the confused politics of the period it was difficult to expect any consistent policy from any power.

The unprovoked attack of Parasaram Bhao on the Mysore forces gave Tipu the pretest to recommence the suspended operations against Nargund and the fort was heavily invested. Kolapant was given one more chance to surrender but he refused being directed by the Poona Government.[22] Tipu's troops pressed the siege and the garrison surrendered on terms of capitulation.[23] The garrison consisted of about 1650 men all of whom were set free by the orders of Tipu except the Desai and his minister.[24] They secured their release only after the closure of the Mysore-Maratha War in 1787. Within a short period not only Nargund but also a number of other small principalities such as Kittur, Hoskote, Dodvadi, Khanpur and Sedam were subjugated by Tipu and the territories were incorporated in Mysore. The action hastened the formation of the Confederacy between the Marathas and the Nizam, and it finally led to the war that lasted for two years. Thus the question of Nargund was the main cuase for this war.

REFERENCES

1. Grant Duff. *History of the Marathas,* Vol. III, p. 2
2. Khare, *Aitihasik Lekha Sangraha,* Vol. VII, No. 2667.
3. Ibid, No. 2668.
4. Duff. *History of the Marathas,* Vol. III, p. 3.
5. Kirmani, *Nishan-e-Haidari,* p. 283.
6. Khare. *Aithihasik Lekha Sangraha,* Vol. VII. No. 3893.
7. Kirkpatrick, *Select Letters of Tipu Sultan,* Letter No. 3.

8. Ibid.
9. Duff. *History of the Marathas,* Vol. III, p. 3.
10. Kirkpatrick. No. 27.
11. Kirmani, *Nishan-e-Haidari,* p. 286-7.
12. Khare. *Aithihasik Sangraha,* Vol. VIII, p. 3894.
13. Krikpatrick. *Select Letters,* No. 15.
14. Grant Duff. Vol. III, p. 4.
15. Ibid.
16. Kirkpatrick. *Select Letters,* No. 15.
17. Ibid.
18. Khare. *Aithihasik Lekha Sangraha,* No. 2820.
19. Ibid, No. 2838.
20. Forrest. *Selections; Maratha Series* Vol. I, p. 518.
21. Duff. Vol. III, p. 4.
22. Khare, Vol. VII, No. 3657.
23. Khare, Vol. VII, No. 2856.
24. Ibid, No. 2869.
25. Ibid, Nos. 2861-2870.

—DR. B. SHEIK ALI

CHAPTER - VII

ANNIE BESANT'S POLITICAL IDEOLOGY IN INDIA

(A STUDY IN INTER-CULTURAL INTERACTION)

Annie Besant propounded an ideology in India based upon the deeper fundamentals of the oriental and western political philosophy and culture. Culture, according to her, was the imprint on the mind of certain forms of knowledge, and was based on them. Unlike education, culture was not the drawing out and training of faculty, but was the result of the exercise of faculties on subjects which aroused sympathetic emotions and imaginations broadening the mind, eliminating personal, local and racial prejudices, acquiring an understanding of human nature in its many aspects, and developing the life-side rather than the form-side of creatures, hence the quick internal response to other lives, and the intuition of the unity of life beneath the diversity of life-expression.[1]

When Annie Besant arrived on the Indian scene in 1893, the country, in common with many other nations, was faced with the problem of adapting and adjusting her ancient cultural heritage to a set of new rapidly altering conditions brought about by immense technological changes.

THE CULTURAL CRISIS

During this period of transition of the Indian history and culture, the creation of a civilization, a true civic order which man could express the collective and individual goals of the good life and set about their realization, stood as the greatest political challenge. The very conception of such a civilization postulated the supersession of the politically disintegrative principles of the industrial revolution by a new politics built upon human needs and functions rather than upon property relationships and industrial needs.

The Industrial Revolution had launched the west upon a wild cultural adventure whose like, measured in turmoil, rapidity of chage, population growth, war, revolution, and the exploitation of resources, the world had never before seen. Among developments of particular significance in politics were two innovations of the modern world; political parties and ideologies.

The scientific revolution carried an import no less disruptive than that of the Industrial Revolution. As a result of it some very direct questions posed themselves:

(1) was there a basis for a development in social classes comparable to that which accompanied the Industrial Revolution?

(2) was there a basis for ideological developments similar to those that accompanied the Industrial Revolution?

Both questions were speculative in the extreme. The most that could be done was to debate the possibilities of the future in the light of the happenings of the past. This required taking a retrospective look at the problem of ideologies and social classes as they first developed.[2]

According to Marx, ideologies developed dialectically out of the conflict between objectively distinct social classes. Objectively distinct classes were said to develop out of relationship to property and production. This idea worked fairly well in explaining European politics. It suggested that medieval aristocracy became threatened by the rising middle classes. The aristocracy responded by developing defensive doctrines proclaiming its own intrinsic governing superiority as the proper guardian of the providential virtue embodied in long-established social institutions. The ebullient middle class replied with its own doctrine of individualism, freedom of economic opportunity, the career open to talent, representative democracy, and criticism of the evil of restrictive social and political barriers. Spokesmen for the newly created working class rallied at their oppression by the middle class, proclaming that the workers should do the same thing to their bosses that the bosses had done to the aristocrats. They criticised the industrial system and demanded that society recognized their right to a fairer share of the goods they produced.[3]

Every social system tends to produce its own belief system or ideology—that is, a body of defensive and conservative beliefs supporting the established goals of the society and explaining away any deviations from those goals as temporary and transient lapses.

The historical European ideologies that surfaced were those of conservatism, liberalism and socialism. As Marx said, they were indeed the products of social classes. But more than that they were products of the way the social systems of 19th century Europe led the three classes (the medieval aristocracy, the middle classes and the working classes) to compete against each other for political power and popular following. The mere presence of an industrial order was not by itself sufficient to produce social classes and ideologies like those native to 19th century Europe. This was seen from the American example, where a rampant industrial society developed without producing the class system or the ideologies typical of Europe.[4]

In both cases a form of imperialism was at work, holding down nations in a self-perpetuating pattern of cultural stagnation just as it held down the lower classes inside nations.[5]

The class revolution of the times was genuinely universal. It was anti-imperialist and it carried the same imperatives within nations as it did between them. The traditional goal of ideological politics in Europe was revolution or counter-revolution.[6]

Nineteenth century 'Capitalism' in America and twentieth century 'Socialism' in Russia and China did not really represent different types of utopianism. Both revolutions aimed at affluent materialist utopias. In the process both suffered considerable violence and injustice. It meant that the advanced industrial nations of East and west were all going through a transitional era in which the goals of the past had lost their relevance and new goals were emerging in their places. With all these built-in situations of diametric conflict, the result was a culture in which every one of the fundamental institutions was capable of being detonated at any moment and of sending explosions throughout society like a pack of fire-crackers ignited by a spark.[7]

East and West were both preoccupied with achieving the conditions of an urbanized mass consumption society. The result was a cultural crisis that pervaded the institutions of the most advanced societies and promised to spread from there throughout the entire world.[8] Annie Besant looked for a new political order that would be tranquil and yet dynamic. She desired it to be a fusion of all that was best both in the western and Indian cultures, and attempted to develop the Indian political ideology on such blending of the two cultures.

DEVELOPMENT OF INDIAN POLITICAL IDEOLOGY

As a result of the British impact, the process of cultural collaboration and conflict set in India. The pulls of caste, of community, of religion, and consciousness of one's heritage conditioned political thinking and action. However one may like to repudiate these factors as narrow and myopic, the fact remains that they accounted for the growth of political consciousness in the first two decades of the twentieth century.[9]

The earliest phase of the interaction of western ideas and traditional Indian society was marked by such features as eclecticism, mutual tolerance and appreciation of the beneficent role of British Raj. The belief began to gain ascendancy that for India's progress, the introduction of western liberal institutions was the only panacea. There was also a mild descent from the tradition, but sufficiently marked. Gradually the uncritical appreciation of British rule was short-lived. The fear of Christianisation led to the reorientation of attitudes.

There followed search for identity, and correspondingly, glorification of the ancient past; and these processes of introspection resulted in the reaffirmation of traditional values and institutions. It seemed as though there supervened some sort of cultural conflict and collaboration. In its struggle for cultural identity, each community went back to its own tradition, to its own institutions, and values.

While in one sense the elite was forward-looking in so far as the process of westernization was concerned; in another sense, it was socially and religiously conservative. This dichotomy was sharpened when men in this period became socially conservative, but politically radical.[10]

Annie Besant stepped on the shores of India at 10.24 a.m. on November 16,1893, we are told, "under the Rishis directions in furtherance of their great plan for a new spiritual impetus to meet the needs of the world."[11] She was to reawaken her true Motherland to knowledge of her age-old purpose.[12] She condemned British imperialism and advocated liberty for India. She sought for Indian ideals which would flower into the national life. She said that every country had its own ideals and the anture of thought was their generating seed. The nature of the national life grew up from them and 'sends forth the branches and bursts into the blossoms which are the products of the National Activity.[13]

Man is created by thought; and what a man thinks upon, that he becomes. So also is with Nations. India, Annie Besant explained, 'flowered out into a civilization unrivalled in the depth of its philosophy, in the spirituality of its Religion and in the perfection of the Dharma of orderly and graded individual and National life, expressing as none other has ever done that balance, that equilibrium which is yoga, that which saved her, when all the contemporaries of her splendid Nationalities have been carried away by Time's tremendous rapids. India shared their past but they did not share her future.'[14] India's secret was her culture or the ideals which created it.

ANNIE BESANT'S POLITICAL IDEOLOGY

We may now come to what Annie Besant believed to be the baslc characteristics of a sound political ideology for a nation. She said, "A national ideal to be useful must be in harmony with the national character, and must grow out of the national past. It must be a native of the soil, not an exotic."[15] Every nation, she said, had its own line of evolution, and any attempt to make it follow the line of evolution of another nation would be disastrous, even if it could be successful; as a matter of fact, any such attempt was doomed to failure, becuase it clashed with the world-plan.

Hence a political ideology of a nation, she ruged, should saturate itself with the past of the nation, distinguish clearly between "root principles" and "passing manifestations"of them, identify itself in thought and feeling with that nation, and hold up before it the ideal which appealed to all that was best in national feeling, and strengthen and reinforce all that was noble in the national intelligence. It should seek to eliminate defects, "to lop off excrescences, to moderate exuberances, but should work within definite limits, not seeking to change its particular types, but to evolve that type to its highest possible expression."[16]

From the point of political history, ideas about the nature of the state and society were equally important. Throughout the ages different views about the duties and rights of the individual and the State had been practised. The nobler ideal that was spreading amongst man was;

> "We live not to assert our rights, but do our duties, and so to make one mighty unit where each shall discharge his functions for the common good of all."

India's ancient system was founded on duty. But India during the nineteenth and twentieth centuries was strange compound of conflicting theories and ideas. It was a strange compound of an ancient nation ruled practically by a modern people. Under such circumstances, she thought, it was part of the necessity of the case that some amongst the people themselves should translate the popular grievances and point out the popular deficits,[18] so that a prudent policy could be followed. Those who had the power needed to be instructed in the knowledge of the wants of the people.

Annie Besant explained : "Therefore while, for my own part, I stand for the ideal of ancient India and look on that as a thousandfold loftier than the mushroom civilisations that have grown up in later days, nonetheless am I bound to admit that we must deal with the country as we have it, and that where you are pushed into western methods you must adopt your own methods somewhat, so as to meet the new conditions, so as to deal with the new ways of thought."[19]

A COMPARATIVE STUDY

The nature and character of the British administration in India were determined both by political ideas prevalent in the United Kingdom and by the structure of the Government of India. The attitude of Englishmen in India was thus described :

> The missionaries of English civilization in India stood openly for a policy of assimilation. Britain was to stamp her image upon India. The physical and mental distance separating East and West was to be annihilated by the discoveries of science, by commercial intercourse, and by transplanting the genius of English laws and English education. It was the attitude of English liberalism in its clear, untroubled dawn, and its most representative figure in both England and India was Macaulay.[20]

The government ideology was best explained by *The Times* London, which wrote :

> The educated classes may find fault with their exclusion from political rights. Political priviliges they can obtain in the degree in which they prove themselves deserving of them. But it was by force that India was won, and it is by force that India must be governed in whatever hands the government of the country may be vested. If we were

> to withdraw, it would be in favour of not the most fluent tongue or of the most ready pen, but the strongest arm and the sharpest sword.[21]

Annie Besant refused to subscribe to the view that India was conquered by sword, and was held by sword. She believed that India was conquered by her own sons siding with Britain against local hereditary enemies, State against State, and British astuteness used Indians to subdue Indians, and, by playing off local jealousies against each other, she conquered each State in turn.

SPIRITUALITY AS THE BASIS OF POLITICAL IDEOLOGY

Annie Besant piloted and participated in many political activities in the seventies and eighties of the nineteenth century in England. Especially her work for the Parliamentary elections of England, had given her a great insight into various aspects of practical politics. But the situation in India was different. Her views had undergone a vital change. Some of the main factors which brought about the change were : (a) Spirituality of India and her growing belief in the greatness of the Indian thought; (b) Her new-found idealism in theosophy; (c) Indo-British friendship.

It was mainly the spirituality of India which had the greatest influence on her political ideology. She believed with Havell that it would not profit India to gain the whole world and lose her own soul.[22] Invasions and even the establishment of a foreign Empire and foreign Kingdoms previous to the invasion and triumph of the East India Company in 1757 had not touched the soul or spirit of India. India had been invaded, but she had assimilated the invaders, and had enriched her own culture by theirs. Portions of her land had been conquered and occupied, but she had turned the conquerors into Indians. But the East India Company attempted to destroy the self-respect of India and jeered at her religions and traditions, it endeavoured to inculcate in them English attitudes and ideals through the study of English literature and history. Indians longed to find Liberty among the blessings of British rule, but they did not find it. After studying Indian history and assimilating its lessons, Annie Besant asserted: "We have resolved to revive the Ancient Ideas of Indian Education and Indian Culture, to make Indian Ideals the basis of Indian Civilization, renouncing the hybrid and sterile ideas of anglicised-Indianism."[23]

Annie Besant believed that the future was not with things material or mundane : it was with the things of soul and spirit,

The body dies but the soul is immortal : civilizations rise and fall, but the spirit of man lives for ever. She held that India was the land of spirituality, and a great civilization.[24] "If religion perishes here, it will perish everywhere, and in India's hand is laid the sacred charge of keeping alight the torch of spirit amid the fogs and storms of increasing materialism. It that torch drops from her lands, its flame will be trampled out by the feet of the hurrying multitudes, eager for worldly goods, and India bareft of spirituality will have no future but will pass on into darkness as Greece and Rome have passed."[25]

In her Anniversary Address in February 1900 she expressed that with the revival of spirituality alone, India could regain her greatness and behind it would follow other things, intellectual strength, material wealth, and all the other things that enter into the growth of national life.[26]

India's ancient character was predominantly spiritual, and the social polity that was its natural expression was shaped to give effect to spiritual ideas and to subordinate the lower nature to the higher, so that the nation might be the "school of souls", and growth and development of the soul might be on every hand aided and encouraged. India, even in her present low state, and despite the loss of spiritual life and the near extinction of spiritual fire, yet remained "the one country where spirituality still hovered in the very atmosphere and where external surroundings helped the soul to rise instead of fettering it to earth."[27]

In a lecture delivered in 1895. Annie Besant expressed the view that if India was agian to hold up her head among nations, India's younger children must begin to lay their own life of the Aryan type of character. These virtues were the most pronounced attributes, and their revival among the Indian youth would presage the rebuilding of the nation. Character makes destiny, and Indian destiny depends on Indian character."[28] Thus, spirituality of India became the keynote of Annie Besant's political ideology.

A THEOSOPHIST'S VISION

The second great influence was her new-found idealism in theosophy. She was convinced that an empire could be founded on brotherhood, on righteousness and on truth, and visualized an empire which was based upon peace and justice, within which a new civilization might gradually grow up, which should stand for peace, not war, cooperation, not competition, education, not cramming, comfort, not pauperism. In a licture that she delivered on "Theosophy and Imperialism", in 1902, she said;

I believe, thoroughly believe, that at the present time to this British nation the possibility of a world Empire is offered, I believe that in the cycle of evolution and the growth of the people the time has come in the vast world-history where this power of serving the world is offered to the British nation—that I believe to be true. I believe it because I am Theosophist, and have studied history in the light of occultism. How vast a destiny for Britain, how magnificent a possibility for the world, if this nation can rise to the greatness of such a destiny, if this nation can be heroic enough to hold and guide and uplift. For it would mean nothing less than a world-peace, amid which a mighty civilization might grow up greater than the past has been. It would mean to the world a federation so strong of peaceloving nations, that they would be able to impose peace upon the world because none should be strong enough to break it. And if the world is for such worldwide peace, so that the problems may be dealt with which are threatening the present civilization, and the nations may have time to look at home instead of always keeping anxious eyes abroad."[29]

Through her daily *New India,* Annie Besant advocated brotherhood and equality between the two people.[30]

Annie Besant was of the view that from the King on his throne to the poorest labourer in the street, the ideal should be the ideal of duty and service, where wisdom ruled and love inspired.[31]

FRIENDSHIP AND UNDERSTANDING

Thus, on the basis of her theosophical belief, Annie Besant worked for the possibility of establishing a world empire based on the brotherhood of man in which she believed the friendship of India and England was indispensable. Therefore, the next point which impressed itself upon her political ideology was to strengthen the bonds of friendship between the two countries.

England and India were bound together, and Annie Besant wanted to strengthen their relations on the basis of equality and brotherhood. She believed that much of the future progress of the world depended on the adjustment of relations between the conquering nation and the subject people. She pointed out that when two nations came into touch with each other, each had something to learn, especially where two such nations as India and England were concerned. India, she said, had been enjoying a high state of civilization long before the seed of western civilization were sown. Relations with such a country, she said, must necessarily be complicated and difficult but highly rewarding, Calling for mutual understanding, she said :

> I know of no greater service that can be rendered, either in this land or that, than the service of those who try to understand the question and to draw the nations closer together by wisdom, instead of driving them further apart by ignorance and by prejudice.[32]

Mrs. Besant then explained the ways in which England and India could help each other. She said that with regard to political conditions both the nations had much to learn in mutual understanding. England needed to adapt herself to the old civilization of India and her methods of thought, of rule, and social conditions even though they were utterly alien from her own conditions. She urged that changes in India, 'if it be wise to introduce, must be brought about with the greatest care, the greatest delicacy, after the longest and most careful consideration.'[33]

Therefore, while emphasizing loyalty to the British throne which stood as the "dignified symbol of a common endeavour", she gave no special place to the English people themselves as the conquering race. She fought for equality of races, friendliness and modesty among those who ruled, and self-respect among those who were ruled.

THE ECONOMIC IDEALS

Annie Besant did not overlook the economic aspects in her political ideology. She felt that the prosperity of a country through a beneficent administration revolved round the latter's financial stability, which was to be based on right economic principles. She said that the Greatest Indian leaders like Naoroji, Ranade and Gokhale had been able to do much good to the country because economics was "the fulcrum of the lever of their activities." They studied the problems of Indian finance, and had thus rendered most efficient help to the rulers. She felt the need of doing further work along these lines.

Mrs. Besant held that young Indians who were eager to jump into "the roaring sea of Indian politics should have learnt beforehand the economic trick of swimming so essential for their safety, as also to the well-being of those to whom they belonged and to whom they owed an obligation, viz. their own countrymen."[34]

The British rule in India had "given her famines and poverty and by cutting at the very roots of its indigenous economic system, by imposing modern "political economy". She said, "to impose English political economy on India was a folly, well-intended folly, but folly nonetheless,"[35] due to which India faced famines and degradation, and destruction of her arts and manufactures. She remarked that "to sell the corn in the years of plenty and to starve in the years of scarcity might be modern political economy but it was pure idiocy." Likewise the arts of India, she pointed out, depended on the social conditions of the country. The artist in India was not a man "who lived by competition, but he was utterly unable to guard himself against that."As a result, the artist was falling back into the "already well-filled agricultural ranks."[36]

Such were the questions, the rulers had to ask and understand and address themselves to. They had to understand the question of Indian taxation; they had to understand the question of taking away from India "seventeen millions a year to meet English charges." They had to consider "the expense of their Government in India and the exhorbitant salaries that were paid to English officers."[37] They had thus to understand the financial exploitation of the people of India. She said :

> It might be possible to form a band of English Experts, who whould be able to make these questions their speciality, and should have weight with the government in India, so that they could advise with wisdom, so that they could point out the most useful path by which improvement could be made.[38]

NATIONAL REGENERATION

Annie Besant believed that the basis of Indian politics should be national and indigenous. It should be based upon the revival of her ancient literature and language, by awakening the youth of the country to the Indian ideals of life, by building up the nation through encouragement of its national dress, manufactures and arts. She pointed out that reforms to be successful in India must be based upon Indian ideals practised in thought and action.[39]

While emphasizing the role of the classics in the life of a nation, she pointed out that for hundreds of years in the West the cultivation of classics, Greek and Latin, was regarded as absolutely necessary for what was called education of a gentleman, and those who were ignorant of the classics were regarded as uneducated. The training of intellect gave a certain definite strength and refinement of expression. India also had her own ancient language which lay at the root of her vernaculars, a knowledge of which opened out to her the greatest literature the world had yet produced and was of vital importance to the development of the nation.[40] She explained :

> If your mental faculties are only directed to the subjects which enable you to keep yourselves alive then you strike at the very root of the development of your nation, and you must sink lower and lower amongst the people of the world.[41]

Her belief in the common language of a nation was not merely a convenience, but was a tie which bound heart to heart and mind to mind. The idea of having a foreign language as a common language was ridiculous proposal. A common language like Sanskrit which was the language of the ancient books, and mother of vernaculars, would make men feel "the tie of brotherhood, instead of different races and tend far more to the national feeling."[42] The education of the children should be based on their ancient language and literature because 'enthusiasm in the young was easily aroused. The young were touched and moved easily by noble ideals. She saw visions of Indian independence through right education of her youth, and wrote :

> If you familiarise them with the past history of their own country, if you wake their devotion to their national faith, the time will come when they will turn away from the west to the motherland. And these boys, grown into men, shall be bound with every bond that link the Indian to his home and from such men will come the salvation of India.[43]

As the future was in the hands of the young, she believed that they should be taught Indian history, Indian literature, and Indian customs, and that would make a real nation.

Thus the entire Indian nation could be built up by the encouragement of national feeling, by maintaining traditional dress, and ways of living. This was the point, she remarked, which went to the very root of Indian revival and was not simply a matter of health, of convenience, and of economy; for the Indian dress suited the Indian climate, not only because it was light, but also because its material could go through water daily, and was more suited to a hot country than the western dress which was worn unwashed over and over again. Hence there was no reason, no common sense, which should make the Indian lay it aside, when the experience of thousands of years had shown it to be the best kind of dress for India. She pointed out the dangers of westernization.

> The inner feeling and outer expression often go together, and he who westernises his outer attire is very likely to grow western inside as well, and therefore instead of strengthening he really tends to weaken his motherland.[44]

Her political ideology was thus based upon India's religious, social, economic and national revival. The influences which shaped her political views were the spitituality of India, the Indo-British friendship and her new found idealism in theosophy for the establishment of a Commonwealth of Nations and a world Empire on the basis of equality, love and brotherhood of man. It would thus be seen that her political ideology was both wider and different than the two main political ideologies prevalent in India, viz. moderate and extremist.

It was wider in the sense that it considered in terms of the salvation of the whole world and not merely of India. Through the revival of India she wanted to elevate the whole world. India was a means but not the end. She thus thought in terms of establishing a Commonwealth of Nations and a World Empire.

Roberts of Manchester had planted the seed of Victorian Radicalism in her. It was nurtured through her contacts with Freethinkers and socialists like Bradlaugh and Bernard Shaw. Indian contacts further added spiritual dimensions to her radicalism in politics. She glorified the past of India, was intolerant of the British methods of government, stood for self-government for India, condemned the violent menas used by the Extremists and had implicit faith in the Moderates' constitutional methods Different stands worked in her and she was radical in politics, eclectic in religion, and patriotic to India's cause while being loyal to the Crown.

Annie Besant evolved a poticial ideology, which was based upon her deep understanding of the Eastern and Western cultures. Her political ideology had a social as well as a religious background. She insisted on the preservation of India's ancient tradition and culture, seeking only to adopt the western democratic culture to suit the changed Indian conditions.

To her the science of politics was an aspect of the Divine Wisdom whose principles were firmly based on the bedrock of humanity's spiritual oneness and not on expediency.

REFERENCES

1. Annie Besant, *Indian Ideals,* Madras, 1930, pp. 3-4.
   Also see Annie Besant's other works on Culture :
   (i) *Hints on the Study of the Bhagvad Gita* (1906);
   (ii) *Wisdom of the Upanishads* (1907);
   (iii) *The Path of Discipleship* (1910); and
   (iv) *The New Civilization* (1928).
2. Annie Besant, *The New Civilization,* Madras, 1928, p. 11.
3. Annie Besant, *An Autobiography,* 1933; reprinted, Madras, 1983, pp. 270-298.
   Annie Besant advocated cause of Match Makers and Dock Workers' Union and in 1885 farmed a society of friends of Russia.
4. Annie Besant, *The New Civilization,* p. 12.
5. Annie Besant, *England, India, Afghanistan, London,* 1879. She wrote against British imperial policies.
6. Annie Besant, *The New Civilization,* pp. 17-19. "The Crumbling Civilization."
7. *Ibid.,* pp. 22-23.
8. *Ibid.,* p. 101.
9. V.N. Datta, *Sita Ram Kohli Memorial Lectures,* 1977, p. 29.
10. *Ibid.*
11. *Besant Spirit Series,* Vol. XI, TPH, Madras, 1943, p. 14.
12. *Ibid.,* p. 19.
13. Annie Besant, *Indian Ideals,* p. 1.
14. *Ibid.*
15. Annie Besant, *India,* Vol. IV : *Essays and Addresses,* Madras, 1913, p. 75, Article "East and West", 1901.
16. *Ibid.,* p. 76.
17. Ibid., p. 131, Article : "The Place of Politics in the Life of a Nation", 1895.
18. *Ibid.*
19. Quoted in Eric Stoks, *The English Utilitarians and India,* Oxford, 1959, pp. xiii-xiv. Also see, K.P. Karunakaran, Indian Political Thought, 1832-1921, New Delhi, 1976, p. 16.
20. *Ibid.*
21. Government of India, *Documents on the History of Freedom Movement,* Vol. II, see Appendix C, quoted ibid.
22. Annie Besant, *Indian Ideals,* Madras, 1930 p. 86.
23. Ibid, p. 38.
24. Annie Besant, *The Path of Discipleship,* Madras, 1980, p. 20.

25. Annie Besant, *Indian Ideals,* p. 1, Article : "India's Mission Among Nations."
26. Ibid., p. 166, "Anniversary Address", February 1900.
27. Ibid., p. 5,"The Aryan Type", 1895.
28. *The Path of Discipleship,* p, 124.
29. Ibid., pp. 197-98 "Theosophy and Imperialism."
30. Quoted in Raj Kumar, *Annie Besant : Rise to power in Indian Politics, 1914-17,* New Delhi, 1981, p. 59.
31. Annie Besant, *Hints on the Study of Bhagavad Gita,* 1973, p. 11.
32. Raj Kumar, *Annie Besant's Rise to Power in Indian Politics.* p. 62.
33. Ibid.
34. *New India,* 28 April 1915, p. 8.
35. *The New Civilization,* pp. 8-9.
36. Ibid., p. 87.
37. Annie Besant, *England, India and Afghanistan, London, 1872;* reprinted Madras, 1931, p. 16.
38. Ibid., p. 235.
39. Ibid., Vol. IV, p. 85, "The Means of India's Regeneration", 1895.
40. Ibid., p. 93.
41. Ibid.
42. Quoted in Raj Kumar, *Annie Besant's Rise to Power in Indian Politics,* pp. 65.66.
43. Ibid., p. 66.
44. Ibid.

—DR. RAJ KUMAR

CHAPTER - VIII

THE ROWLATT SATYAGRAHA OF 1919

To raise a problem associated with Gandhi is to rush where angels would fear to tread. This is so because of the attention which historians have already bestowed upon Gandhi, upon his style of politics and upon his influence on nationalism in India. We all know that the advent of Gandhi marked a revolutionary change in politics in the country. We also know that this change was reflected both in the values which inspired the political community and in the social background of the men and women who participated in political agitations. Apart from fleeting moments of heightened emotion or moral aberration, politics before the advent of Gandhi was a tame and respectable activity. It seldom involved defiance of the law, or violation of constitutional proprieties, and it equally seldom involved social groups other than those who had received their education through the medium of English. All this was dramatically transformed by the charismatic personaiity of Gandhi. Politics, under his aegis, involved frontal collisions with the British Raj and it reflected the hopes and the aspirations of the common people of India.

While such reflections about Gandhi's influence upon politics rest upon irrefutable evidence, I nevertheless believe that the questions which historians have hitherto asked themselves obscure rather than illumine the nature and the quality of this influence. To assert, for instance, that the agitations launched by Gandhi gained widespread support in the cities and in the villages conveys very little, more particularly when we bear in mind the complex structure of society in India, and the conflicting ideologies which battled for the allegiance of men's minds. Would it not be pertinent for the historian to ask himself which social groups participated in the agitations launched by Gandhi? Would it also not be pertinent for him to inquire into the identity of these social groups, to unfathom their interest and motivations, and to ascertain why they accepted Gandhi's leadership? By raising such questions we can not only know who participated in the movements led by Gandhi, and why, but we may also gain an insight into his vision of the political community, and be in a position to assess his legacy to politics in India.

I

To answer some of the questions we have posed above, I propose to focus on the agitations launched by Gandhi between 1919 and 1921, when he first appeared on the national stage, and espoused causes which were of the most intimate concern to the entire country. I shall focus in particular on the Rewlatt *Satyagraha* of 1919, for the very good reason that I have studied this movement in considerable detail with some of my colleagues.

The background to the Rowlatt *Satyagraha* can be outlined in a few brief sentences. During the course of the first World War the British Government in India was obliged to assume extraordinary powers in order to control the terrorist movement in Bengal and other places. To legitimise these powers under conditions of peace, the Government of India introduced two Bills, in January 1919, one of which sought to amend the Penal Code, and the other to shortcircuit the processes of law in question concerning revolutionary crime. Gandhi reacted to these Bills with feelings of acute horror. He looked upon them as measures which sought to subject the people to the arbitrary authority of government, and which were opposed to basic British notions of fairplay and justice. He, therefore, issued an appeal to the people of India to observe Sunday, the 6th April 1919, as a day of 'humiliation and prayer' in protest against the Rowlatt Act.

The response to Gandhi's appeal to different parts of the country throws interesting light on the extent to which he was successful in bringing about popular participation in politics. The protest against the Rowlatt Act was observed throughout the country, although it was confined to the cities and the towns. However, the depth of feeling with which the people responded to Gandhi's call, and the events which followed the *hartal* of the 6th, varied in a most significant way from region to region. In cities like Madras and Calcutta, the *hartal* was observed in a quiet and orderly fashion, and local leaders who owed personal allegiance to Gandhi harangued substantial crowds on the iniquities of the British Government in India. In cities like Bombay, Ahmedabad, particularly the latter, the temper of the people was pitched to a higher key, and the *hartal* of the 6th led to serious friction between the authorities and the *satyagrahis*. This friction expressed itself through acts of violence and arson, and through sanguinary conflicts between the custodians of the law and crowds of demonstrators.

But it was in the cities of the North like Lahore and Amritsar that the Rowlatt *Satyagraha* evoked the most violent protest from the people, and the most brutal repression from the British Government. The *hartal* of the 6th passed off relatively peacefully in these cities. But a few indiscriminate arrests of local leaders, and a few violent encounters, between the custodians of the law and crowds of excited demonstrators, rapidly transformed in innocuous movement of protest into something perilously close to rebellion. For practically a week the Government of the Punjab exercised a most precarious authority over the principal cities of the province, and its impotence was highlighted by the spontaneous growth of Soviet-like institutions, which were called 'Popular Committees' by their creators and 'Revolutionary Committees' by their detractors, and which took upon themselves during their brief existence the tasks of political negotiation and civil administration. Nothing comparable to the 'Popular Committees' of 1919 flourished in India till the events of 1942 presented an even more serious challenge to the British authority in India.

The explosive violence with which the cities of the Punjab responded to the Rowlatt *Satyagraha* probably came as a complete surprise to Gandhi. We have little reason to believe that his concepts of *satya* and *ahimsa* tied him with any special bonds of affection to the people of the Punjab; and we have equally little reason to believe that the institutions through which he organised the Rowlatt *Satyagraha* were particularly powerful in the cities of the North. Indeed, as we shall presently see, the position was actually the reverse, and if at all the historian is to explain the passion with which the cities of the North supported the Rowlatt *Satyagraha,* then he must seek an explanation in the local politics of the Punjab, rather than in the ideals preached by Gandhi, or in the political institutions created by him.

A brief digression into the intellectual influences on Gandhi, and into the institutions through which he organised the Rowlatt *Satyagraha,* is necessary to underscore the seeming irrationality of the enthusiasm with which the Punjab supported the movement.

In an essay which highlights the 'Traditional Influences on Gandhi', Professor Basham draws our attention to the extent to which Gandhian concepts like *satya* and *ahimsa* were "strongly influenced by later devotional Hinduism and Jainism, [and] by ideas of strict nonviolence and vegetarianism [which] dominated the ethical systems of the middle classes....in the 19th century Gujerat."

> We suggest [Professor Basham points out] that... Gandhi's concepts are fully in keeping with Indian tradition, and were probably developed from ideas which he absorbed in his childhood and youth fertilised and brought to fruition by his contact with the West......It is possible that if he had never read the Gospels, Tolstoy, Ruskin and such western literature, Gandhi would not have entered politics at all, or, if he had done so, would have devised techniques and politics different from those which he actually did devise. But if he had not been brought up in a middle-class Hindu-Jaina enviornment of the type that was to be found in 19th century Porbunder and Rajkot his techniques and policies would have been very different indeed.[1]

The Hindu-Jaina ethos of the Gujerati *bourgeoisie* which exercised so decisive an influence upon Gandhi was hardly designed to help him in establishing rapport with the people of the Punjab. Any explanation, therefore, which attributes the violence of the Rowlatt *Satyagraha* in the North to an identity in outlook and values between Gandhi and the people of the Punjab is unlikely to carry much conviction. Nor can the events of 1919 in cities like Lahore and Amritsar be explained on the basis of any special efforts in organisation on the part of Gandhi. Indeed, when we look to the institutions through which the Rowlatt *Satyagraha* was organised, we obgserve that the movement evoked the maximum response in precisely those parts of the country where such institutions were weak to the points of being non-existent.[2] The Home Rule Leagues of Besant and Tilak provided Gandhi with the principal means to whip up popular feeling against the Rowlatt Act. The radical members of the League, men like the brothers Dwarkadas, or Shankerlal Banker, had by the end of 1918 become critical of Besant's moderation, and they were, therefore, all too willing to accept a radical programme of direct action against the British Government. Having accepted such a radical programme, they threw into the campaign against the Rowlatt Act a well organised network of Leagues, and a well disciplined cadre of leaders. When Gandhi organised his *Satyagraha Sabhas* in March 1919, to guide the people during the course of the struggle, the men prominent in the *Sabhas* were those who had already been prominent in the Home Rule Leagues, and the *Sabhas* were able to act to any purpose only in those parts of the country where the Leagues were already well established. In the cities of the Punjab, for instance, the Home Rule Leagues had not made much headway, and Gandhi, therefore, found it quite difficult to gain influential and dedicated members for his *Satyagraha Sabha.*

II

If neither the values nor the institutions created by Gandhi in 1919 evoked any sympathetic response in the North, then we can clearly conclude that the citizens of Lahore and Amritsar Participated in the Rowlatt *Satyagraha* to express local frustrations and to secure parochial interests. It is, indeed, my belief that the Rowlatt *Satyagraha,* like other agitations launched by Gandhi, provided an umbrella under which numerous classes and communities could pursue their distinct, and often contradictory, interests without doing any damage to the wider and more romantic objectives of the movement. It is also my belief that because such movements served primarily as channels for the articulation of local and sectional interests, they can be fully understood only when the historian turns his attention to the local movements which were subsumed under the wider movements.

To what extent do our assumptions illumine the course of the Rowlatt *Satyagraha* in a city like Lahore? To answer this question we shall recapitulate in brief the events associated with the heroic days of April 1919, in the capital of the Punjab. During the months of February and March the local leaders of Lahore conducted a vigorous campaign against the Rowlatt Act under the aegis of local bodies like the Lahore Association or the Provincial Congress Committee. This agitation affected the middle classes in general, and the student community in particular, with the result that the *hartal* of 6 April was a complete triumph for the *satyagrahis* in the city. But while the *hartal* of the 6th was a triumph for the *satyagrahis,* the temper of the city was subdued and restrained. The crowds which demonstrated against the Rowlatt Act acted with considerable moderation, probably because they were drawn from the respectable classes, although we should remember that the very substantial student community of Lahore had thrown its weight in favour of the movement right from the outset. The crowds of the 6th avoided any collision with the custodians of the law, although even at this stage they could not resist innocuous displays of temper, as when they obliged a petty representative of the local administration "to take off my turban, which I did, because I knew that if I did not do so there would be trouble...."[3]

All this was to be dramatically transformed in the days which followed, at least partly in response to the challenge thrown out by Sir Michael O'Dwyer, the Lieutenant-Governor of the Punjab, who threatened the local leaders with dire consequences if they persisted in preaching disloyalty to the people. Sir Michael's challenge was immediately taken up by the local leaders, and on the occasion of *Ram Naumi,* which fell on 9 April, they appealed to the Muslims of Lahore to join the Hindus in demostrating against the repressive laws of the British Government. The Muslims of Lahore, particularly those belonging to the poorer classes, responded with considerable enthusiasm to the appeal. The 9th of April, therefore, witnessed fraternisation between Hindus and Muslims on a scale which was never to be repeated thereafter. But the crowds which demonstrated on the 9th, and which were drawn from Hindus and Muslims, from business and professional men, from students and the *petite bourgeoisie,* and finally from the artisan and the working classes, not only represented an impressive display of communal harmony, but they also revealed the extent to which the authority of the British Raj had come to be held in contempt by the people :

> Generally we know that the people give us due respect, and the mob always obeys our orders, but on that day we were altogether absolutely ignored [an Honorary Magistrate of Lahore pointed out]. On that occasion of *Ram Naumi* generally, processions were formed with the object of explaining certain historical events, and certain prayers were recited, but nothing of the kind was done in this procession. Instead of all this the attitude of the people was so rude that they did not allow any Honorary Magistrate or respectable gentleman of the town to join them....When I went there I saw none of the city fathers were there. Instead, all the leaders who had signed the

> notice to protest against the Rowlatt Bills were there in place of the old leaders, and these leaders were garlanded, and they led the procession.[4]

Despite the truculent mood of the people, the 9th passed off without any bloodshed. But on the 10th, Lahore was up in arms, and a wild mood of excitement seized the city, when it learnt of Gandhi's detention, and of unlovely happening in Amritser, which had been triggered off by the arrest of some local leaders. Within an hour of the arrival of this news, the shopkeepers of the city declared a state of *hartal,* and excited groups of people poured out into the bazars, disorganised, leaderless, and not knowing what to do, but determined to express their indignation at Gandhi's arrest, and at the Amritsar outrages. To conjure the mood of Lahore on the 10th, I can do no better than quote the recollections of an obscure student who was caught up in these turbulent event :

> On April 10, as I was going to the bazar for shopping in the evening I saw shops being suddenly closed, and a multitude of people came crying, 'Hai Hai Rowlatt Bill', 'Black Bill', 'Gandhi Ki Jail' and so forth. I was asked by one in the crowd to put off my cap. I asked him what the matter was. He told me that Gandhiji had been imprisoned, and people were sorrowing on that account. He further inquired of me whether I was willing to participate in the general sorrow. I spontaneously expressed my willingness........
>
> I followed the multitude silently, asking many questions as to why and where the mob was going. It appeared to me that no one knew precisely where the crowd was going. Some said that they would probably go all over the city to show their sorrow, and others, that the people would probably go to the Mall to show their sorrow to the Englishmen.[5]

Since the citizens of Lahore were in an excited frame of mind, and because O'Dwyer was convinced that the crowds had assembled "with the object of invading the civil station, where there were several thousands of Europeans, the majority being women and children",[6] bloodshed was more or less inevitable. The police fired twice on the crowds of demonstrators, presumably to prevent invasions of the civil station where the European lived, as a rcsult of which a large number of Hindus and Muslims were wounded and killed. The firings a of the 10th enraged an already excited populace, and completely undermined the control which the British Government exercised within the walled city of Lahore. "On the 11th....(the) city was actually out of hand",[7] a British Officer later confessed. A large congregation of 35,000 converged on the Badshahi Mosque in the heartof the city, and like the crowds of the 9th, this congregation was drawn from all classes and communities of Lahore : Hindus and Muslims, shopkeepers and professional men, students and clerks, and artisans and workers. The unity between the Hindus and the Muslims on the occassion was highlighted by the solid phalanx of local leaders men like Harkishen Lal, Rambhuj Dutt Choudhry, Duni Chand, Pir Tajuddin, Mohsin Shah and Khalifa Shujauddin who stood around the pulpit of the Badshahi Mosque and harangued the congregation on the wickedness of O'Dwyer's administration. At Rambhuj Dutt's suggestion the crowd elected by popular acclaim a Committee to represent the city in negotiations with the administration, and to attend to civic matters in the absence of the established authority.

The 'Popular Committee', which the British Government insisted upon calling the 'Revolutionary Committee', posed a serious threat to the British authority, since it was an important focus of power in Lahore during its brief existence from the 11th to the 14th. The Committee comprised 50 members, and it met daily to review the political situation in Lahore. Its power was recognised even by O'Dwyer, since he conducted negotiations with its leading members with a view to end the *hartal* in the city. But despite the influence of its leading members, the Committee could function effectively only when it reflected the popular mood, and was guided by, instead of attempting to guide, the citizens of Lahore. Thus, when the Committee tried to negotiate a settlement with O'Dwyer on the 13th, its leading members found themselves out of favour with the people, and were even accused of trying 'to get land-grants from the Governments'.[8] The leaders of the Popular Committee did not, in fact, know how to exploit the power which popular initiative had thrust into their hands, and when O'Dwyer called in the army to restore order in Lahore, they surrendered their persons to the authorities without any protest.

III

Our brief recapitulation of the course of the Rowlatt *Satyagraha* in Lahore brings out the extent to which all the major classes and communities in the city were drawn into the movement of protest against the Rowlatt Act. I would like to draw attention in particular to the congregation which assembled at the Badshahi Mosque on the 11th, on which occasion rich and poor and Hindus and Muslims joined hands in a most impressive demonstration of unity. That the local leaders of Lahore could persuade 35,000 souls in a city with a total population of 2,80,000 to attend a meeting held in protest against the Rowlatt Act, speaks eloquently of their success in drawing the masses into the movement.

But how much of this enthusiasm was due to Gandhi? And to what extent were the citizens of Lahore exploiting the opportunity offered by him to voice frustrations which were in no way related to the Rowlatt *Satyagraha* ?

We must first of all concede that any attempt to displace Gandhi from his central position in the stage would do serious violence to the political temper of India in 1919. Indeed, in focussing on the reaction of the citizens of Lahore to Gandhi's detention on April 10 we have given some indication of his charismatic hold upon the popular imagination. But having made such a concession, we must also draw attention to the startling fact that few of the leaders of Lahore who participated in the Rowlatt *Satyagraha* owed personal allegiance to Gandhi, or were influenced by his ideas, or subsequently followed his lead in politics.

A majority of the Hindu leaders who led the Rowlatt *Satyagraha* in Lahore possessed a middle class background, and they were drawn from vigorous and enterprising castes like the Khatris, the Aroras and the Banias. These castes had special reason to be disaffected towards the British Government in 1919. Not that this had always been so. The annexation of the Punjab had, in the first instance, proved a blessing for the Khatris, the Aroras and the Banias, since it had opened to them opportunities which had not been open to them under the Sikhs. Because they were generously endowed with enterprise and acumen, the Khatris and the associated castes exploited such opportunities to the full, and soon established for themselves substantial bridgeheads in business, in the liberal professions and in the civil service. So remarkable was the progress made by these castes in the decades which followed 1849 that they looked upon the British Government with sentiments of loyalty and affection.

It is generally believed that the Land Alienation Act of 1901 was a measure designed to inhibit the progress of the middle classes, and it, therefore, encouraged them to adopt an anti-British stance. This may well have been so. But instead of putting a brake upon their progress, the Act merely encouraged the middle classes to invest their savings in urban instead of rural enterprises. The decade which followed 1901, therefore, witnessed a most remarkable growth of financial and industrial institutions in the Punjab, and men like Harkishen Lal owed their spectacular rise in the world of high finance and industry largely due to the restrictions imposed by the Alienation Act upon the purchase of rural properties by the urban castes.

The cleavage between the middle classes and the British Government of the Punjab came about in 1913, rather than in 1901. The occasion for this cleavage was the appointment of Sir Michael O'Dwyer as the Governor of the Punjab. O'Dwyer came to Lahore with the firm conviction that the urban classes were responsible for the exploitation of the peasants, and he, therefore, looked upon the former with feelings of undisguised hostility. He also took every opportunity to remind the urban classes of their selfishness, and to impress upon them how little they deserved any share in political power. In addition to all this, O'Dwyer also involved himself in a sordid intrigue which destroyed the financial and industrial empire of Harkishen Lal in 1913, and in doing so initiated an economic recession which affected virtually every substantial Hindu family in Lahore.

Although O'Dwyer's policies concerned only prosperous businessmen or substantial men in the professions, the hostility generated by them affected a significantly wider section of the Hindu community in Lahore. This was so because of the ties of interest and sentiment generated by the institution of caste. As we have already pointed out, the middle classes of Lahore were drawn from castes like the Khatris, the Aroras and the Banias. Each one of these castes consisted of a social pyramid, with a few successful lawyers, or doctors, or civil servants, or businessmen perched at the apex, while a vast horde of petty shopkeepers, or junior civil servants, or men in the lower rungs of the professions, formed the base of the pyramid. Despite a significant gulf in wealth and status, the men who occupied the base of a caste pyramid were tied with strong bonds of loyalty to their successful caste-fellows at the apex, and shared with them their aspirations and their ambitions as well as their prejudices and their frustrations. Because of the existence of such loyalties, the relatively small number of rich and influential men whose interests were adversely affected by O'Dwyer's policies were able to infect a large proportion of the Hindus of Lahore with feelings of hostility towards the British Government.

If the rich and the poor Hindus of Lahore detested O'Dwyer's administration because of the damage it had done to their interests, the Muslims of the city, a large proportion of whom were employed in industrial establishments, or in declining crafts like weaving, were equally hostile towards the British Government, though their hostility stemmed from an altogether different set of reasons. The sentiments of the Muslims were shaped, on the one hand, by the belief that the followers of Islam all over the world formed an indissoluble community, and on the other, by the suspicion that Great Britain was involved with other Christian Powers in an intrigue to undermine the power and glory of Islam through dismembering the Ottoman Empire.

The most striking feature of Muslim concern for the integrity of the brotherhood of Islam and the Ottoman Empire was the extent to which such a sentiment bound the rich and the poor, the orthodox and the liberal, and finally the educated and the untutored in a common bond of hostility towards the British Government. The educated Muslims of Lahore were influenced by the poetical writings of Iqbal, who disseminated new values through the medium of his verse; and by the polemical writings of Mohamed Ali, whose editorials in the *Comrade* and the *Hamdard* were avidly read by the intelligentsia all over the country. But so far as the poor Muslims were concerned, their mentor was Zafar Ali, who represented a new political style in Lahore. A shrewd journalist and a clever demagogue, Zafar Ali addressed himself to the poor Muslims through the columns of his newspaper, the *Zamindar*, whose editorials were couched in a style and dwelt upon themes that inflamed the passions instead of widening the outlook. Zafar Ali commenced his career as a demagogue by creating a sense of identity among the Muslims through the primitive expedient of heaping abuse upon the Hindus. At this stage the *Zamindar* was sold in the bazars of Lahore by vendors who described it as the *Hinduaon ka bera gharak Karnewala Zamindar.*[9] Next, Zafar Ali attacked the British Government, and described as completely hypocritical British policy towards Turkey and towards the Muslim community in India. The style of the *Zamindar* can be gauged from the following extract from an editorial which expressed Muslims indignation at the demolition of a section of a mosque in Kanpur in 1913.

> A sacred portion of the Cawnpore Mosque was demolished in the midst of guns and bayonets. In this way the funeral of that religious liberty, whose effigy has been shown as living and moaning for more than a century, was performed with full millitary honours. Similarly, the memory of that bloody 3rd of August cannot be effaced from the page of our heart, on which date the sun appeared over the horizon of Cawnpore shedding sorrowful tears over the fountains of blood, over writhing dead bodies, over the bleeding wounds of innocent children, and over aggrieved and helpless humanity, and which was the day on which the corpse of British justice.....was at last laid on the banks of the Ganges.....[10]

Whatever opinion we might entertain about the quality of such polemics, its success among the poor and unsophisticated Muslims of Lahore was most striking. According to a contemporary account, "as soon as this paper, i.e., the *Zamindar* was brought into the bazar, large crowds of people surrounded the news-shops, and the copies were soon sold out".[11] The popularity of the *Zamindar* is also reflected in the fact that under Zafar Ali its circulation rose from 1,200 in 1910 to 15,000 in 1913.

It took more than just the propaganda of the *Zamindar*, however, to alienate the poor Muslims of Lahore from the British Government. Indeed, Zafar Ali's phenomenal success in activating Muslim artisans and workers can be attributed in no insignificant measure to the stresses and strains to which they were exposed in earning their livelihood, and to their consequent readiness to accept a romantic body if ideas which pointed to the British Government as the single source of all their unhappiness. Cities like Lahore possessed a considerable population of artisans and workers, some of whom, like the weavers, were finding it increasingly difficult to compete with goods produced by the machine. Their misery was heightened during the years of the war, when the prices of foodgrains and other essential commodities rose by substantial margins without corresponding increases in wages. The situation became particularly acute in the opening months of 1919, due to the complete failure fo the *kharif* crops in the winter of 1918.

On the eve of the Rowlatt *Satyagraha,* therefore, almost the entire population of Lahore was disaffected for reasons which varied from class to class, and community to community. The prosperous Hindu middle classes, for instance, felt that they had been denied a proper share in political and economic power. Their sentiments were fully shared by their poorer caste-fellows, who also suffered from acute economic distress owing to the inflationary conditions generated by the war. The Muslim artisans and workers were even more agitated than the Hindu *petite bourgeoisie,* because they had been led to believe that their religion was in danger, and because the rise in prices had drastically reduced their standard of living, which was never significantly above the level of subsistence.

In the spring of 1919, therefore, Lahore was ripe for 'rebellion'; and the movement of protest initiated by Gandhi enabled the citizens of Lahore to give expression to the accumulated tensions and frustrations of more than a decade.

IV

While the course of the Rowlatt *Satyagraha* in Lahore represents a considerable triumph for Gandhi, precisely the reverse is true of Bombay, where the movement of protest against the Rowlatt Act failed to touch the imagination of large and significant sections of the community. The comparative failure of the Rowlatt *Satyagraha* in Bombay appears at first blush to be somewhat of a paradox. The city was, after all, an important centre of political activity in India. It possessed a rich, cultured and influential Gujerati community which subscribed to the 'Hindu-Jaina' ethic that lay behind Gandhian ideals and Gandhian practice. Both the Home Rule League and the *Satyagraha Sabha,* the two organisations through which Gandhi controlled the agitation, were more powerful in Bombay than they were in any other city in the country. Despite all this, however, the Rowlatt *Satyagraha* never assumed the character of a mass movement in Bombay.

Why it did not do so is, I believe, susceptible to rational analysis. And if I may anticipate the results of such an analysis, I would like to emphasise that these results reinforce the conclusions we have by implication drawn about Gandhi's conception of the political community, and his vision of political action, in our recapitulation of the Rowlatt *Satyagraha* in Lahore.

Briefly if not very elegantly put, the Rowlatt *Satyagraha,* like other agitations launched by Gandhi, rested upon the politics of the social pyramid and the ideology of romanticism. Both these terms can be easily explained. In describing the structure of society in Lahore, we emphasised the fact that the loyalties of the individual and his sense of identity were shaped by community and religion, rather than by class and occupation. We further held that a caste could be looked upon as a social pyramid, with a few successful Individuals perched at the apex, while the vast majority formed the base of the pyramid. It was also pointed out that despite differences in wealth and status, the ties of interest and sentiment between the members of a caste were so strong that they acted as cohesive social units in situations of political crisis.

Gandhi looked upon the social pyramid as the legitimate basis of political action in India. If at all, he interfered with such pyramids, then his interference was confined to challenging the established leaders within them, and substituting in their place new leaders who were sympathetic to his social ideals and his political objectives. In the case of Lahore in 1919, however, tensions within the various communities stemmed from factors which had very little to do with Gandhi. The ideal of the Pan-Islamic community, for instance, had created a serious turbulence in Muslim society, and enabled upstarts like Zafar Ali to make a bid for the leadership of the community. Similarly, the retrogressive policies of O'Dwyer alienated the middle class Hindus from the British Government and encouraged them to make an alliance with Gandhi, and to persuade their caste-fellows to participate in the movement of protest against the Rowlatt Act.

What I have described as the ideology of romanticism was a logical extension of the politics of the social pyramid. Since Gandhi accepted the distinct identity of different castes, communities and religious groups, and because he looked upon his movements as broad-based alliances between such social units, he never elaborated a concrete body of ideas as the basis of his political action. Instead, he looked upon his movements as romantic gestures of protest against specific acts, like the repressive legislation of 1919, or the moral myopia of the Hunter Commission, or the tax on salt. Finally, because Gandhi's movements were romantic gestures of protest, they rendered possible the co-existence on the same platform of classes and communities with conflicting interests and different styles of life.

The principles and preconceptions which formed the agitations launched by Gandhi can be of considerable help to us in understanding the relative failure of the Rowlatt *Satyagraha* in

Bombay.[12] As we have already pointed out, the Gujeratis of Bombay, who were drawn mainly from the Brahman and Bania castes, and who held dominant positions both in the liberal professions and in trade and industry, constituted a natural base of support for the movement of protest against the Rowlatt Acts. This was particularly so because the Gujerati *bourgeoisie,* after having made substantial progress in the 19th century, was finding the British presence an obstacle rather than a help in the flowering of its cultural creativity, and in the expansion of its industrial and commercial activities. The frustration of the Gujerati middle classes, a frustration born of achievement and ambition rather than poverty and suffering, is all to evident in the readiness with which the young men of the community adopted, what were by contemporary standards, radical stances in politics. The Home Rule agitation in Bombay, for instance, rested largely upon Gujerati young men like the brothers Dwarkadas, or Shankerlal Banker, and the militancy of the movement reflected their mood rather than the mood of Annie Besant.

When Gandhi organised the Rowlatt *Satyagraha* in Bombay, he leaned heavily upon the Home Rule League, and the core of his *Satyagraha Sabha* consisted of millitant members of the League. Gandhi's dependence upon the League was to prove a double-edged weapon. For while the Home Rulers had organised an intensive, and a largely successful, agitation among the middle classes and the *petite bourgeoisie* of Bombay, they had also left substantial and important sections of the city unaffected by their propaganda.

The mill-workers of Bombay, who constituted 20 per cent of the population of the city, were the most significant of the classes which were unaffected by the propaganda of the Home Rule League. These mill-workers were Marathas of low-caste from the Konkan or the Desh; and since they were first generation immigrants, their style of life and their values were rural than urban, while the unlovely conditions of their existence heightened their nostalgia for the village. A deep gulf of class, caste, language and culture separated the mill-workers from the *bourgeois* redicals of the League, and even though individuals like the brothers Dwarkadas had discovered the working class of Bombay during the influenza epidemic of 1918, they were unsuccessful in establishing rapport with it. Thus, the successful strike which the workers of Bombay waged in January1919, was completely free of political influences, and rested exclusively upon economic issues. Indeed, the naivety of the mill-workers at this stage is vividly reflected in an encounter with the custodians of the law in the course of which they hailed the Commissioner of Police as 'Our Namadeva and our Tukarama.'[13]

Because Gandhi depended upon Gujerati radiclas hailing from the middle classes, he was unable to make any impression upon the Maratha mill-workers of Bombay. The *haratal* of April 6, therefore, was a relatively tame affair in the city, and devolved upon a predominantly Gujerati middle class and lower middle class crowd of 10,000 which assembled at Chowpatty to hear Gandhi denounce the Rowlatt Act. Even the hooliganism of the 11th, when news of Gandhi's detention had reached Bombay, did not involve any new section of the community. The closure of shops and markets in response to the detention spilled large numbers of shopkeepers, retailers and their employees on to the streets, and their numbers gained in strength because the 11th was a Friday, and a day of rest and prayer for the Muslims. All these sections of the community congregated into mobs in the streets, and indulged in disorderly behaviour. But it is important to note that lawlessness did not spread to the working class districts like Parel or Chinchpokli, and all except two of the city's 85 mills continued working right through the agitation.

V

By adopting the politics of the social pyramid and the ideology of romanticism, Gandhi, as our brief survey of the Rowlatt *Satyagraha* indicates, was remarkably successful in drawing into politics social groups which had been inactive before 1919. He was able to do so, first, because he did not tamper with the social loyalties of the people, and secondly, because his agitations permitted different social groups to join hands with one another without giving up their distinct, and even contradictory, interests. But if Gandhi was successful in drawing the masses into politics, he did so at a considerable price. Under his leadership, since different castes, communities and religious groups constituted the active units of a broad based alliance, these units acquired a heightened awareness of their distinct identities, and in doing so weakened those very bonds which held them together in a single political community.

We end, therefore, on a strange note of paradox : Gandhi, who did more than anyone else to fashion India into a nation, simultaneously created a style in politics which will put to a severe test the concept of national unity in India.

REFERENCES

1. *Vide* a paper presented by Professor A.L. Basham on "Traditional Influences on Gandhi" at a seminar on 'India in 1919' held at the Australian National University, Canberra, in 1966.
2. For information on the Home Rule Leagues I am indebted to Dr. Hugh Owen's paper entitled "The Organisation of the Rowlatt Satyagraha" which was also presented at the seminar on 'India in 1919' in Canberra.
3. Evidence by Sayad Muhammad Shah, Extra Assistant Commissioner, Lahore : *Hunter Commission Report,* Volme IV.
4. Ibid.
5. Evidence by an Unknown Student : *Report of the Punjab Sub-Committee of the Indian National Congress,* Volume II, p. 284.
6. Sir Michael O'Dwyer, *India As I Knew It* (London, 1925), p. 275.
7. Evidence by E.P. Broadway, Senior Superintendent of Police, Lahore : *Hunter Commission Report,* Volume IV.
8. Evidence by Lala Dharam Das: *Report of the Punjab Sub-Committee of the Indian National Congress.*
9. *NAI* (National Archives of India) : *Vide* sketch of Zafar Ali in letter from C.A. Barron, Chief Secretary to the Government of the Punjab, to H. Wheeler, Secretary to the Government of India, Home Department, Dated 16 December 1916 : Home Department, Political A Proceedings No. 127/137, March 1914.
10. The *Zamindar,* 20 April 1913.
11. *NAI* : O.M.'s Report dated 28 January 1916 : Home Department, Political A Proceedings No. 173, May 1916.
12. For an appreciation of the Rowlatt *Satyagraha* in Bombay I have drawn heavily from Dr. Jim Masselos' paper entitled "Some Aspects of Bombay City Politics in 1919" which was presented at the seminar on 'India in 1919' in Canberra.
13. *Vide* the Bombay *Chronicle,* 21 January 1919.

—RAVINDER KUMAR

CHAPTER - IX

ENGLAND AND INDIA

The demission of empire in India was the greatest transfer of power in modern times. The process, inaugurated in 1917 largely as a means of rallying support in war-time, was only completed thirty years later, when a second war had exposed the palpable inadequacy of Britain's resources to sustain an empire. In the end Britain quit quickly, for only in 1946 was there any devolution of responsibility in the Central Government of India. The consequence of Britain's unwillingness or inability to transfer central authority earlier was that when the main Indian parties confronted the problem of governing the old united empire they could not agree upon a solution. The price of freedom became partition.

The problem of demission may be defined in terms of reconciling the principles of freedom and unity, of preserving in freedom the unity that empire had imposed. Whilst the Indian adversaries of the Raj claimed that Britain's real object during the ostensible age of devolution was *divide et impera,* British statesmen and officials held that their constant purpose was to transfer power progressively by constitutional steps designed to bring together the disparate elements of a deeply divided dependency.

It is important to trace the development of Britain's commitment to the principle of freedom and to consider the bearing of the series of devolutionary stages upon the problem of unity. The second section of this article argues that Britain's intentions with regard to India's eventual status remained obscure until the Second World War, that declarations of purpose were never until then unequivocal on the key question of equality. The third section suggests that at both of the major stages in the devolution of responsibility, the Montagu-Chelmsford reforms of 1919 and the India Act of 1935, the constitutional arrangements exacerbated the dualities in Indian political society, between the princely states and the British Indian provinces, and between the Hindu majority and the Muslim majority provinces. Until 1939 Britain's vague purpose of freedom awaited clarification, while the collapse of the putative all-India federation in that year left Britain bereft of a policy for giving effect to it.

It is also important to discover how the consequent constitutional impasse was bridged. The fourth and fifth sections of this article follow the British responses to the early war-time Congress demands for a clarification of purpose and for the immediate concession of appropriate right and reforms. The evidence reveals that the Cripps Mission to India in March 1942 marks the point in time at which Britain's purpose clearly became complete freedom, within or without the empire as India wished, as soon as the war was over. These sections also trace the revision of Britain's policy that freedom should be granted only to a united India. Again, the Cripps Mission marks the turning-point, by accepting that freedom might be achieved either through unity or partition. It is argued that after 1942 British policy was to transfer power to viable successor authorities as soon as possible, though the policy break was masked for some time by an unwillingness to move during the war.

A final section reviews some of the determinants of London's policy, in particular the effect of the Congress movement, the cast of the imperial mind, and the importance of British interests.

If the argument of the article is sometimes cryptic, or the evidence scant, this is probably because, in the interests of a concise synthesis, a paraphrase has been made to stand for an analysis published elsewhere. The footnotes draw attention to several such instances.

II

The earliest official statement on India's eventual status was the declaration of Edwin Montagu (Secretary of State, 1917-22) on 20 August 1917 that Britain's policy was 'the progressive realization of responsible government'.[1] It was incorporated in the Preamble to the India Act of 1919, with the condition that Parliament was to decide the time and nature of each successive advance. For some five years after Montagu's declaration the full range of policies, external as well as internal, was referred to the purpose that it avowed. The Indianization of the civil and military services, the tolerable level of political dissent and the dermination of appropriate tariffs; Indian representation at the Versailles Peace Conference, at Dominions' conferences, in London and at the League of Nations; all reflected the glow of eventual freedom. It was commonly assumed that the 1917 declaration promised dominionhood. In 1929 the Reforms Branch of the Government of India submitted that Britain's own actions supported the assumption.[2]

However, in 1924 the assumption was repudiated. In a statement to the Indian Legislative Assembly that had been vetted by the Secretary of State, the Home Member of the Government of India (Sir Malcolm Hailey) argued that 'full self-governing Dominion status' might be a step beyond responsible self-government.[3] The obstacles to the step were Britain's responsibilities for defence, the minorities and the princely states. Later, Hailey insisted that his main concern had been to deny the possibility of the step being taken at the time of the decennial review for which the 1919 Act had provided.[4] Still, it came at a time when there was evidence of tergiversation in London. The Viceroy, Lord Reading (1921-6), who had himself equated Montagu's purpose and Dominion status, had been rebuffed for his liberal intentions towards further constitutional change and the Indianisation of the services.

Three years later, the all-white complexion of the decennial review body, the Statutory Commission (1927-30), revealed only too clearly Britain's persistent assumption of superiority. In recollection, Hailey's statement seemed sinister, and in 1928-9 Indian Liberals, Congressmen and Muslims pressed Lord Irwin (Viceroy, 1926-31) hard for a clarification of Britain's purpose.

In July 1929 Irwin came to London with the intention of securing the British parties' *imprimatur* for the equation of responsible self-government with Dominion status. His announcement of 31 October did affirm the equation, but it was not the definitive statement upon equality that he intended. The difficulty was not so much its lack of a time limit to British control as the extraordinary context in which it was made. For though it was upheld by the minority Labour Government it was contested vigorously by the Liberal and Conservative leaders, save only Baldwin. The evidence requires a brief rehearsal.[5]

The Prime Minister, Ramsay MacDonald, supported Irwin's initiative but he referred it to Baldwin and Lloyd George, partly because he lacked a parliamentary majority but mainly because India was not then a partyissue. The 1919 Act had been framed by a coalition and the Statutory Commission was deliberating as an all-parties parliamentary inquiry. When Baldwin received MacDonald's notice of Irwin's initiative he was at Bourges, en route to Aix-les-Bains. Without reference to his colleagues he approved the plan (Irwin was not only a friend but had gone to India at his own nomination) on the understanding that the Statutory Commission agreed. The Commission had not seen the draft statement, but as its chairman, Sir John Simon, knew of it the Government assumed its acquiescense. Similarly, when the Government proceeded with the initiative Simon assumed Baldwin's approval. During the week preceding the announcement Baldwin was made aware that the Conservative experts on Indian abominated the initiative, and that their dislike was shared by the Liberals' Indian expert, Lord Reading, and his leader, Lloyd George, as well as by all but the Labour members of the Statutory Commission. Baldwin demanded the postponement of the declaration pending all-party consultation, but as copies of it had already been released to Indian leaders the Government remained obdurate. On 31 October Irwin's announcement would have commanded the support of only the Labour Party if it had been put to the vote in Parliament.

The opposition leaders' objection was based upon an apprehension that Dominion status was an advance upon responsible self-government. On 25 October, after luncheon with two recent Secretaries of State (Lords Birkenhead and Peel), Lord Winterton, himself a former Under-Secretary, noted :

> Now 'Dominion Status' has a very special meaning (especially since the Imperial Conference of 1926), and use of the term would be in advance of any definitions hitherto attempted, such as 'self-government within the Empire', because of that meaning.[6]

Before 1926 'Dominion status' had still implied a measure of subordination to the British Parliament, but then Balfour had explicitly defined the Dominions as 'autonomous communities within the British Empire, equal in status, in no way subordinate one to another in any aspect of their domestic or external affairs, though united by a common allegiance to the Crown, and freely associated as members of the British Commonwealth of Nations.'[7] Birkenhead therefore described the Irwin declaration as making 'an indication never made before'.[8] Reading, adhering to his Government's statements of 1924, objected to the declaration chiefly because Indians would view it as an advance in policy and demand its early implementation.

The Parliamentary debates on the declaration in Novermber did not bring down the Government. For reasons of their own, neither Baldwin nor Simon joined the opposition chorus. Simon was now fighting to preserve his Commission, which party warfare must destroy. Baldwin was personally in favour of Irwin's policy, and he became committed to defending it when his leadership was challenged by a coalition of Conservative and Liberal leaders that charged him with jettisoning the empire. In the event, the Irwin line was held against a combined assault from the foremost constitutional experts of the day.

However, the opposition forced Baldwin to require and MacDonald to concede a written assurance that the declaration marked no advance on the Preamble to the 1919 Act.[9] In effect, the rearguard action was intended to establish that notwithstanding Balfour's definition of 1926, in 1929 Dominion status meant no more than had responsible self-government within the empire ten years previously. This face-saving dodge could scarcely erase the purport of the Irwin announcement : that the Montagu declaration implied that India should enjoy Dominion status as defined in 1929. The opposition leaders' awareness of the weakness of their ground is revealed by their refusal to countenance the repetition of the Dominion status pledge in Parliament when Irwin requested it in June 1930 (although he was allowed to make the reaffirmation in India as a *quid pro quo* for MacDonald's agreement to opposition representation at the impending Round Table Conference).

During the decade that followed Irwin's announcement, the term 'Dominion status' was sedulously avoided in official documents and speeches on the constitution. The reports of the Statutory Commission and the Joint Parliamentary Committee on the India Bill were silent on the matter. The opposition delegations to the Round Table Conference refused to contemplate the use of the expression, even 'with safeguards', which Simon considered a contradiction in terms. At the close of the first Conference session MacDonald spoke merely of 'central responsibility with safeguards'. Dissension within the National Government prevented the preparation of a Preamble to the 1935 Act, for unless it simply repeated that of 1919 it could, in the words of the Secretary of State, Sir Samuel Hoare (1931-5), 'possibly prejudice the whole passage of the Bill'.[10] At the Bill's second reading Hoare proposed to speak of the goal of 'self-government within the Empire'.[11] Only after the Viceroy, Lord Willingdon (1931-6), objected did he state that Indian would 'ultimately....take her place among the fully self-governing members of the British Commonwealth of Nations',[12] but without defining what 'her place' was. Lord Lintithgow, chairman of the Joint Parliamentary Committee on the 1935 Bill and later Viceroy (1936-43), described the spirit of legislation :

> ....we framed the constitution as it stands in the Act of 1935, because we thought that way the best way.....of maintaining British influence in India. It is no part of our policy, I take it, to expedite in India constitutional changes for their own sake, or gratuitously to hurry the handing over of the controls to Indian hands at any pace faster than that which we regard as best calculated, on a long view, to hold India to the Empire.[13]

The passage dates from December 1939, when Linlithgow's articulation of policy was lagging behind Whitehall's. But certainly until the outbreak of the Second World War British cabinets shrank from defining in unequivocal terms their intention to extend to India Dominion status of the Balfour declaration or Statute of Westminster variety.

III

Whatever their intentions towards India's eventual status, British statesmen applied them to all-India, to the united India of the Raj.[14] The Montagu declaration spoke of 'the progressive realization of responsible government in India as an integral part of the British Empire'. In 1929 the Reforms Branch of the Government of India observed that since 1917 British policies in the international field assumed an eventual single Dominion of provinces and princely states. However the difficulty of conveying a united India towards dominionhood was formidable. In 1917 the states were virtual autocracies whereas the provinces enjoyed representative government. Moreover the political development of the disparate elements in provincial societies was highly uneven, and, in particular, the relatively backward Muslim minority of British India apprehended that democratic rule by the Hindu majority would leave it permanently subject. The 1919 Preamble's provision for advance by 'progressive successive stages' was logical approach to the problem of constitutional and social heterogeneity. Responsibility must be devolved gradually, for Britain was obliged to protect the princes and the minorities until they were prepared to entrust their interests to a self-governing Dominion. From 1917 the future unity of India turned on the question whether the princes and the Muslims could be accommodated to a polity acceptable to the increasingly dominant party of British India, the essentially Hindu and ostensibly democratic Congress. The first stage of devolution set up severe strains.

Under the Montagu-Chelmsford constitution the separateness of the princely states was emphasised by their exclusion. Nothing was done to encourage the princes to bring their states into constitutional harmony with the proveinces. Their response to the reforms was to seek freedom from the operation of paramountcy, or British intervention in their affairs, and assurance that the paramount power would never transfer its sovereignty to a responsible Indianised central authority. By the late 1920s 'two Indians' had emerged, and, in the judgement of the Government of India, the Statutory Commission and the Indian States Committee (1928-9), there was little prospect of bringing them together in the near future.

In relation to British India the Montford reforms left the Central Government intact, with the Governor-General presiding over a predominantly official executive, the Indian members of which were no more than 'responsive' to the overwhelmingly Indian and elected legislature. At the centre the principle of unitary government was retained, and though there were separate electorates to protect certain minority interests and communities the generality of legislative members were returned through direct territorial, not indirect provincial, electorates. However, the provinces divided along communal lines. Aided by separate electorates even in their majority provinces, Muslim parties were able to enjoy ministerial power, most notably in the Punjab and Bengal. In so doing they soon realized the advantage to them of a federal form of constitutional development. By the late 1920s Muslim leaders had subscribed to a strong-province-but-weak-federation strategy. Their platform included : separate electorates; strong sovereign provinces; the separation of Sind and its elevation, together with the reformed North-West Frontier

Province and Baluchistan, to full provincial status; the cession, on a voluntary basis, of appropriate provincial powers to a federal government in which Muslims enjoyed weighted representation and guarantees of their separate identity.

By 1929, when the decennial revision of the Montford constitutions was in progress, the princes had emerged as opponents of a fully responsible self-governing Dominion, and the Muslims as enemies of a unitary self-governing British India. At the same time these powerful antagonists of Congress-style democratic freedom (as expressed, say, in the Nehru Report's essentially unitary constitution in 1928) had become natural allies of their trustee, the British Raj. From 1920 Congress had rejected devolution by stages and demanded immediate *Swaraj*. Britain was prepared neither to recognise Congress as the representative of India at large, nor to accept the possibility of India providing for its own defence, nor to jettison its own financial and commercial interests. The stability, security and solvency of India continued to demand a gradual demission of empire. As the Congress would not co-operate the Raj must look to the minorities and the princes to help with the work of constitutional devolution.

In the absence of the Congress, the constitution that was made between 1930 and 1935 favoured the princes and the Muslims. It seemed to take India a step closer to responsible self-government but it really contributed to disunity. While it did provide for central responsibility within a strong federation (except that defence and political relations were reserved, and finance, the services, commerce, the minorities, and the safety, tranquillity and interest of British India were subject to safeguards), it allowed the princes to veto this step and the Muslims to entrench themselves against it.

In the first place, the India Act of 1935 replaced the unitary central legislature of British India with a federal legislature of all-India. The princes and the Muslims were both to receive weighted representation, so that Congress could hope to secure only about a third of the seats. British statesmen believed that the experience of the princes and their ministers would stabilize an assembly that might otherwise be dominated by popular demagogues. The accession of sufficient princes to fill half of the states' seats was therefore made a condition of the advance to central responsibility with reserves and safeguards. The princes had flirted with federation at the first Round Table Conference in order to further their own concerns : the enhancement of their sovereignty through the reduction of paramountcy, the redress of some of their grievances, and the reaffirmation by the Crown of its treaty obligations to protect them. As they came to realize that Britain would not bargain away paramountcy in return for their cooperation with the federal scheme, and that any all-India federation involved the diminution of their sovereignty and the revision of their treaty rights, their reluctance to accede became increasingly manifest. On the eve of the war their substantial rejection of the federal offer was apparent. It had been confirmed by a Congress campaign for the return of the states' federal representatives by popular election rather than princely nomination.

Secondly, the 1935 Act provided for the introduction of provincial autonomy prior to the creation of federation. In consequence, when provincial elections were held in 1937 Muslim parties were able to consolidate their control over the Punjab, Bengal and Sind. Moreover, Congress was able to secure control of the Muslim minority provinces and to deny the Muslim population any say in their government. A sense of exclusion and even persecution drove the Muslims into hostility against the Act for the scope that it afforded to Hindu raj. The experience of Hindu provincial government stimulated the growth of Muslim separatism. Congress attempts to overturn the balance of the federal constitution, first by bringing pressure to bear on the princes, and secondly by seeking (though with doubtful success) to impose uniform policies upon the Congress provinces through the Working Committee, had the same effect. By the outbreak of war the resurgent Muslim League was calling for the reconsideration of the constitution *de novo*. The League's secretary, Liaquat Ali Khan, argued the need for a constitutional structure that would prevent Congress from governing India alone. He expounded three alternatives : Pakistan, or the partition of India; Dominion status for each province, with the option of acceding to or abstain from a federation; a confederation of Muslim provinces and Hindu provinces.[15] The League now condemned responsible self-government as a constitutional ideal unsuited to the realities of Indian politics.

The devolution of power by stages, coupled with the uncooperative or unconciliatory policies of the Congress, enlarged the obstacles to the achievement of dominionhood by a united

India. Between 1917 and 1939 the phased demission of empire produced a crisis of unity. As Britain had never contemplated dominionhood for any entity other than a united India the collapse of the paper federation in 1939 precipitated a crisis of freedom.

IV

It was the Second World War that drove Whitehall to clarify its intentions with regard to Indian freedom, and to decide the bearing that the problem of unity should have upon their implementation.[16] The relationship between events and the making of policy must now be traced in some detail.

On 14 September 1939, a few days after Linlithgow committed India to the war, the Congress Working Committee demanded a declaration of Britain's 'war aims in regard to democracy and imperialism', and of how these aims would 'apply to India and so be given effect to in the present'.[17] Congress sought the right of Indians to frame their own constitution through a Constituent Assembly and to participate in the war effort through representation in the Viceroy's Executive Council. Linlithgow recommended and the Cabinet approved the reiteration of the purpose of Dominion status, an intimation that after the war Britain would consult Indians about modifying the 1935 Act, and the offer of Indian membership of an advisory war committee. The statement was issued on 18 October. Four days later the Congress Working Committee, rejecting it as a reiteration of 'the old Imperialist policy', called for the resignation of the Congress provincial ministries. On 26 October, Hoare, speaking for the Government in the House of Commons, argued that Britain's pledge of Dominion status 'did not mean some system of government that deprived India of the full status of equality within the British Commonwealth'. It meant 'the Dominion status of 1926'. On 7 November the Secretary of State, Lord Zetland (1935-40), reaffirmed in the House of Lords that Britain meant India to have Dominion status of the Statute of Westminster variety. At the same time, Linlithgow secured Cabinet approval to offer the enlargement of his executive to accommodate representative Indians. Congress was unconvinced by these new promises of eventual equality and aggrieved by the denial of India's right to make its own constitution at the end of the war. By mid-November all of the provincial Congress ministries had resigned.

Though dominionhood had been interpreted as equality of status the Cabinet still distinguished it from independence. Early in 1940 the Cabinet required Linlithgow to substitute the phrase 'self-government within the Empire' for 'independence within the Empire' in a speech to the Orient Club, Bombay, that explained the meaning of Dominion status. Zetland conveyed to him the opinion of Sir Thomas Inskip, as the Attorney-General during the making of the 1935 Act, that Dominion status assumed membership of the empire and carried no right to repudiate the allegiance to the Crown.[18] Linlithgow's speech, which repeated Zetland's earlier reference to 'Dominion status of the Statute of Westminster variety', led Gandhi to request further discussions. Early in February Linlithgow offered him the following package : a reaffirmation of the object to grant Dominion status at the earliest possible date; the addition of representative politicians to the central executive; the inauguration of federation as soon as the necessary princely accessions were secured; 'at some time in the future, at all events after the war, consultation with Indians on the revision of the constitution'.[19] The offer fell too far short of self-determination to induce Congress to negotiate.

Linlithgow's three offers during the first six months of the war did not amount to a new approach to the constitutional problem. Neither he, nor the Chamberlain Cabinet that approved them, would go beyond the policy of Dominion status within the empire, all-India federation, and consultation (but without responsibility) through a body set up to revise the 1935 Act and in the existing central government. Democratic concessions were inhibited by the continued defence of the princes and the minorities. Trusteeship remained. Linlithgow insisted that even the admission of the Indian parties to his executive must be conditional upon their prior agreement to a reconstitution of the provincial Governments.

Almost from the beginning of the war a non-official initiative began to develop in London. On 3 October Clement Attlee criticized the Viceroy's lack of tact in not seeking to bring India into the war 'on a level with us'.[20] He called for 'more imaginative insight in dealing with the Indian people'. A deputation of Labour and Liberal Members of Parliament waited on Zetland to secure a debate that would elicit an official statement, going as far as possible to meet Congress claims and enlist it as a willing partner in the war. When the debate occurred on 26 October the most remarkable speech was delivered by Sir Stafford Cripps.

Cripps had first encountered the Indian problem in 1932, when he was briefed by a firm of London solicitors to advise the Nizam of Hyderabad on the implications of the federal scheme for his sovereignty. In 1938 he met Nehru in London. The two socialists had much in common. Cripps sympathised with Congress aspirations to democratic self-government. He corresponded sporadically with Nehru, was in touch with Krishna Menon and wrote articles on Indian freedom for the *Tribune*. At the outbreak of war he was an independent Member of Parliament and had given up his bar practice to devote himself to public affairs. On 28 September he visited the Foreign Secretary, Lord Halifax (formerly Lord Irwin), about a proposed tour of Russia and the East. He argued that Nehru was not unreasonable and Halifax, somewhat impressed, arranged for him to visit Zetland the next day. Claiming 'a very close knowledge of Nehru' (derived from conversation with Menon), he told Zetland that with regard to immediate reform Nehru would settle for a reconstitution of the Central Assembly (which was still operating under the 1919 Act) and the association of selected members of it with the Viceroy's executive.[21] On 11 October he advised Nehru that Congress should 'stand firm as a rock upon its demands', accepting nothing short of 'action which proves conclusively the faith behind words'.[22] On 23 October, the day after Congress rejected Linlithgow's offer of a consultative war committee, he saw Halifax again. Whereas Halifax argued that Congress was not the only Indian party and that Britain could not go beyond its first offer, Cripps held that Congress spoke for the majority of British India and that to concede consultation on war matters alone was insulting.

In his Commons speech of 26 October Cripps claimed that the 'new cricumstances which have inevitably arisen with the coming of the struggle in Europe' made India 'a test question in the eyes of the world'. The war object of freedom must be applied to India. He expounded a bold plan to win India's cooperation 'in our effort to establish democracy and freedom in the world'. Britain should pledge itself to grant 'full self-government after the war'; all-India federation should be abandoned, as it was anathema to both the Congress and the League; a new Central Legislative Assembly should be elected on the basis of the existing provincial registers; the Viceroy should then ask the majority party in the Assembly to form a government and appoint it as his executive. Cripps' proposed reconstitution of the Viceroy's

Executive is of particular interest, for it bears upon his negotiations in 1942 :

> It is true that, technically and in accordance with the constitution, the Executive Council would not be a Cabinet, but there is no reason on earth why our Government should not give an undertaking that the Veceroy would deal with the Executive Council.....as if it were a Cabinet on all major matters; that is to say he would accept their advice as the Crown here accepts the advice of the Cabinet when duly tendered to it.

During November Cripps' proposed private tour of India won moral support from several Members of Parliament who favoured sending out a non-parliamentary mission to explore the demands of the Indian parties. They included Halifax, R.A. Butler (a former Under-Secretary of State for India), Lord Snell (Labour's leader in the Lords), Wedgwood Benn (Labour Secretary of State for India, 1929-31), R.W. Sorensen (Labour), Sir Stanley Reed (Unionist), Sir George Schuster (Liberal, Finance Member of the Viceroy's Executive, 1928-34), and even Zetland himself (to whom the elder statesman, Raghavendra Rao, commended the notion). At a dinner party to which Schuster invited a number of them, as well as Lord (formerly Sir Malcolm) Hailey, Cripps' explanation of his ideas 'made a considerable impression'. Encouraged by the apparent receptiveness to his proposed new initiative, Cripps wrote to Nehru on 16 November of 'a quite remarkable change of opinion even among Conservatives, which is most remarkable, and may have its influence on Government action'.[23] This was wishful thinking. Only ten days earlier the Cabinet had agreed unanimously that Britain should not make a statement such as Congress demanded. Nehru assessed Cripps correctly at this stage as a man whose 'judgement is not always to be relied upon'.[24] Cripps probably mistook interest for agreement. This was certainly the case a little later when, at the behest of Schuster and Butler (the latter urging 'the unity of India is at stake'[25]), Sir Findlater Stewart, Permanent Under-Secretary for India, saw him twice for discussions.[26]

By about 22-24 November Cripps had decided upon the heads of a scheme that he would take to India.[27] Britain should declare its willingness to grant 'Dominion status', by which it meant 'complete self-government and absolute liberty to terminate partnership in the British Commonwealth of Nations'. This involved deciding 'to implement forthwith its promises of Dominion status in the form of complete self-government for India', and carried the right of Indians to frame their own constitution through a Constituent Assembly. As an Act of Parliament was necessary to set up the Assembly some delay was unavoidable, but the Government would bind itself to introduce a bill 'immediately the war is over, or before that time if opportunity occurs'. Cripps envisaged an Assembly of some 2000 members, chosen on the basis of the existing provincial electorates and with the proportional representation of the states' people. But he was prepared to accept any alternative Assembly agreeable to the Indian parties. Britain would endorse decisions taken by the Assembly on a three-fifths vote, provided only that the Assembly agreed to enter into a fixed term treaty (he suggested fifteen years), whereby Britain could discharge its obligations to the princes, the minorities and the services, and for defence, finance and commerce. Consistently with its avowed purpose, Britain would immediately 'do its utmost in association with the representatives of the Indian people to arrange such expedients as are possible under the existing constitution to give the Indian people a larger measure of self-government during the war'.

During December Cripps met Gandhi, Nehru, A.K. Azad, and many other Congressmen both at Allahabad and Wardha, Liaquat Ali Khan at Delhi, Jinnah at Bombay and the Viceroy at Calcutta. The Congress leaders were sceptical of Britain promising complete independence by any particular date, while the Muslims were opposed to the democretic mechinery of a Constituent Assembly. The Viceroy listened without confiding his views, but his letters to Zetland reveal his hostility. He thought that in the existing conditions of communal animosity it would be hopeless to get the Muslims into any Hindu-dominated assembly. He abominated Cripps'acceptance of the central Congress demands and advised persevering with his own more limited courses. After meeting Linlithgow Cripps concluded that there was no hope of the Hindus and the Muslims being brought together while he was Viceroy. As far as Cripps personally was concerned this first private initiative lapsed when he left India at the end of the year.

However, first Zetland and later his successor, L.S. Amery (May 1940-July 1945), pressed the Viceroy and the Cabinet to accept some of the major aspects of the scheme, until in almost unrecognisably adulterated form it appeared as the August offer of 1940. These aspects included allowing a Constituent Assembly to make a Dominion constitution as soon as the war was over, the negotiation of a fixed term treaty for the discharge of Britain's remaining obligations, and the admission of representative Indians to the Viceroy's executive. Neither Zetland nor Amery advocated two other aspects of the scheme : the definition of Dominion status in terms of the right to secede, and the conversion of the Viceroy's executive into a quasi-responsible Cabinet.

The attraction of the immediate post-war date for Dominion status was that it established Britain *bona fides* with regard to freedom. The advantage of the Constituent Assembly plan was that it placed upon Indians themselves the responsibility of removing the main obstacle of post-war freedom : disunity. If the Indian parties could agree upon the form of a constituent body to settle safeguards for the Muslims and terms of accession for the princes then instant dominionhood was theirs. Congress would have to realize that the way to freedom lay through their accommodation of the Muslims and the princes. Britain would neither impose a constitution agreeable to the majority but anathema to the minorities and the princes, nor interfere to secure its own interests under the constitution. A treaty for a relatively short transitional period, and negotiated by a co-equal Indian Dominion, was the only condition.

Zetland urged the merits of the scheme upon the Prime Minister in December and put it before the Cabinet in January 1940. However, Linlithgow scotched advance along such 'radical' lines by insisting upon his own conservative approaches. He was highly sceptical of the prospect of a post-war communal agreement, and believed that Britain must stay on 'for many years'. Further concessions to Congress would only encourage their recalcitrance over the communal problem, at the same time alienating important Muslim collaborators. Britain could not bind itself to accept the decisions of a Constituent Assembly as long as it desired a connection with India. After Linlithgow's February talks with Gandhi failed, Zetland again put the scheme to the Cabinet. Like independent observers of the Indian scene at the time he was appalled at the hardening of the divisions between Congress and League, and Congress and Government.[28] Indian was silding toward disunity and civil disobedience. While the Government could suppress satyagraha, its methods would 'expose our motives in the war to the most effective criticism'. Before he could budge the Cabinet, both Congress (by claiming complete independence at Ramgarh on 20 March 1940) and the League (by claiming Pakistan at Lahore on 24 March 1940) adopted unapproachable postures.

Amery peppered Linlithgow to take up the scheme almost as soon as the Churchill Government was formed. Then, on 17 June, 1940 he urged him 'most strongly' to support its incorporation in an invitation to the party leaders to reconstitute the provincial Governments and join the central Executive.[29] Though Linlithgow was still unconvinced of the case for change, the gravity of the war situation after the fall of France induced him to arrange meetings with Gandhi and Jinnah. At this time, a Congress Working Committee resolution at Wardha recognised that, with the fall of France, 'the problem of the achievement of national freedom has now to be considered along with the one of its maintenance and the defence of the country'.[30] Gandhi was effectively set aside as leader. On 1 July 1940 Linlithgow proposed the 'somewhat revolutionary scheme' that he had resisted for months.[31] On 7 July 1940 the Congress Working Committee added a plank to its complete independence platform that might facilitate its cooperation with the war effort : '......a provisional National Government should be constituted at the Centre, which, though formed as a transitory measure, should be such as to command the confidence of all the elected elements in the Central Legislature, and secure the closest cooperation of the responsible Governments in the Provinces'.[32]

On 12 July1940 Amery placed before Cabinet a draft declaration, based on Linlithgow's cabled proposals. Briefly, it promised : membership of the Commonwealth as an equal partner within a year of the war ending; the right of Indians to frame their own constitution provided that they agreed upon machinery for doing so; a treaty for handling Britain's obligations during a transitional period; the addition of representative Indians to the Viceroy's executive and the creation of an advisory war council. Only Attlee gave Amery strong support. The main critics were Churchill, Lord Lloyd and Simon. No objection was taken to the short-term changes. However, Churchill abhorred such a 'far reaching departure' in policy for the future, while the Cabinet generally wished to emphasize Britain's continuing obligations rather than India's rights. Amery was asked to redraft the declaration, while Churchill individually questioned the Viceroy direct about the wisdom of making any declaration at all. Linlithgow's response was to retrace his steps, claiming, somewhat unfairly, that he would not have gone so far had not Amery's entreaties led him to assume Cabinet support for a declaration going beyond past statements. He modified his recommendation, now playing down the freshness of the proposed declaration's policy, suppressing the suggested treaty, emphasizing Britain's obligations, and leaving Britain's hands free in the future.

Amery feared the collapse of the initiative. He called upon Attlee and Halifax to help with the Cabinet, and struggled to defend himself against Churchill's unjust accusation that he had gone behind the Cabinet's back, misleading the Viceroy in order to inspire a novel policy departure. It had always been customary for the Secretary of State to develop his personal views in correspondence with the Viceroy prior to placing them before Cabinet. Amery pleaded (in vain) for Churchill to realize that with Britain's acceptance of the principle of self-government, the principle of trusteeship became an anachronism. Britain must now say to India : 'We are prepared to implement immediately after the war any agreement which you may by then have reached among yourselves.'[33]

The declaration survived, but in much weakened form. Linlithgow's modifications were incorporated, while Churchill himself revised the text, excising the one year's time limit and the pledge to accept in advance the decisions of a constituent assembly. Britain merely undertook to assist the creation of a body, 'with the least possible delay' after the war, to devise a constitutional framework, which, through 'primarily the responsibility of Indians themselves', must be 'subject to the due fulfilment of the obligations which Britain's long connection with India has imposed upon her'. Furthermore, the pre-requisite to advance was that Indians must agree on the form of the constituent body and the principles of the constitution that it devised. In other words, there was no provision for Indian dominionhood on any basis other than unity.

When Linlithgow announced the offer on 8th August all parties rejected it without hesitation. At once Churchill counselled Linlithgow against further change : 'Declaration represented the farthest Cabinet was prepared to go.'[34] It was agreed not to proceed with the short-term reforms.

The first year of war-time negotiations to bridge the constitutional impasse had ended in stalemate. A new individual satyagraha was soon launched and soon crushed. By September 1941 some 23,000 Indians had been convicted in connection with it. During the second year of war no further constitutional initiative was taken. In May 1941, in response to pressure from a gathering of Indian moderates, reinforced by Amery's reading of sentiment in the House of Commons, Linlithgow proposed and the Cabinet approved the addition of three non-official Indians to the Viceroy's executive and the creation of a war advisory committee. The enlarged executive's first action in November was to secure the release of the satyagraha prisoners whose sentences had not expired. This was a necessary but by no means sufficient condition of further negotiations. On both the short-term reforms and the gaol delivery Amery had to overcome Churchillian hostility. Moreover, in September Churchill had denied the applicablility of the Atlantic Charter to India.

V

Towards the end of 1941 opinion in London was becoming favourable to a new initiative. In September, Ernest Bevin (Minister of Labour and National Service in the War Cabinet) wrote to Amery :

> I must confess that leaving the settlement of the Indian problem until after the war fills me with alarm......We made certain definite promises in the last war and practically a quarter of a century has gone, and, though there has been an extension of self-government, we have not, in my view, 'delivered the goods'in a broad and generous way. It is quite understandable that neither Muslim nor Hindu places much confidence in our 'after war promises'. It seems to me that the time to take action to establish Dominion Status is now—to develop or improvise the form of Government to carry us through the war but to remove from all doubt the question of Indian freedom at the end of the war. I firmly believe that a bold step now would rally Indian opinion behind us.[35]

Bevin had previously expressed interest in India in conversation with Amery, and earlier in the year had pressed him to have an Indian Labour member added to the Viceroy's executive in order to win over the American Labour press. In October Schuster began to inform Amery that among all parties in the Commons there were members who favoured an initiative, perhaps by an all-parties' delegation visiting India to discuss the details of a new constitution with the leaders. At the same time American opposition to aid to Britain was making much of the persecution of Indian patriots and the insincerity of British 'intentions of applying to her the democratic principles for which she professed to be fighting'.[36]

On 19 December, thirteen days after Pearl Harbour, at a Cabinet meeting presided over by Attlee, Bevin questioned whether present policy was 'calculated to get the fullest war effort from India'.[37] As Churchill was then in Washington he was well palced to relate the Pacific war situation to India, but, as usual, he was hostile to 'raising constitutional issue'.[38] Attlee replied that it was bound to be raised in Parliament soon. Early in 1942 a group of Indian moderate elder statesmen appealed to Churchill for 'some bold stroke [of] far-sighted statesmanship'. Labour and American pressures upon him soon became irresistible. In January Attlee argued for 'someone' to be sent out to bring the Indian leaders together.[39] He was echoed by a Labour peer, Lord Faringdon, early in February. At this time, Cripps, returning from a successful ambassadorship in Moscow and about to become Lord Privy Seal and leader of the Commons, told the press that he might visit India 'later on'.[40] Meanwhile he bacame a member of an India Committee of the War Cabinet charged with drafting a new constitutional statement. Churchill set it up on 26 February, the same day that Mr. W.A. Harriman, the President's Special Representative on Lend Lease to the British Empire, raised the Indian question with him.[41]

The 'draft declaration' that eventually issued from the India Committee, and Cripps' exposition of it in India from 22 March to 12 April, mark an historic departure in British policy, indeed the moment of decision in the problem of freedom with unity.

The draft declaration defined Britain's object as 'the creation of a new Indian Union which shall constitute a Dominion, associated with the United Kingdom and other Dominions by a common allegiance to the Crown, but equal to them in every respect, in no way subordinate in any aspect of its domestic or external affairs'. It laid down in precise and clear terms the steps by which self-government was to be achieved. Immediately after the war an assembly of British Indians would be elected by the provincial assemblies on the basis of proportional representation, and charged with making a new constitution. The states would be asked to send delegates on the same proportionate basis as British India. Alternatively, Britain would accept any other constituent body that Indians themselves agreed upon. Britain undertook to accept and implement the new constitution forthwith, subject to two conditions : first, the conclusion of a treaty covering all matters arising from a complete transfer of power (including the protection of minorities) but imposing no 'restriction on the power of the Indian Union to decide in the future its relationship to the other Member States of the British Commonwealth'; secondly, the right of any province to stand out of the Union and become a separate Dominion. In the immediate future, that is during the war and the post-war period of constitution making, Britain would retain control of the defence of India but the organization of India's resources would be the responsibility of 'the Government of India with the cooperation of the peoples of India'. The declaration ended with an invitation to the leaders of the principal sections of Indian opinion to participate 'in the counsels of their country', and so help with 'a task which is vital and essential for the future freedom of India'.

The declaration contained the essential aspects of Cripps' scheme of November 1939, but with one vital difference for which Amery was responsible.

First, complete independence was conceded. While the language of the Balfour declaration was used, once the treaty between the Dominion of India and Britain was signed India was free to stay in or leave the Commonwealth. Cripps expounded the point at press conferences. When a questioner put it to him that 'what is required is one word, "freedom", Cripps replied : 'There is no conceivable doubt that [the declaration] allows complete and absolute self-determination and self-government for India.'[42] R.G. Coupland, the eminent constitutional historian who joined the Cripps Mission, aptly dates the 'Declaration of Indian Independence' to the publication of Cripps' offer on 29 March 1942.[43]

Secondly, Indians secured the right to frame their own constitution immediately after the war, subject to the treaty provision. The treaty method of handling transitional arrangements underlined India's equality. Further, with Cabinet approval Cripps stated that Britain would not attempt to protect its commercial interests in the treaty.

Thirdly, representative Indians were invited to participate in wartime government, which meant the provinces and the Veceroy's executive.

The vital difference between the 1939 and 1942 schemes was the departure from constituion-making by a three-fifths majority vote of delegates drawn from all of the provinces. In 1939 Cripps wa prepared to impose a democratically devised constitution upon the Muslims. In 1942 Muslim majority provinces might opt out of the new Union. Indeed, as the declaration provided for an alternative assembly on any agreed basis, it was possible for the redistribution of provincial boundaries, or partition, to precede the transfer of power. Probably Cripps accepted this new departure, for which Amery was responsible, because of his first-hand acquaintance with the views of Jinnah and Liaquat, together with their success since 1939 in making the Muslim League the mouthpiece of Muslim nationalism.

The contrast between the declaration and the August offer is strong. Independence, not only Dominion status, was now conceded, while the time and method of its achievement were defined. Indians would no longer be merely 'primarily' responsible for making the constitution, subject to Britain fulfilling its obligations. They would be solely responsible, and Britain's obligations would be handled in a separate treaty. However, the really decisive policy advance was Amery's answer to the problem of freedom with unity. For the first time Britain conceded India's right to freedom without imposing the condition of unity. No longer was the accession of the states or the agreement of all of the provinces made a prerequisite to dominionhood. The declaration cut the ground from beneath the feet of critics who accused Britain of pursuing *divide et impera.*[44] The answer to the problem of freedom with unity was to admit that it might be insoluble, and to accept the possible consequence : plural dominionhood.

It is necessary to despatch three objections to the argument that the Cripps offer marks the culminating stage in the evolution of London policies for freedom and unity.

First, it may be argued that the offer was contingent upon its acceptance as a whole, and that its rejection by the Indian parties in April 1942 rendered it null and void. But there could be no back step in imperial policy. Once enunciated, the doctrine of independence for one or more Indian nations could not be retracted. In July 1942 Churchill told the King that all British parties were reconciled to giving up India after the war. That month the Cabinet considered the Viceroy's suggestion for the need to affirm that a policy no less liberal than the draft declaration would apply to India after the war. Amery drafted a suitable parliamentary question and the following reply :

> His Majesty's Government stand firmly by the broad intention of their offer, which is that on the conclusion of hostilities India shall have it within her power to attain complete self-government through such method of arriving at a constitutional solution and under such form of government as may be agreed among themselves by the principal elements in India's national life.[45]

Churchill was defeated when he sought to retract the draft declaration and return to the language of the Balfour declaration, expunging the former's reference to secession. On 30 July Amery reaffirmed in Parliament that 'the broad intentions of the Government [i.e. 'complete self-government'] remained the same, irrespective of the immediate conduct of the Congress Party'. Pledged now to post-war independence, Britain's problem would be to secure agreement among successor authorities upon the form that it should take.

Secondly, it has been argued that whatever the declaration said about the future, its limited application to the present betrayed a persistent unwillingness to transfer responsibility to Indians. It has been suggested that the Cabinet intended the offer of participation in wartime government to be rejected by Congress, that there was no will to enlist Congress as an ally, and that the Mission was a clever propaganda exercise : 'a "plant" merely devised so as to range world opinion against India'; 'just "bluff" to influence American opinion.'[46]

The truth is that London opinion was divided on the key question of reconstituting the Viceroy's executive, with Churchill and Cripps at opposite poles, and that Linlithgow's opposition to Cripps' negotiations was sufficient to secure Cripps' repudiation.[47] Cripps' position on the reconstruction of the Viceroy's executive had not changed in substance since October 1939 : the constitution could not be changed in war-time but party representatives could be empanelled and treated as if they were Cabinet ministers. The Viceroy would normally accept their advice, as the Crown accepted that of His Majesty's Government, but he could not, of course, divest himself of his statutory responsibility to veto measures affecting 'the safety, tranquillity or interest of British India'.

Cripps left London with a brief, written by himself and approved by the Cabinet, which required him 'to negotiate some scheme' for the Indian leaders' participation 'in an advisory or consultative manner in the counsels of their country'.[48] He could offer Indians seats on the executive to any extent consistent with 'defence and good government', while the 'advisory or consultative manner' in which the Viceroy might employ them was not circumscribed. He was required to consult the Viceroy and the Commander-in-Chief. Cripps negotiated with the leaders chosen by the Congress, Azad and Nehru, in terms of a fully Indianised executive (save for the Viceroy and the Commander-in-Chief) that would normally operate as a Cabinet. They welcomed the proposal. It was broadly consistent with the July 1940 plea for a 'provincial National Government', while in December 1941 January 1942 the Congress Working Committee and the All-India Congress Committee had agreed a resolution that removed defence from the operation of Gandhi's policy of non-violence, thus paving the way for Congress cooperation in the war effort if suitable opportunity arose. Linlithgow, who believed any reorganization of the executive to be his own affair, was opposed to offering full Indianisation as part of a political deal and hostile to the application of Cabinet conventions to his Government. Cripps' Mission was doomed from 6 April, when Linlithgow won the support of Amery and Churchill on the latter point. Cripps' freedom to negotiate on the executive was withdrawn. On 9 April, at his last meeting with Azad and Nehru, Cripps could only say that they must discuss the reconstruction of the executive with the Viceroy. Linlithgow's reputation among Congressmen now became the decisive point in the rejection of the Cripps' offer. Nehru's view was that 'with a more accessible person with whom the Congress leaders could have talked around the table and discussed actually how the Executive worked, they might possibly have accepted'.[49]

The truth of London's tergiversation has been masked by Cripp's loyal denials that there was any change to his brief, or even that he had offered a quasi-Cabinet to Azad and Nehru. However, it was known at the time by Roosevelt's circle (for the President's representative Lousis Johnson had become involved in the defence aspect of the negotiations), by a member of the Mission's staff (F.F. Turnbull, Amery's secretary) and by Amery's acting secretary (Miles Clauson).[50]

The change to Cripps' brief was effected in London despite the presence of such strong supporters as Attlee and Bevin in the War Cabinet. The progress of negotiations was reviewed by the India Committee, normally chaired by Attlee. Its members were the wavering and uncertain Amery, the essentially illiberal Simon, Sir James Grigg, a recent Finance Member of the Viceroy's executive who had found Linlithgow too conciliatory towards Congress, and Sir John Anderson, a former Governor of Bengal and an opponent of centralization in India. What enabled Churchill to destroy the Mission after 6 April, and to deliver the *coup de grace* from the chair of the India Committee four days later, was Linlithgow's antagonism, together with Cripps' injudicious failure to keep the Viceroy informed of the detail of negotiations on the defence question in which he, Louis Johnson and Nehru were involved. Attlee found it difficult to stand his ground once the Viceroy's hostility to Cripps became apparent, and impossible to do so when it seemed that Cripps was negotiating behind the Viceroy's back.

On 10 April 1942 the Congress, aggrieved at Cripps' retraction of his earlier offer, raised its demand to government by a Cabinet with full power. Later in the year it again resorted to civil disobedience, indeed to the less than civil Quit India movement. Cripps' plan for a provisional National Government ceased to be practical politics. The India Committee consistently rejected the proposals of Linlithgow's successor, Lord Wavell (October1943-March 1947) to revive the plan.[51] Only at the end of the war was the Viceroy permitted to arrange a conference at Simla in an attempt to set up an interim Indian government.

The third objection to accepting Cripps' offer as the final breakthrough to Indian freedom is the argument that the offer implied a new imperialist policy, empire by treaty.[52] It is suggested that Cripps' provision for the opting out of provinces, and for the abstention under British protection of states unwilling to accede to the Union, would make a parody of freedom , leaving imperial forces to hold the ring. With regard to the princes, Cripps did undertake that Britain would honour its treaties to protect them, even if that meant maintaining forces in Ceylon. However, as the Resident to Hyderabad, the largest of the states, realized as early as 1930, it would scarcely be practicable for Britain to defend a prince against aggression by a self-governing India, which, in many cases would encircle his state. Cripps acknowledged that the states' defence would require the concurrence of the Indian Union, and he never envisaged that the treaty whereby Britain discharged its obligations should be more than transitional. In 1939 he had made it clear that the treaty was, in effect, a means of serving the princes with fifteen years' notice. Certainly in 1942 Cripps denied Britain's intention to confer dominionhood upon a state or group of states. As for the provinces, the opting out provision was intended to make Congress face the necessity for conciliation, while Cripps (like Wavell after him) hoped that the creation of a National Government would countervail the drift to disunity. But even if some of the Cabinet looked forward to a plurality of Indian Dominions, could they realistically have expected Britain to bear the burden of their defence? Such an arrangement must have depended upon the Dominions' agreement to meet the costs, for already by 1942 India's sterling balances had grown alarmingly. The empire was indeed, as Gandhi perceived, a failing bank. True, Amery doodled with plans for a continuing imperial presence in a federal Indian enclave, and even after the war Churchill wistfully told Wavell to 'keep a bit of India'.[53] But how could Britain, against the wishes of a nation or nations to whom she had given freedom, retain forces on Indian territory to serve imperial interests?

After the declaration of 29 March 1942 it was inevitable that at the end of the war, the pressure of Indian, British and world opinion would force His Majesty's Government to quit India as soon as viable successors could be found.

VI

The relationships between events in India and London policies are, of course, complex. As long as Britain remained in India, tactics and strategies for winning and holding collaborators were necessary. Together with the preservation of interests and the influence of moral and political principles they explain the timing and the form of the stages in the devolution of empire.

The 1917 and 1929 declarations were undoubtedly attempts to 'rally the moderates' behind the Raj. On the former occasion Britain needed war-time allies at a stage when the 'extremist' home rulers had gained control of the Congress. On the latter occasion Irwin and the Labour Government wanted to break the solid unity of the Hindu nationalists who were boycotting the Statutory Commission. At both stages Britain needed to win enough support to make the coming reforms work. But neither declaration was merely tactical. In 1917 the principle of responsibility exceeded the Congress demand for self-government. The war-time and early post-war shibboleth of self-determination was certainly influential in the general re-orientation of London's India policy from 1917 to 1922. Again, Irwin, Baldwin and the Labour Cabinet believed sincerely in the principle of India's equality within the Commonwealth, behind which lay their acceptance of the moral right of a new brown Dominion to the status of the old white ones. It was a tenet of the Montford reforms that India should enjoy fiscal autonomy, while Irwin and the Labour Secretary of State, Wedgwood Benn, resisted attempts to manipulate tariffs to Britain's advantage during the slump. The 1939, 1940 and 1942 declarations were clearly intended to win Indian support for the war, and were prompted or influenced by Labour pressures and world, especially American, opinion.

What is remarkable is that London was not responsive to the Congress satyagrahas in protest against the inadequacies of declarations or reforms. The 1920-2 non-co-operation movement evoked no London offer to advance beyond the 1919 Act. Though in December 1921 the Viceroy contemplated moving at once from provincial dyarchy to full responsibility a Committee of Cabinet refused him power to negotiate. The 1930-1 Civil Disobedience movement gave rise to the Gandhi-Irwin Pact, but that won Gandhi no modification to the all-India federation scheme that had emerged at the first Round Table Conference. The revival of the movement in 1932-4 was suppressed ruthlessly, leaving Willingdon feeling like an imperial Mussolini and disposed to make concessions. Whitehall over-ruled him firmly both when he pressed for a British Indian federation to be granted central responsibility if the princes became a ball-and-chain, and even when he proposed to appoint an Indian to the traditionally British Commerce membership of his executive. The muted satyagraha that followed the rejection of the August 1940 offer was crushed in 1932 style. When, a few months later, Linlithgow proposed a more limited expansion of his executive than the offer had allowed, some members of the Cabinet now demurred. The Quit India movement was a major reason for the India Committee's disallowance of Wavell's proposals for the reconstruction of his executive.

Once a declaration was made, or reforms were in progress, satyagraha simply led Britain to rely upon the non-Congress parties and the princes. As the Congress protest movements were largely an attempt to win a national mandate by direct action, it is scarcely surprising that Indians who could not subscribe to Congress policies sought Brtitish protection under the constitution. Separate electorates After 1909; Muslim ministries in the Punjab and Bengal under dyarchy; provincial autonomy, the separation of Sind, and weightage in an all India federation, under the 1935 Act; the recognition of Jinnah as a nationalist leader in 1939; all were the natural consequence of Congress tactics and Britain's need for collaborators. All worked towards separatism, until the possibility of Pakistan was officially conceded in 1942, and, three years later at Simla Jinnah was able to reject the countervailing machinery of a National Government. Similarly, Congress frightened the princes into the welcoming arms of the Raj, until the princes' exercise of their veto in British Indian progress wrecked the possibility of central responsibility in the 1930s.

This is not to argue that satyagraha was responsible for disunity. The periods of constitutional activity by Congress parties saw a diminution of Congress unity and national coherence. In the 1920s the proliferation of essentially Hindu parties (Liberals, no-changers, Swarajists, responsive co-operators, Mahasabhites) was a function of participation in the parliamentary game. In the 1930s proliferation followed the end of civil disobedience, as the Swrajists, Malaviya's Nationalists and the Congress Socialists emerged. The exercise of office by provincial Congress ministries weakened the central control of the Working Committee and helps to explain the apparently cavalier resignations of November 1939. As Gandhi knew, participation in government reduced an organization that claimed to speak for all India to one among many competing parties.

It was not so much that Britain pursued a policy of divide and rule as that the process of devolving power by stages in a politically and socially disparate country was inherently divisive.

Devolution by stages seemed appropriate when political and social development was so uneven that the transfer of power at a stroke would contravene the cardinal doctrine of trusteeship. Effete princes with loyal subjects, the historically important but often backward Muslim minority, the scheduled castes, these and others required special protection under the constitution, which the more precocious, more westernized and primarily high caste Hindu Congress was not trusted to provide. Devolution by stages would enable the elements of modern politics, in particular parties based upon principles and interests, to supplant the divisions of caste and creed.[54] The difficulty with such a policy was the time-scale that it assumed. Before India secured self-government it must pass through the stages of evolution that Britain had experienced since the Middle Ages. Lord Curzon, the draftsman of the term 'responsible government' in the Montagu declaration, noted : 'When the Cabinet used the expression 'ultimate self-government' they probably contemplated an intervening period of 500 years.'[55] Birkenhead thought it 'frankly inconceivable that India will ever be fit for Dominion self-Government'.[56] Simon anticipated that the emergence of Indian nationhood would involve a 'prolonged evolution'.[57] In an article on 'The Evolution of Political Life in India', Irwin followed Stubbs's account of 'the gradual unfolding of the primitive institutions of our forefathers who made the England which William conquered, in to the parliamentary government which our country knew on the eve of the modern age', as if to suggest that India must pass through a similar succession of stages under British tutelage.[58] Churchill charged the National Government that introduced the 1935 Act with running 'counter to nature', with 'trying to put the clock forward without regard to the true march of solar events'.[59]

The main flaw in London's inter-war India policy is that it was cast in the evolutionary mould characteristic of late-Victorian thought, of the stable era in which the statesmen of the 1920s and 1930s were reading Stubbs and Maine at Oxford and Cambridge. Policy was essentially unconstructive. As Zetland realized in 1939 the follies of the princes were Britain's reward for thirty years of *laissez-faire.* They had not been pressed to introduce parliamentary government, which Britain might have made a condition of continued protection. Again, programmes for social and economic reform were insufficient to the task of modernization, the normal concomitant of democracy. It was not until December 1942 that the India Office had before it a comprehensive plan for the mobilization of India's resources (the work of Cripps and an unknown colleague.)

This is not to deny that the advantages of empire acted as a powerful brake on London's initiative. As long as India was major area of trade and investment, a large contributor to the costs of imperial defence, and a fair field for the employment of British civil and military officers, the policy of gradual devolution was bound to seem a rationalization of self-interest. In the early 1930s, at a time of economic crisis, a National Government could still manipulate Indian tariffs and the exchange rate to Britain's advantage. Yet between the wars the relative importance of the India trade declined sharply. In the year preceding the First World War India took £83.5 m worth of British goods, in the year before the Second, £35m worth. The corresponding years' Indian exports to Britain were £39m and £ 41.25m. By 1939 India had a favourable balance of trade with Britain. At the time of the Joint Parliamentary Committee on Indian reform (1933-4), Lancashire interests, their cotton trade with India virtually lost, refused to join with Churchill in his attack upon central responsibility . Certainly, the Indian Army reamined vital to imperial defence between the wars. However, the process of Indianisation made the civil services less of a haven for Britain's youth, and indeed, the decimation brought by the First World War opened up so many opportunities at home that an Indian career was often no longer the necessity that it had once been. It has recently been suggested that the transfer of power in India was largely the result of a manpower shortage.[60]

On the eve of the Second World War, while some tendencies in imperial relations pointed towards a transfer of power, London's policy of constitutional gradualism, together with the deepening of divisions in India, made early self-government seem unlikely. The most likely policy after the princes' rejection of the federal offer in September 1939, was that favoured by Linlithgow and Hoare : the application of further pressure upon the princes to secure their accession.[61] But that would scarcely have solved the problem of freedom with unity. The Congress Working Committee, already concerned at the provincialization of politics under the Act, would scarcely cooperate in a central government that it could not hope to control. Neither the princes nor the Muslims were likely to participate in central government that it *could* hope to control.

The war created the necessity for a change in British policy. By 1942 the underpinning of the empire was gone. Special arrangements for trade no longer seemed necessary. India's sterling debt was fast being obliterated by its sterling balances (credits earned by contributions to the war effort). Lend lease had given America a voice in imperial affairs. Labour leaders demanded an equal place for India in the new order for which the free world was fighting. It was in these circumstances that, twenty-five years after Montagu's declaration and in the third year of a second war, London cut the Gordian knot of the problem of freedom with unity. The departure was so inconsistent with inter-war policy that it would scarcely have been made so early in peace time.

REFERENCES

1. M. Gwyer and A. Appadorai (eds.), *Speeches and Documents on the Indian Constitution,* 1921-47, 2 vols. (London, 1957), I, xxvii. Unless otherwise noted, the declarations mentioned in the present article may be consulted in this collection.
2. 'Dominion Status and Responsible Government', 4 June 1929, Government of India 100/Notes, NAI.
3. Indian Legislative Assembly Debates, IV, pt. I, 349.
4. Hailey's Memorandum of 27 Oct 1928, Hailey P., 30, IOL.
5. A detailed account appears in the author's *The Crisis of Indian Unity,* 1917-40 (Oxford and Delhi, 1974), ch. 2.
6. Winterton's dairy for 25 Oct. 1929, in *Orders of the day* (London, 1953), p. 158.
7. D.L. Keir, *The Constitutional History of Modern Britain,* 1485-1937 (London, 1948), p. 543.
8. *Lords' Debates,* 5 Nov 1929.
9. *Daily Telegraph,* 12 Nov 1929.
10. Hoare to Willingdon, 17 Feb 1935 (cable), Templewood P. IOL.
11. Willingdon to Hoare, 31 Jan 1935 (cable), *ibid.*
12. *Commons' Debates,* 6 Feb 1935.
13. Linlithgow to Zetlant, 21 Dec 1939, Zetland P., IOL.
14. The argument of this section paraphrases the author's *The Crisis of Indian Unity* 1917-40, and 'The Demission of Empire in South Asia : Some Perspectives', *Journal of Imperial and Commonwealth History,* II (Oct 1973), 79-94.
15. Cripps' record of a conversation with Liaquat, Dec. 1939, In E. Estorick, *Stafford Cripps, A Biography,* (London, 1949), p. 198. At this time Zetland observed that Jinnah seemed 'to have got back to the position taken up by Minto and Morley thirty years ago', Zetland to Linlithgow, 22 Nov 1939, Zetland P.
16. An account of negotiations during the early war months appears in the author's 'British Policy and the Indian Problem, 1936-40', in C.H. Philips and M.D. Wainwright (eds.), *The partition of India* (London, 1970), pp. 79-94, esp. 85ff.
17. Gwyer and Appadorai, II, 484-7.
18. Zetland to Linlithgow, 24 Jan 1940 (cable), L/PO/252/16, IOL.
19. Zetland to Linlithgow, 2 Feb 1940 (cable), *ibid.*
20. *Commons' Debates,* 3 Oct 1939.
21. Zetland to Linlithgow, 2 Oct 1939, Zetland P.

22. Cripps to Nehru, 11 Oct 1939, in J.N. Nehru (ed.), *A Bunch of Old Letters* (Bombay, 1958).
23. Cripps to Nehru, 16 Nov 1939, J. Nehru P., NML.
24. Nehru to Mahadev Desai, 9 Dec. 1939, in *A Bunch of Old Latters.*
25. R.A. Butler of S.F. Stewart, 17 Nov 1939, L/PO/258, IOL.
26. Stewart complained that Cripps had unjustifiably claimed his support for the scheme that Cripps took to India in December 1939: 'At best he has been guilty of wishful thinking to the point of crookedness' (Stewart to Laithwaite, 13 Jan 1940, L/PO/258, IOL).
27. Enclosure in Cripps to Stewart, 24 Nov 1939, L/PO/252/16, IOL.
28. Zetland's memo, for War Cabinet, 31 Jan 1940, WP (G) (40) 37, in L/PO/252/16. For non-official appreciations, arguing the need for urgent action to meet a dangerous situation, see (i) the report by a small sub-committee of the National Labour Organization, 7 Feb 1940, encl. to M. MacDonald to Zetland, 20 Mar 1940, L/PO/77; (ii) Guy Wint's letters to Schuster, Mar-May 1940, L/PO/6/105d.
29. Amery to Linlithgow, 17 June 1940 (cable), L/PO/6/105 d.
30. Gwyer and Appadorai, II, 500.
31. Linlithgow to Zetland, 1 July 1940 (cable), L/PO/6/105 d.
32. Gwyer and Appadorai, II, 500-1.
33. Amery to Churchill, 14 July 1940, L/PO/6/105 d.
34. Churchill to Linlithgow, 14 Aug 1940 (cable), *ibid.* Certainly Amery was prepared to go further (see, e.g., his letters to Linlithgow, 4 July; Attlee, 21, 23 July; Halifax 23, 30 July; Churchill, 23 July; Zetland, 3 Aug; also Churchill's Cabinet Paper 'remodelling' the already revised draft of the statement that Amery had originally prepared, WP (40)295, 30 July 1940; all in L/PO/6/105d). In 1942 Amery was some-what misleadingly apt to read the germ of the Cripps Mission's offer into the August offer. In particular, he extrapolated the 1942 provision for separate Muslim dominionhood from the 1940 promises: that India would secure dominion status 'with the least possible delay after the war', and that Britain would not transfer power 'to any system of government whose authority is directly denied by large and powerful elements in India's national life'. In other words, the 1940 offer's insistence upon agreement among the Indian parties was not intended to delay dominionhood. This may have been Amery's own position in 1940 but in view of this difficulty with the August offer it can scarcely be claimed that the Cabinet then contemplated Indian freedom on any basis other than for a single united dominion. Only in March 1942, when he secured Cabinet approval for the principle of separate Muslim dominionhood, was the precondition of unity waived. See Amery to Linlithgow, 21 Feb 1942; Amery to Churchill, 25 Feb 1942; Amery's Note,? Apr 1942; all in N. Mansergh and E.W.R. Lumby (eds.), *The Transfer of Power,*

1942-7, Vol. I. *The Cripps Mission* (London, 1970), pp. 217-78, 240-1, 838-41. In the light of the evidence now available for 1940, the author's present argument reverses his earlier acceptance of Amery's claims (in 'The Mystery of the Cripps Mission', *Journal of Commonwealth Political Studies*, XI. 3 (1973), 207; and 'The Stopgap Viceroy', *South Asian Review* VII, (October 1973), 57).

35. Bevin to Amery, 24 Sept 1941, Bevin P., Churchill College, Cambridge.
36. G.S. Bajpai to Linlithgow, 1 Dec 1941, Linlithgow P., F 125/130, IOL.
37. Cabinet Conclusion 131 of 1941, Mansergh and Lumby, p. 14n.
38. Churchill to Attlee, 7 Jan 1942, *ibid.*, 14.
39. Attlee to Amery, 24 Jan 1942, *ibid.*, 75.
40. *Ibid.*, 127.
41. G.R. Hess, *America Encounters India*, 1941-7 (Baltimore, 1971), pp. 36-7.
42. Mansergh and Lumby, pp. 576-7.
43. *The Cripps Mission* (London, 1942), p. 34.
44. Amery to Linlithgow, 21 Feb 1942, Mansergh and Lumby, p. 218.
45. War Cabinet (42) 321, 28 July 1942, L/PO/77, IOL.
46. *E.g.* Memo by Sir E. Villiers on a meeting with Nehru, 5 July 1942, L/PO/6/105 e. Also notes by Graham Spry (Cripps' secretary during his Mission) on his propaganda visit to America, 22 April-30 May 1942, L/PO/6/105 d-f; see esp. note on meeting with L. Currie, Executive Assistant to the President, 9 May.
47. A detailed account appears in the author's 'The Mystery of the Cripps Mission', *loc. cit.*
48. Mansergh and Lumby, p. 306.
49. D. Monteath's note on a conversation with Sir E. Villiers about his meeting with Nehru, 13 Aug 1942, L/PO/6/105e.
50. Spry's Notes, esp. of meetings with A.A. Berle, Assistant Under-Secretary of State, 11 May; Mr Justice Frankfurter, 13 May; Dr Stanley Hornbeck of the State Department, 13 May; the President, 15 May; all in L/PO/6/105 e-f. Clauson's note on R.I. Campbell to Sir D. Scott, 17 July 1942, L/PO/6/105 e. F.F. Turnbull to A.H. Joyce, D. Monteath and P.J. Patrick, 21 Sept 1942, *ibid.*
51. Wavell's attempted initiatives appear in P. Moon (ed.), *Wavell: The Viceroy's Journal* (London, 1973). Some Labour opinion also favoured a further war-time initiative (e.g. Labour Party International Department Report No. 265, 'Advisory Committee on Imperial Questions: The Indian Deadlock', Mar 1944, in Bevin P., 2/11, Churchill College, Cambridge).
52. E.g. Eric Stokes, 'Cripps in India', *Historical Journal*, XIV (1971), 427-34.
53. *Wavell's Journal*, 31 Aug 1945.
54. The point is developed in C. Bridge, 'Conservatives and Indian Reform (1929-39) : Towards a Pre-requisites Model in Imperial

Constitution-Making?', *Journal of Imperial and Commonwealth History,* IV, 2, (Jan 1976).

55. Quoted in R. Danzig, 'The Announcement of August 20th, 1917', *Journal of Asian Studies,* XXVIII (1968), 31.
56. Birkenhead to Reading, 4 Dec 1924, in F.W.F. Smith (Lord Birkenhead), *Frederick Edwin, Earl of Birkenhead* (London, 1935), p. 245.
57. *Indian Statutory Commission Report,* 2 vols. (Cd. 3568-9, 1930), I, para. 460.
58. J.G. Cumming (ed.), *Political India,* 1832-1932 (London, 1932), pp. 1-21, see pp. 4-5.
59. Speech of 11 Feb 1935, in C.H. Phillips (ed.), *The Evolution of India and Pakistan,* 1858-1947: *Select Documents* (London, 1962), p. 316.
60. D.C. Potter, 'Manpower Shortage and the End of Colonialism : The Case of the Indian Civil Service', *Modern Asian Studies,* VII (1973), pp. 47-73.
61. For Hoare, see Templewood P., XI. 1 (Nov. 1939), Cambridge University Library; Zetland to Linlithgow, 8 Nov 1939, Zetland P.

—R.J. MOORE

CHAPTER - X

THE GURUKUL KANGRI AS AN EXPERIMENT IN NATIONAL EDUCATION

> "As education is the mother of character and as the strength or weakness of a person or people lies in the character, it is not illogical to say, that nowadays the fortune of a nation is not decided on the battlefield, but in the schoolroom where the children are educated."[1]

I

One of the most important fields of activity for the socio-religious reform movements that emerged in late 19th century India was education. Not only could they spread their religous ideas through the channel of educational institutions—but schools and universities were also ideal instruments to give a voice to their social and political agenda and helped to disseminate their respective visions of an Indian nation. It is hardly surprising then that educational endeavours were at the core of many influential religious and nationalist projects at the time : The brand of Islamic reform represented by Syed Ahmad Khan for instance was centred around the famous Anglo Muhamaddan College in Aligarh, the Islamic seminary in Deoband was pivotal for Muslim reformers with less modernist ambitions, Tagore's Shantiniketan was a project that caused tremendous stir all-over India, prominent representatives of what was later to be labelled as the Hindu right joined the campaign for the foundation of 'national schools' in Bengal 1905-10 and of a Hindu university in the 1910s,[2] and later Gandhi came up with his scheme of *naī tālīm*.[3] Indeed, it has even been argued that the partition of India was in a way anticipated by the strife to establish separate Hindu and a Muslim Universities.[4]

The impact of the above mentioned institutions and projects on diverse Indian nationalisms has been highlighted by many authors and their histories have been reconstructed and analysed in great detail in the past decades.[5] Strangely enough, the *Gurukul*[6] Kangri, one of the most controversial and radical attempts of making a school to the nucleus of 'national regeneration', has been largely overlooked so far. In 1902 the 'vegetarian wing' of the Punjab Arya Samaj founded the Gurukul in Kangri near the holy city of Hardwar with the avowed aim of "making an experiment in truly national education"[7] which would rekindle the spirit of the "virile civilisation of the ancients", thereby encouraging a complete reconstruction of society and finally allowing India to rise again to "the position of the queen of the civilised world".[8]

That this important facet of the Aryas' work has been hitherto neglected by critical research is astonishing since the Samaj is not only considered to have been the most influential Hindu reform movement in late 19th and early 20th centuries,[9] it is also regarded as an important 'ancestor' of today's Hindu nationalist organisations.[10] Christophe Jaffrelot, for instance, claims that the ideological essence of a militant, overtly political Hinduism had already been in existence albeit "in a latent state" in the Samaj.[11] If the movement did in fact play such a crucial role for the development of Hindu nationalism, one could also expect new insights into the nature of the so-called 'Hindu fundamentalist' ideology by analysing the ideals and values transmitted through this particular type of 'Arya' education.

Notwithstanding this, most of the research on the Arya Samaj—including Kenneth Jones' pioneering work[12]—has concentrated on the politically active so-called 'moderate wing' of the Arya movement. The Gurukul wing has not drawn the same attention[13] since it has often been regarded as 'apolitical' or 'devotional'.[14] My aim in this paper is to show that, first, the Gurukul did indeed have a highly elaborated political agenda and, secondly, in spite of its relative insignificance in terms of sheer numbers of its graduates, the school has had a considerable impact on contemporary Indian nationalist projects.

What, then, did the school actually contribute to the process of nation building? What were the sepcifically 'national' elements in the Gurukul brand of education and to whom did they appeal? I want to show that it is by applying the model of the 'nation of intent' as developed by Tønesson and Antlöv, that we might best understand the political significance of the vision of an 'Aryan nation' that was inculcated in the brahmacharies[15] through their training in the Gurukul :

> A nation of intent is a vision of territorial entity, a set of institutions, an ideal type of citizen and an identity profile that a group of 'social engineers' have in mind and try to implement. It will often be an idealistic form shared by a number of people who indentify themselves [....] with a whole nation whose other members, they hope, will join their vision.[16]

I argue that the Gurukul students were trained precisely to become such social engineers and to form the core of the proposed nation. In order to verify this assumption, I will concentrate on the activities of the institution in three particular fields which are generally regarded as being crucial for the construction of a national identity : historiography, language policy and homogenisation through the moulding of an ideal citizen and 'inventing' the image of an ideal society. In the specific case of creating a homogenous Hindu society, the overcome of caste barriers and other 'social evils' played a crucial role. The Gurukul's efforts in regard to these problems will also be discussed. To put these points into perspective, however, it is helpful to start with a brief description of the general educational situation in India at the turn of the 19th century, and to provide a short outline of the history and general features of the Gurukul.

II

THE STATE OF EDUCATION IN LATE 19TH CENTURY INDIA

Towards the end of the 19th century, the shadow of Macauly's famous 'Minute on Education' was still looming large on the minds of the intelligentsia in India. Although it had never been fully implemented, distrust towards oriental learning and cultural arrogance dominated by educational institutions run either directly by the British or at least "on western lines"[17] by missionaries or private carriers. At the level of primary education, missionaries were much more active than the government and many Hindus feared that an education in a Christian school would finally lead to cultural alienation of their children or was even part of a conspiracy that would lead to a "wholesale conversion to christianity".[18]

On the level of higher education the problems were of a slightly different kind. The curriculum taught in colleges and high schools that prepared students for the university entrance examination was modelled after its British counterpart and had almost nothing to do with the everyday experience of Indian students.[19] Krishna Kumar has explained this circumstance convincingly with the assumption that the main purpose of British educational efforts in India was not the transmission of useful knowledge but rather the production of reliable colonial citizens through moral upliftment and 'character training'.[20] The resulting alienation was catalysed by the fact that higher education was imparted exclusively through the midium of English which was, after all, a foreign language. Moreover, in the 1880s the growing number of graduates could no longer be absorbed by the above-mentioned professions and unemployment became a serious problem.[21] The resulting frustration and discontent made the educational system the target for severe criticism especially by those with nationalist leanings. Some of the defects commonly attributed to the prevailing system were :[22]

(1) The curricula with their stress on the English language, literature and history led to cultural alienation. Worse, the colleges were anti-national because they inculcate contempt for the indigenous culture and uncritical admiration for western culture;
(2) the vernaculars were completely neglected;
(3) physical exercise was not encouraged sufficiently;
(4) practical and technical education were lacking;
(5) the same was true for moral and religious instruction.

Yet, one basic assumption that the critics shared with the criticised was the tremendous optimism that the right type of education would not only produce morally and physically superior individuals but also solve economic problems and wipe out all 'social evils' and *ergo* contribute to the strengthening of the 'race' or 'nation'.[23] As a consequence, the decades from 1880 to 1930 witnessed quite a few initiatives mostly form socio-religious reform organisations to establish idiosyncratic educational institutions that had to be modern in the sense that they included instruction in natural sciences and English in their scheme of studies and were at the same time 'national', avoiding all the above-mentioned shortcomings of the governmental system and equipping their graduates with a sense of self-respect and pride for their 'national heritage'. It is obvious that in the heterogenous cultural, religious and linguistic landscape of India the ideas of what actually constituted this cultural heritage were as diverse as the different group that referred to it. It is in this context that we are now going to analyse in some detail the specific conceptions of the Arya Samaj.

EARLY ARYA EFFORTS IN EDUCATION

The firm belief that education was an individual right for everyone including women and *śūdras* and that it should be made compulsory, had already found exspression in the teachings of Swami Dayanand (1824-83). In his *Satyārth Prakāś* he had devoted one full chapter to this question,[24] where he gave detailed instructions about the nature of the schools he had in mind and the course of studies the brahmacharies ought to follow. Though the founders of the Gurukul and their successors always refer to Dayanand's precepts on educational matters as their guiding principles, interestingly the term Gurukul was never used by him. And indeed, the few educational experiments undertaken by the Swami himself during his lifetime were of a completely different type than the Kangri Gurukul.[25] Nonetheless, there are a few features in his proposed schools that became important for the institution founded in 1902 and are therefore worth being mentioned here.[26]

The first characteristic is the strict observation of *brahmacharya* during the whole period of education. i.e. until the age of 25 for boys and 16 for girls. To prevent the students from the "indulgence in lascivious thoughts", girls' and boys' schools were to be located at a distance of at least three miles from each other. The second point that was implemented was the idea, that education ought not be merely intellectual but also physical and spiritual. The third essential feature of the scheme was absolute equality of treatment of the students "be they princes or sons of paupers."[27] This provoking statement reoccurred almost literally decades later in the various reports and prospectus of the Gurukul.[28] A last element that became important was the special relationship between teachers and students (*guru-sisya sambandh*) that Dayanand laid stress upon. According to him and the Gurukul founders, successful education could only be accomplished if every external impact (including that of the children's parents) was strictly excluded.

THE ESTABLISHMENT OF THE KANGRI *GURUKUL*

The Dayanand Anglo-Vedic High School,[29] the first serious attempt to turn Dayanand's concept into reality, however, was far less radical than the founder of the Arya Samaj had suggested. The prominent role of English and western sciences and the neglect of Sanskrit and religious education soon provoked harsh criticism by the hardliners within the movement, and after the formal split of the Punjab Arya Samaj in 1893, the 'radicals', led by Lala Munshiram (1857-1926), started an agitation for the foundation of their own educational institution, the Gurukul. The actual fund-raising campaign lasted from 1897 to 1900, but it took another two years to find a proper place near the pilgrimage centre of Hardwar where Munshiram, who was appointed governor, wanted the institution to be situated. The *vidyālay* (high school) section of the Gurukul Kangri was opened in March 1902 with 53 brahmacharies.[30]A college section (mahāvidyālay) followed in 1907 and in 1917 there were already 340 students.[31] The teaching staff consisted of c. 15 professors and teachers in the latter year.

The whole course of studies extended over 14 years:[32] ten classes in the high school section and four in the college. The curriculum focussed on Sanskrit and Vedic literature but English and the sciences were also taught from the beginning. Later, additional courses in agriculture and traditional medicine (*āyurveda*) were introduced. All subjects—except for English—were taught through the medium of Hindi. The Gurukul even awarded its own degrees[33] to the brahmacharies who had successfully undergone the final examination, but these degrees were not recognised by the government and the institution voluntarily stayed outside the official system of education. In a pamphlet published in 1911 it was stated that :

> Under the present circumstances of our country, a seat of learning that aspires to become a centre of Arya (Hindu) culture and to give the first place to any methods of juvenile training must perforce forego official recognition; for you cannot dovetail into an occidental system [*sic*] a system which is based upon entirely different and in some respects opposite principles. All lovers of the indigenious [*sic*]system cannot therefore [*sic*], but fall back upon the Gurukula as the sole national educational centre of the ancient Aryan-race.[34]

This anti-colonial stance had several consequences that decisively influenced the institution's history: First: it earned the Gurukul both the sympathy of militant nationalists[35] and the suspicion of the government who kept the school under surveillance and closely watched every move of its teachers. Secondly: it kept the scope of the school very limited. Not too many parents were ready to send their boys away for such a long period when all lucrative jobs remained out of reach for them afterwards. As a result, the number of graduates from the college section between 1912 and 1932 rarely exceeded 15 per annum.[36] Most of the students' guardians belonged to the lower urban middle classes and came from a background which would have made it difficult to afford an education in one of the western colleges. Apart from the financial advantages, the decision to have one's son sent to the Gurukul—tuition was free and only a nominal fee for food, shelter, and clothes of Rs. 10 was charged[37]—it also brought about a considerable gain in religious prestige since the institution soon became very famous and was respected and even copied by "orthodox" Hindus.[38] The symbolic importance of the Kangri school is also evident by the extraordinarily vivid public debate on the pros and cons of such an institution throughtout the 1910s.[39] Moreover, the list of guests and visitors of the Gurukul demonstrates that its significance can hardly be overestimated. Apart from British officials like Lieutenant Governor James Meston and Viceroy Hardinge and considerable number of western politicians and intellectuals[40] were attracted by the academy, and leading figures of the national movement like Gandhi, Jawaharlal Nehru, M.M. Malviya, Lala Lajpat Rai, Rajendra Prasad, S.P. Mookerjee, Vinoba Bhave et al. paid a visit to the remote school and gave speeches before the school's staff and students. All of them expressed their admiration for what they saw.[41]

THE AIMS OF THE GURUKUL

The general criticism levelled against education on western lines referred to in the intoductory section, was fully shared by the adherents of the Gurukul concept. They were convinced that modern education or "slavish imitation of western models" were "extremely unnationalising in [their] effects"[42] and threatened the very existence of the Hindu 'race'.[43] The *gurukul śikṣā praṇālī*[44] was developed to counter this threat; it was a brand of education that was religious in its rhetoric and political in its goals. It was designed to produce a well trained and highly motivated avant-garde that would serve as multiplicators of Arya ideals and were expected to guide the "indifferent, unenthusiastic, inactive mass of Hinduism"[45] on their way to reform and regeneration, thereby "welding it into one coherent mass". [46] Once the first goal, i.e. the unification of the nation, was achieved, in a second step, the supporters of the Gurukul aspired to the spiritual conquest of the west :[47]

> If the Brahmacharies fulfil the fond hopes [....] the day is not far off when captive Ind[ia] will by the force of her Brahmacharya take captive her conqueror and London will become the diffusive centre of Vedic thought.[48]

The national scale, however, definitely had priority and the advocates of the Gurukul system concentrated their efforts accordingly on the strengthening and homogenising the Hindu community. With its emphasis on religious regeneration, the institution was supposed to provide an ideological tonic as well. The spread of 'dharmic values', would not only help to "deny the seven devils of secularity entrance" in (Hindu) India,[49] it would also prevent the suspected mass conversion to Christianity referred to above.

In the logic of the *ārya dharma* the *gurukul śikṣā praṇālī* was portrayed as being in continuity with the educational system that had prevailed among the Aryans in vedic times and yet at the same time was more scientfic, rational and advanced than the latest western pedagogical theories.[50] In this scheme, the Gurukul Kangri played the role of a model institution that was intended to serve as an example for similar schools and universities. The final goal of the Arya efforts was to establish a network of hundreds of Gurukuls all over India and thus completely replace the existing educational system.

After having thus laid down the broad aims and strategies of the Gurukul system, the following section is dedicated to a closer analysis of the actual process of 'welding together the community', the key activities in nation-building as practised in the Kagri school.

III

THE CREATION OF A NATIONAL HISTORY

The pitiable state of Hindu society and its lack of self confidence and pride was seen as being partly caused by "distorted representations" of Indian history.[51] The rewriting of ancient Indian history with the avowed aim of correcting the mistakes and misrepresentations by western orientalist scholars, therefore, was a crucial point in the programme of the Gurukul movement right from the outset.[52] It took seven years after the opening of the school for the project of an alternative historiography to be commenced by Ramdev,[53] then headmaster of the Gurukul. A programmatical article that appeared in the *Vedic Magazine* shortly before the first volume of his comprehensive history of ancient India was published, shows that the perception of the role of history and historiography was not only largely influenced by the well known ideas of a 'national history' prevalent in Europe in the 19th century but was also moulded by the ever recurring theme of being 'uncivilised' and backward compared to the West :

> Natioanl History is that golden chain which links the past with the present and the future. It keeps alive in a people the spirit of unity; inspires them with common ideals; infuses in them common interests and common sentiments [....] The nation whose history is alive is never in danger of decay from internal causes. Hence all civilized nations look upon the preservation of history as their sacred and paramount duty.[54]

With these ideals in mind, Ramdev wrote *Bhāratvarṣ kā itihās*. The book became one of the most widely ever circulated publications of the Gurukul and also received considerable attention even outside Arya circles.[55] It was used in the institution as the standard history textbook until the 1970s.[56] As pointed out, the book was considered to be a corrective to Western representations of Indian history, hence its aggressively assertive character throughout. Almost every page contains a quotation from or a reference to the statements of historians and indologists like W. Jones, H.H. Wilson, J. Todd, F.M.Müller, V.A. Smith et al. Which are subsequently debunked.[57]

In the first section the author vigorously refutes the Western assumption that the Aryans had no historiography worth the name and attempts to prove instead that the Vedas and the books of the Rishis (*ārṣ granth*)were important historiographical accounts and not merely fiction.[58]

Subsequently he proceeds to divide ancient Indian history according to his main sources into five periods:[59] of the *Brāhmaṇas*, of the *Manusmṛti*, of the *Rāmāyaṇa*, the *Mahā-bhārata* and the *Sukranitisāra.*[60] In line with Dayanand's interpre-tation and that of Ramdev's contemporary Harbilas Sarda,[61] he devotes the major part of the second volume to demonstrate that the Aryan culture had strongly influenced all major civilisations of the world including China, Greece, Rome, Africa, and America.[62] Through-out the book, not only the incommensurable glory of the ancient ' Aryan empire' but also its modern and rational outlook are constantly highlighted. All major achieve-ments of modern European history had already been realised in Bharatvars; for example:

> The King had a House of Parliament built in his Capital. He passed resolutions after consulting the representatives of the people and on the basis of the *vedas* and *dharmaśāstras.* In matters, the representatives[...] could not agree upon, he would decide after consulting the *brāhmaṇ sabhā.* Whoever has only a trifle of historical understanding and reads the evidences given above, will agree with us on the statement, that the government in ancient Bhāratvarṣ was democratic.[63]

According to Ramdev, apart from a democratic form of government far superior to the English system[64] complete with separation of judicial, executive and legislative functions, an advanced system of education had also been part of the magnificent Aryan civilisation.

When it comes to an analysis of the political implications of the Arya brand of nationalist historiography, the question about the attitude towards Islam inevitably arises. Originally, a fourth volume was planned to cover the medieval and modern periods but unfortunately it was never completed and we can only get an idea of the assessment of the so-called Muslim period of Indian History through the preface, where Ramdev describes the general purpose of the book. As one would expect, Indian History is understood exclusively as Hindu-history. The establishment of the Muslim empires is presented as a catastrophe for the glorious Hindu civilisation which was caused just by treason and the "stupidity and egoism of some of its leaders"[65] and not by the fact that they had been defeated on the battlefield.

Ramdev's magnum opus was not the only contribution of the Gurukul Kangri to the rewriting of Indian history[66] but by far the most comprehensive. For the brahmacharies the book was compulsory reading. Their interpretation of the past was additionally influenced by the so-called *sarasvati yātras* (educational tours) that took the advanced students to "ancient and historical places"[67] where the relics of former times were explained to them according to the Arya view of history.[68]

Thus, the Gurukul teachers provided their students with an understanding of history that was supposed to give them pride and self esteem. Past defeats and weaknesses were turned into victories by a revisionist construction of the past. The Aryan nation they hoped to build was projected into an ancient golden age, complete with a state that displayed all the features of modernity and was at the same time based on the firm foundations of *dharma*. This historical knowledge, they hoped, would guide their actions in the present, by inspiring them with a sense of "national pride" (*jātīya abhimān*)and making them "proceed even more firmly on their way to progress."[69]

THE CREATION OF A NATIONAL LANGUAGE

The question of language had been a cornerstone of the Arya reform scheme ever since the time Swami Dayanand had adopted aryabhasa—the heavily Sankritised form of Hindi that the Samajis cherished—for his writings and speeches in 1873. As the participation in the Hindi agitation in the U.P. had gained them sympathies in the wider world of Hinduism, it was only natural that the propagation of Hindi as national language would also be a prominent feature of the Gurukul's programme for 'national regeneration'. In fact, the step-motherly treatment accorded to Hindi and Sanskrit in the D.A.V. College had been one of the causes for the breakaway of the Gurukul faction in 1893.[70] Two decades later, the Gurukul founder Munshiram summed up his position on the language question during a programmatic speech held in Bhagalpur on the occasion of the fourth *Hindī sāhitya sammelan* :

> To unite a country without the propagation of a national language [*rāṣtrabhāṣā*] is as impossible a task as to survive without water. How can the integration of a society progress, if its members possess no means to understand the inner feelings of their fellow members. The political leaders of Bhāratvarṣ have realized by now that the nation cannot be built without a national language. But the opinions still differ when it comes to

> the question as to which language should be chosen. I am convinced that only *āryabhāṣā* can become the national language.[71]

The Gurukul was to contribute to this propagation in three different ways. The first was that the whole course of instruction over fourteen years including 'modern sciences' like physics (*bhautikī*) and chemistry (*rasāyan*), was conducted in Hindi. For that purpose standard textbooks were translated from English into Hindi[72] and a good deal of textbook literature was originally produced in that language by Gurukul teachers. In the Government system the use of Hindi—like that of other 'vernaculars'—had almost exclusively been restricted to primary and lower secondary education. This emancipation of Hindi from its image of being nothing but 'rustic speech', a language appropriate mostly for private communication, into a medium of higher education, containing countless newly created technical terms, was well-acclaimed even by people from outside the Samaj.[73]

Next to this emancipatory impetus it was also the nature of the type of language used in the Gurukul that was relevant for the national project of the Gurukul spokesman. The preface of the standard *āryabhāṣā* textbook written exclusively for use in the Gurukul[74] gives us clues as to what ideal Hindi should look like. While explaining why none of the twenty other Hindustani textbooks in use in the Government schools of the United Provinces could be adopted in Kangri, the author remarks :

> All the Hindi textbooks accepted by the Board of Instruction of this province are written in a language that cannot be called Hindi or *āryabhāṣā* [....] All Sanskrit words have been banned from this language, ignoring the rule, that without the help of a classical language vernaculars cannot exist. Classical languages only can give life to vernaculars.[75]

The demand that purity (*śuddhtā*), i.e. the use of Sanskritised neologisms often with clear religious connotations for all abstract terms[76] should be the dominant quality of a language propagated as 'national' shows the exclusive character of the proposed nation. Muslims and adherents of all other religions except Hinduism could not but feel alienated by such an idiom. And even the ordinary Hindu population had difficulties in following the Arya brand of Hindi: an undercover agent of the Intelligence Department observes about the speeches given during the annual festival of the school that they "were made in Arya Bhasha, a form of Hindi which few but themselves understand."[77]

The Gurukul served as a testing ground[78] for the planned spread of this artificial idiom over the whole subcontinent since it drew its students also from outside the Hindi speaking areas. An article in the *saddharm Pracārak,* a Hindi newspaper edited by Munshiram, describes how new students from differnt regions of the country arrive at the Gurukul and start to quarrel for they have no common language to communicate in and comments :

> This is the disastrous state of affairs in the mutual relationship of the sons of Aryavarta. But only one week in the Gurukul and they are all moulded into a uniform Gurukuli shape. All of them become *āryya bhāṣā* speaking sons of Aryavarta.[79]

However, the propaganda work was not confined to the teaching of Hindi to the brahmacharies in the classes. The fostering of Hindi language and literture was also one the foremost aims of the *sāhitya pariṣad* (literary council) founded in 1908.[80] It was a voluntary forum for teachers and advanced students of the institution. The *pariṣad* met every fortnight to discuss a paper that one of its members had given on a literary or philosophical topic. On special occasions it organised competitions in Hindi poetry writing as well.[81] That the club "produce[d] good and finished writers in Sanskrit [sic] and Arya Bhasha"[82] was a desired side-effect for the Gurukul authorities, as graduates who had undergone this additional training would be most useful for the proposed propaganda work.

The wider public was to be reached by the various books published from the Gurukul and by the *ārya bhāṣā* sammelan (Hindi conference) that was held together with the annual festival of the school (*varṣikotsav*). These annual festivals drew up to 90,000 visitors[83] and thus were an ideal platform for the Hindi conference that not seldom was attended by famous poets, scholars and intellectuals from outside the Arya world.[84] The main work of the conference consisted of the passing of resolutions for the promotion of Hindi. These usually included the following:

(1) Hindi should be adopted as the national language
(2) The *devanāgrī* script should be used for all Indian languages
(3) Libraries and reading rooms supplying books and papers in *āryabhāṣā* should be opened

(4) All national institutions should conduct all their affairs in the national language.[85]

The lively participation of non-Arya writers in these *sammelans* suggests that (in contradistinction to the delicate issues of caste reform, women's upliftment and conversion) the commitment for the cause of Hindi as national language was a sphere of Arya activities where they met with the approval of most other organised Hindu forces. Their work in this field not solely contributed considerably to the development of what was later to become the idiom of Hindu nationalism.[86] The so-called *sarkārī*-Hindi[87] finally adopted by the Congress led government of independent India is also clearly Sanskrit biased and in fact very close to the ideal of a pure *āryabhāṣā*.

THE CREATION OF AN IDEAL TYPE OF CITIZEN

It has already been hinted at above that the production of the 'perfectly socialised individual' was at the core of the Gurukul's educational mission. In the Arya ideology society was imagined as an organism, whose different limbs had to acknowledge their responsibilities for the whole and fulfil their respective duties. This conception, doubtless, had a basis in various Hindu traditions, where the imagination of society as a body is well known, but it was influenced at least to the same extent by the theories of Herbert Spencer, as the countless quotations from his works in articles and pamphlets published from the Gurukul suggest. The Spencer quote chosen as a motto for the Gurukul newslatter tells much about the self perception of the institution:

> The welfare of society and the justice of its arrangements are at bottom dependent on the characters of its members.....there is no political alchemy by which you can get golden conduct out of leaden instincts.[88]

The ideal of social responsibility was blended with the colonial postulation of moral and physical superiority through education. The self perception as being weak, degenerated and effeminated was a stereotype in the Hindu reformist discourse in late 19th and early 20th centuries.[89] Hence the final goal of the instruction in the Gurukul was "to breed a nobler race of men [....] who might stand the battle of life with the courage of heroes",[90] and *cāritra nirmāṇ* (character building) was among the most important aims of Arya education. As the mere choice of this term suggests, the influence of contemporary British educational concepts was omnipresentl. The stress laid on sportsmanship and physical exercise, the revulsion from sexuality and sensual pleasures, the contempt for the "emasculate bookworm", the ideal of selfless service for the community with its underlying anti-individualism,[91] the militarised language[92] were all as much part of the Gurukul as they were for instance of the Boy Scout movement that emerged in Britain a few years after the Gurukul had been inaugurated.[93] All these points found expression in the curriculum as well as in the organisation of the daily routine in the school.

The ties with society were fostered already on the occasion of the initiation ceremony (*vedarambh saṃskār*), through the symbolical act of a begging tour through the nearby Kangri village. This procedure (*bhikṣā*) had a long tradition but as a reversal to the ancient practice where the public supported the sons of brahmins to earn religious merit, it became now a metaphor for the brahmacharies' obligation to pay back for the help received during the time of studies with their commitment to the cause of the upliftment of society as a whole.[94] Like the rigid discipline that prevailed in Kangri, the ideal of self denial (*ātma-tyāg*) in the service of the community propagated by the Gurukul authorities was one of the features that appealed very strongly to the public and brought the school even the admiration of government officials and Muslim.[95]

The brahmacharies had to wear yellow *dhotīs* and white *kurtās*. Shoes or sandals were forbidden and so were caps and umbrellas.[96] Additional clothing items were not allowed. The strict prohibition to keep any personal belongings was another point that added to this equalising tendency.

The moral improvement, the "cultivation of will and spiritual culture" was expected to be realised through leading "a simple and hard life [sic!] and through control in the matters eating drinking and sex"[97]—in short—through the keeping of *brahmacarya*. To effectively implement this concept, the Gurukul authorities had introduced a rigid system of control. Apart from the teachers, the *vidyālay* pupils were supervised by more than a dozen of *adhiṣṭhātās* (superintendents)that accompanied them every minute of the day apart from the time they were under the control of the teachers during classes. They had to keep track whether they dedicated enough time to their studies, kept their rooms in order, ate with discipline and eschewed "inappropriate thoughts and deeds" during the night.[98] The superintendents were also present on the rare occasions when they were entitled to see their parents or other relatives. Other than that, the students were strictly prohibited to leave the Gurukul or keep in touch with the world outside through writing letters. The isolation was reinforced by the fact that the school was situated in the middle of the jungle about eight kilometres from the outskirts of the city and could only be reached on foot.

The strategy of its implementation might have been radical but the concept of *brahmačarya* understood as "complete control of the lower self" was in fact very close to the Gandhian concept of inner *svarāj,*[99] and indeed the Mahatama who visited the school several times,[100] not only expressed his admiration for "spirit of self sacrifice" and praised it as "democratic and national institution" but also sent the pupils of his South African Phoenix farm to the school twice and had been spend several months there. He was especially fascinated by the organisational capacities of the Gurukul leaders and the school's experiments in agriculture and practical teaching.

Notwithstanding this common ground, the understanding of *brahmačarya* as it prevailed in Kangri included one feature that distinguished the Gurukul clearly from the Gandhian stance: its emphasis of physical culture, military virtues and the cult of virility. The Samajis missed no opportunity to emphasise that "exercises and manly games [we]re compulsory" in the Gurukul[101] and that it offered the better alternative to government colleges considered as institutions in which the pupils only underwent lessons "in the grand science of being a book-worm":[102]

> The Gurukul has a claim [....] on Indians [....] who are filled with horror when they look at the bloated and wasted looks of our students who are fathers before they are out of their teens—and whose flabby muscles and hectic glances proclaim the degeneracy of our race—who know that there is a tragic lack of grit, self assertion and virility in our public life and that most of our public workers are incapable of sustained effort and united work.[103]

All these deficiencies were supposed to be removed through two compulsory sports lessons a day which consisted of working with dumb bells, wrestling, swimming etc. in the morning and games (cricket, hockey, football, *kabaḍḍī*) in the evening.[104] In addition, there were regular drill exercises and lessons in fencing and horseback riding. The success of the training was demonstrated on the occasion of annual festivals where the brahmacharies broke chains and bamboo sticks by sheer physical force and displayed feats of swordsmanship with the result "that the people in thousands were convulsed with commotion and everybody was talking on the wonderful system of physical culture followed in this institution."[105]

The ideal citizen, then, as produced in Kangri was not merely intellectually cultivated and spiritually raised, he was also physically strong. All three fields were interconnected and again subordinated to the underlying ideal of service to the community. Especially the essential role that physical culture and the constant stress of 'manliness and virility' play in the schedule deserves our attention.

TOWARDS AN IDEAL SOCIETY : THE PROBLEMS OF CASTE AND CHILD MARRIAGES

The vision of a model citizen was of course closely linked with that of a homogeneous society functioning on the lines of rationality and efficiency. The proposed reshaping of Hindu society according to these principles was centred around the Arya Samaj interpretation of the *varṇāśrama* system and was conceived to work on various levels. Dayanand had regarded the *varṇa vyavasthā* as being not based on birth but on *guṇ, karm* and *svabhāv* (abilities, behaviour and nature).[106] The respective *varṇa* was only ascribed to the individual after his education had been completed. The Gurukul was originally thought of as being the institution responsible for the implementation of this meritocratic concept. If everybody, including the children of *śūdras* and outcastes had an equal opportunity to receive the best type of education and thus 'earn' his later position in the society, the basis of untouchability (*chūt chāt*) was destroyed. As untouchability and the division into castes and subcaste was perceived—and not only by the Samaj—as being largely responsible for the 'deplorable state' of Hinduism, its abolition was considered to be of the utmost importance:

> The Hindu race can never acquire the place due to it under the sun as long as it is not welded into one nationality and nationality can never be formed, as long as castes and their iron rules are not broken; but they can never be successfully and willingly broken without the Gurukula system of education.[107]

The egalitarian way of life that should bind together the heterogenous elements of Hindu society and prevent a possible breakaway of the untouchables from the fold of Hinduism was demostrated in the model institution where brahmin and *śūdra* boys ate at the same table and slept in the same room. That way, the brahmacharies were supposed to develop a sense of mutual responsibility and finally become "perfectly socialised individuals".[108]

The abolition of caste and untouchability was on the agenda of most Hindu reform organisations of the time. Many of them, however, had tried to throw overboard the concept of *varṇa* altogether and had been excommunicated by the authorities of brahmanical Hinduism. In their endeavour to reform the entire Hindu community, the Arya Samajis themselves had experienced more than once that they were rejected by the Hindu majority for being too radical. By sticking to the *varṇa* concept—though in a completely modified manner—and employing religious symbols that were widely accepted, the adherents of the Gurukul-faction hoped to gain "favourable access to old orthodox Hindu heart"[109] and eventually to be able to act as the unifiers of Hinduism.

In a similar way the *āśrama* system was also seen as an ideal instrument to check the presumed decline of the 'Hindu race' without alienating its more traditional members. A revival of the virtue of *brahmacarya* was to solve two of the most virulent problems that—according to the Samaji perception—threatened the existence of the Aryan race. The decreasing number of Hindus, evident from the decennial census carried out by the British, was seen as being mainly caused by three phenomena: conversion, the prohibition of widow remarriage and child marriages which again resulted in infant mortality and a general degradation of the virile power of the offspring. Whereas the former two should be contained by the Arya inventions of *śuddhi* and *niyog*,[110] the latter was to be stopped through the application of *brahmacarya* which would also guarantee the asmelioration of the genetic stock of the Hindu 'race'. Since the principle prescribed sixteen and twenty-five as the proper ages of consent for women and men respectively, child marriages would disappear as a natural result once it was generally followed, and "the sad spectacle of prematurely worn out and early dying Indian manhood"[111] could be stopped. This biological argument also included references to the science of eugenics[112] which was popular in Europe at the time.

The Gurukul was regarded by its founders as the only institution that could succeed in making the revised *varṇāśrama* system work and thus solve a whole bundle of problems that resulted from the specific structure of Hindu society.

IV

As we have seen, the effort to establish a 'national' school like the Gurukul Kangri was to some extent a result of the educational situation in late 19th century India. It was particularly the Hindu intelligentsia that felt jeopardised by the onslaught of missionary educational activities and the cultural alienation through a 'spread of materialism' in western colleges. However, among the many efforts to amalgamate western educational concepts and contents with instruction in (selected and reformulated) parts of the indigenous cultural traditions the Gurukul was unique in its encompassing approach. Few other projects had such a clear cut and comprehensive idea of the nation they wanted to build, and fewer even implemented their ideology so radically. We have shown, that the institution was perceived by its founders not merely as a testing ground for Arya ideals but as the nation *en miniature*. In the logic of the model of the 'nation of intent' the founders of the Gurukul hoped to produce 'social engineers', a *minorité agissante* that would carry their national values to the 'ignorant and passive masses'. In this manner, the school would not only train the élite of the proposed nation, it would also provide all the other features that—in an adoption of western criteria—were regarded as essential for a national community:

> First : a national history which allowed the members of the nation to be proud of their forefathers by retelling the deeds of the ancient Aryan heroes and at the same time to be rational and 'modern' by projecting all the important features of a 19th century European nation state into the Hindu empires of the past. *En passant* it also defined national territory (*āryavarta*) and the relevant canon of national literature (*veda, ārṣ granth*).

Secondly : A 'purified' and modernised national language (*āryabhāṣa*) which would be suitable for the needs of the 20th century together with a national script (*devanāgarī*).

Thirdly : An ideal type of citizen who would be mentally, spiritually and physically equipped to serve society, having internalised quasi religious values such as selflessness, discipline and devotion to the cuase of the nation.

Fourthly : A remedy for the 'social evils' which divided and weakened Hindu society, (the reformulated *varṇāśrama vyavasthā*).

When it comes to an assessment of the whole project, to inherent problems of the scheme have to be mentioned, one regarding its relationship to the colonial power and one regarding its effect on non-Hindus. Our study of Gurukuli vision of an ideal citizen has shown that, in spite of their religious and sometimes even aggressively anti-colonial rhethoric, the Gurukul founders tacitly accepted some essential assumptions of their masters, e.g. that education was the cure for all diseases and that the masses of society needed moral and physical upliftment from their paternal well wishers—be they English or Arya. The emphasis placed on discipline and self control is also perfectly in accordance with the British ideal of a 'colonial citizen', and one has to raise the question of whether the whole project indeed brought about an emancipation from the intellectual hegemony of the British.

As to its capacities as a model for national integration, particularly the analysis of the Gurukuli brand of historiography and its language policy can leave no doubt that the nationalist ideology as implemented by the institution not only failed to integrate non-Hindu elements (most importantly the Muslims) but risked contributing actively to tensions between the different communities of British India. It must be stated that, during the time covered by the present study, the Gurukul certainly was not a militant anti-Muslim institution. Nonetheless, it was among the first Hindu institutions that directly linked *body building* with *character building* which was again seen as a prerequisite for *nation building* and employed exclusively Hindu sysbols in its vision of national virility. In this respect it paved the way for overtly militant Hindu organisations like the Arya Vir Dal and the RSS. Thus, our assumption that a detailed study of the Gurukul would enhance our knowledge about the role of the Arya Samaj in the emergence of militant Hindu nationalism has been confirmed. All the same, contrary to the widespread assessment that places the Arya Samaj exclusively in this context, we have found some indications that the influence of the school went much further. Especially a study of the impact of the 'Gurukuli values' on the allegedly secular brand of nationalism propagated by the Indian National Congress seems to be a promising project for the future.

REFERENCES

1. Indra Vedalankar, first graduate and later headmaster of the Gurukul Kangri, in a speech entitled "The Vedic Guru and his Pupil", delivered on the occasion of the school's 12th anniversary in March 1914 (*The Vedic Magazine & Gurukula Samachar 7* (9/10), Apr.-May 1914, p. 719-24).
2. There were numerous other educational projects with a clear nationalistic bias in other parts of India; the Satyabadi schools in Orissa and the Fergusson College in Maharashtra may be mentioned here as examples.
3. *Nai talim,* Urdu for 'new education'; for an outline of Gandhi's educational ideas see K.N. Sen, *Education and the Nation. An Indian Perspective,* Calcutta 1970, p. 163-204.
4. J Lutt, *Religion und Politik in Indien. Pandit Malaviyas Vermittlerrolle im politischen Hinduismus des frühen 20. Jahrhunderts,* Heidelberg (unpubl. Habilitation thesis) 1976, p. 10.
5. Cf. G. Minault/D. Lelyveld, "The Campaign for a Muslim University 1898-1920," *Modern Asian Studies 8* (1) 1974, p. 145-89; Metcalf, B., "The Madrasa at Deoband: A Model for Religious Education in India," *Modern Asian Studies* 12 (1), 1978, p. 111-34; D. Lelyveld, *Aligarh's first Generation. Muslim Solidarity in British India,* Princeton 1978; B.D. Metcalf, *Islamic Revival in British India. Deoband 1860-1900,* Princeton 1982; J.Lütt, "The Movement for the Foundation of the Benares Hindu University," Cultural Dept. of the German Embassy in India (ed.), *German Scholars on India. Contributions to Indian Studies,* Vol. 2, Delhi 1974, p. 160-95, and K. Kumar, "Hindu Revivalism and Education in North Central India," in K.N. Panikkar (ed.), *Communalism in India. History Politics and Culture,* New Delhi 1991, p. 173-95. Of course there have been several publications on the educational activities of Gandhi and Tagore but they are mostly concerned with strictly educational and psychological questions while ignoring the political dimension of the problem. Cf. for instance W. Cenkner, *The Hindu Personality in Education. Tagore—Gandhi—Aurobindo,* Delhi 1976. The best example for such a

completely a historical approach in M.M. Krischke-Ramaswamy, *Revitalisierende Pädagogik: Knozepte zur kulturellen Erneuerung im Indien des 20. Jahrhunderts, Göttingen* (unpubl. 1977 Ph.D. thesis).

6. Gurukul literally means 'the line (or family)of the teacher'. It was used to denote the traditional system of educating the sons of brahmins who lived with their teacher's families during their education. For details cf. A.S. Altekar, *Education in Ancient India,* Benares 1934, p. 92-101.

7. Arya Pratinidhi Sabha, Punjab (ed.), *The Rules and the Schemes of Study of the Gurukula, sanctioned by the Arya Pratinidhi Sabha, Punjab, together with an Introduction by Lala Ralla Ram*, Lahore 1902, p. 8.

8. *The Vedic Magazine & Gurukula Samachar* 5 (10), 1911, p. 64.

9. C. Heimsath, *Indian Nationalism and Hindu Social Reform* Princeton 1964, p. 292.

10. The most eloquent elaboration of this theory is found in the well-acclaimed work of the French political scientist Christophe Jaffrelot: *The Hindu Nationalist Movement and Indian Politics 1925 to the 1990ies. Strategies of Identity Building, Implantation and Mobilisation (with Special Reference to Central India),* London 1996. A similar view is presented by D. Gold, "Organized Hinduisms: From Vedic Truth to Hindu Nation," in: M. Marty/ R.S. Appleby (eds.), *Fundamentalism Observed,* Chicago 1991, p. 531-91.

11. Cf. C. Jaffrelot, "The Growth and Development of Hindu Nationalism in the Punjab: From the Arya Samaj to the Hindu Sabha (1875-1910)," *Indo British Review* 21 (1), 1993, p. 3-39, especially p. 29.

12. K.W. Jones, *Arya Dharm. Hindu Consciousness in 19th Century Punjab,* Berkeley 1976. Besides this book Jones has about a dozen articles on the Arya Samaj to his credit.

13. The only exception is Jordens who devotes a few pages to the Gurukul in his biography of the school's founder, Munshiram alias Swami Shraddhananda. J.T.F. Jordens, *Swami Shraddhananda. His Life and Causes,* Delhi et al 1981.

14. Cf. I. Talbot, *Punjab and the Raj,* New Delhi 1988, p. 72f.

15. In allusion to the first stage in a male brahmin's life according to the *varnasrama* concept, students in the Gurukul were called brahmacharies; besides, *brahmacarya* (chasity) was the guiding principle of their student's life. Note: I use the spelling common in the English sources instead of the Hindi *brahmacari.*

16. S. Tonesson/H. Antlöv, "Asia in Theories of Nationalism and National Identity," in: idem (eds.), *Asian Forms of the Nation,* Richmond 1996, p. 1-39, esp. p. 37f. The term 'nation of intent'

has been coined with slightly different connotations in the late sixties by the Africanist P. Rotberg, "African Nationalism: Concept or Confusion," *Journal of Modern African Studies* 4(1) 1967, p. 33-46.

17. R. Nathan (ed.), *Progress of Education in India 1897/98-1901/02,* Vol. 1, Calcutta, 1904, p. 4.

18. *Singh Sahai,* 12-4-1895; *Selections from the Vernacular Newspapers Published in the Punjab* 1895 (hereafter)quoted as *SVNP*), p. 2. Similar statements can be found in countless newspaper articles of the 1880ies and 1890ies all over Northern India.

19. Cf. E. McDonald, "English Education and Social Reform in Late Nineteenth Century Bombay: A Case Study in the Transmission of a Cultural Ideal," *Journal of Asian Studies* 25 (1), 1966, p. 453-70, *passim.*

20. Cf. Kumar, *Political Agenda of Education. A study of Colonialist and Nationalist Ideas,* Delhi etc. 1991. especially p. 23-46.

21. S.C. Ghosh, *The History of Education in Modern India 1757-1986.* Delhi 1995, p. 101f.

22. One of the most Influential voices to utter this critique was that of Rabindranath Tagore in his 1892 article *Shikhṣār her fer.* cf. *Ibid.*, p. 131f, and U Dasgupta, "Santiniketan: The school of a Poet," in: M. Hasan (ed.) *Knowledge. Power & Politics. Educational Institutions in India.* Delhi 1998, p. 258-303, p. 264f. See also Lütt, "The Movement for the Foundation of the Beneres Hindu University," p.162.

23. Cf. also C.A. Watt, "Education for National Efficiency : Contructive Nationalism in North India - 1916," *Modern Asian Studies* 31 (2), 1997, p. 339-74, p. 342.

24. D. Sarasvatī, *Satyārth prakāś.* (ed. Sārvdeśik Ārya Pratinidhi Sabhā, Delhi (repr.)) 1993 [[2]Lāhaur 1884], p. 36-75. The Formal aspect of initiation to student's life is also touched upon in the same author's *Saṃskār vidhi,* Naī Dillī (repr.) 1995; see esp. p. 93-113.

25. Dayanand founded two Sanskrit *pāṭhśālās* which did not have much in common with the comprehensive reformist scheme of the Kangri school. They were concerned solely with the teaching of *deva vāṇī,* as the religious prestige language was called by the Samajis, and remained largely within the framework of traditional religious eudcation. They were not all too successful either and had to be close down before long because of the corruption of the teaching staff. Cf. Jordens, *Swāmī Dayānanda Sarasvatī. His Life and Ideas,* Delhi 1978, p. 64ff and Mukhopādhyāy, *Mahārṣi Dayānand kā jīvan carit* (transl. from Bengali into Hindi by Ghāsīrām, repr.), Dillī 2050 VS, p. 195f [[1]1933].

26. For early 20th century accounts on Dayanand's educational views cf. Ram Rattan, "Swami Dayanand as Educationist," in H.B. Sarda

(ed.), *Dayananda Commemoration Volume,* Ajmer 1933, p. 129-34. A more recent outline is given in S.P. Chaube, *Recent Educational Philosophies in India,* Agra 1993, p. 20-45. A more detailed but similarly uncritical account can be found in: R Safaya/ D. Bhan, *Educational Philosophy of Swami Dayanand,* Ambala 1977.

27. Sarsvatī, D., *Satyārth prakāś,* p. 37.
28. Cf. for instance Arya Pratinidhi Sabha, Punjab (ed.), *The Rules and the Scheme of Study of the Gurukula 1902*, p. 18.
29. The D.A.V. High School was inaugurated in 1886 and followed by a college section three years later. For a detailed analysis of the D.A.V. movement cf. K.W. Jones, *The Arya Samaj in the Punjab. A study of Social Reform and Religious Revivalism,* Berkeley (unpubl. Ph. D. thesis) 1966, chs. 3 and 4, and S.K. Gupta, "Dayanand Anglo-Vedic College Movement (1886-1986)," *The Punjab Past and Present* 20 (1) 1986, p. 226-41.
30. Gurukula Vishvavidyalaya Hardwar (ed.), *Prospectus and Rules Regarding Examinations, Admission etc.*, Lahore 1912, p. ix.
31. G. Pāṭhak, *Gurukul Kāṃgṛī kā itihās,* Kāṃgṛī n.d. [c. 1935], p. 32f. Out of the 340 enrolled, 276 studied in the high school (*vidyālay*) and 64 in the college (*mahāvidyālay*) section.
32. Originally 18 years had been envisaged but the Gurukul authorities had to cut down the schedule due to economic constraints.
33. The degree of *vidyālaṃkār* was equivalent to B.A., *vedālaṃkār* was for those who had specialised in Vedic literature, *siddhāntālaṃkār* for philosophy. Later *ayurvedālaṃkār* for traditional medicine, *vidyāvācaspati,* (Ph. D.) and *vidyāmarṭanḍ* (D. Litt.) were introduced.
34. Gurukula Kangri Vishvavidyalaya (ed.), *The Aims Ideals and Needs of the Gurukula Vishvavidyalaya Kangri,* Kangri 1971 VS [1914], p. liif. In 1914 James Meston, the Lieutenant Governor of the United Provinces, had even offered Munshiram to include the Gurukul in the Government's grnt-in-aid scheme and to recognise the diploma if the curricula were slightly altered. In spite of the school's critical funding situation, Munshiram refused to cooperate with the British. Cf. I. Viyāvācaspati, *Amar śahLd svāmī Sradhānand, mere pitā,* Dillī, n.d. [1953], p. 113f.
35. *Karmayogi,* 18-1-1910; *SNNUP,* 1910, p. 132.
36. Cf. Vidyāsāgar Vidyālaṃkār, *Gurukul Snātak paricāyikā,* Dillī 1977, p. 1-70. The number of the neophytes was around 30 per annum.
37. The project was chiefly financed through donations by the Arya public. In 1912 for instance 57.6% of the school's budget was supplied from the various funds and fund-raising delegations. Cf. Munśīrām (ed.), *Gurukul Kāṃgṛī kā vṛttānt jismeṃ saṃvat 1966-*

1967 kā vṛttānt ādhikārī ādhikārī parkṣā etc., Kāṃgṛī 1911, p. 80f.

38. In 1906 a 'Rishikul', apparently modelled after the Kangri institution, was founded in Hardwar by the Sanatan Dharm Sabha. Cf. Parmanand, *Mahamana Madan Mohan Malviya, A Historical Biography,* Vol.1, Varanasi 1985, p. 243.

39. Dozens of articles referring to the Gurukul Kangri can be found in the selections of the vernacular newspapers of both the Panjab and the United Provinces.

40. The list of Western visitors includes C.F. Andrews, Beatrice and Sindney Webb, later British prime minister Ramsay Macdonald, the American educationist Myron Phelps and the German indologist Otto Strauss, to name just the more illustrious.

41. Cf. Viṣṇudatt Rākeś (ed.), *Dīkṣālok [Gurukul Kāṃgṛī viśvavidyālay meṃ pradatt dīkṣānt bhāṣaṇoṃ evaṃ sārasvat vyākhyānoṃ kā saṇgrah]* Haridvār 1997, *passim.*

42. Alakh Dhari, "Essential Elements of Sound Education," *The Vedic Magazine & Gurukula Samachar* 2 (2), 1907, p. 21-6, p. 26.

43. In the early years of the Gurukul-movement, the term 'Hindu' was rejected because of its foreign origin and negative connotations and the word 'Arya' was used instead. However, as it became evident that the "ignorant dharmic brethren" refused to accept the Arya suggestion the Samajis began to employ the word 'Hindu' in the period after 1910-12 to foster solidarity within the community. Cf. for instance *Sadharm Pracārak,* 11. jyeṣth 1970, p. 3.

44. *Sikṣā praṇālī* (Hindi): educational system.

45. M.C. Sinha, "Gurukula as a System of Education," *The Vedic Magazine & Gurukula Samachar* 8 (11/12), 1915, p. 1063-83, p. 1070.

46. "The *Round Table* on the Arya Samaj," *The Vedic Magazine & Gurukula Samachar* 7 (5) 1913, p. 400-10, p. 409.

47. The effort towards universal dissemination of their ideologies seems to be a common feature of this type of religious nationalism. Similar ideas can be found in Swami Vivekananda who tried to spread his political Vedanta in England and America, Bipin Chandra Pal and many others.

48. Ratan Lal: "A Glimpse on Rishi Dayanand's Revived System of Education, The Gurukula," *The Vedic Magazine & Gurukula Samachar* 6(7), 1911, p. 525-35, p. 535.

49. Ratan Lal, "A Glimpse," p. 534f.

50. See for example Balkrishna, *The Gurukula System of Education and its Critics,* Kangri 1911, p. 6-18, and, Ratan Lal, "A Glimpse", p. 531.

51. This view was shared by a considerable part of the Hindu intelligentsia both within and outside the Arya Samaj. Cf. for example the articles by Lala Hardayal on national education: in *Hindustan,* 15-5-1908,

SNNUP 1908, p. 318f, *Hindustan*, 23-9-1908, *Ibid.*, p. 591 and *The Vedic Magazine & Gurukula Samachar* 4(6), Dec. 1910, p. 30-3.

52. In several speeches given in Lahore in January 1900, Munshiram mentioned this point as one of the eight foremost goals of the Gurukul. Cf. G.R. Garg, "The Gurukul Movement of Education," Vedic Path, 53 (4) 1981, p. 52-6, p. 56. It reappears in Ralla Ram's first prospectus for the school written the following year.

53. Ācārya Ramdev (1881-1939) had started his education in the D.A.V. High School in Lahore and joined the Gurukul-wing led by Munshiram around 1899. He held an B.A. degree and refused a job as district school inspector in order to work as a teacher of English, western philosophy and history. He replaced Munshiram as principal in 1917. For further details of his work and biography Cf. Rāmgopāl Vidyālaṃkār, "Ācārya Rāmdev," in: Dharmpāl (ed.), *Ācārya Rāmdev jī ādvarṣvād ke Jyotistambh. Vyaktitva evaṃ kṛtitva*, Naī Dillī 1991, p. 9-32.

54. "National History," *loc. cit.*, p. 30f.

55. Rāmdev, *Bhāratvarṣ kā Itihās (BVKI)*, Vol. 1, Kāmgṛī 1910, vol. 2, 1914, vol. 3, Kāmgṛī 1933; among the admirers of the book were V.D. Savarkar and the Hindi poet Maithili Sharan Gupta who allegedly was inspired by the work to write his famous *mahākāvya*-poem *Bhārat Bhāratī*. Cf. Sankar Dev Vidyālaṃkār, "Jñānyogī ācārya Rāmdev jī," in: Dharmpāl, op. cit., p. 51-60, pl. 56. Immediately after its publication it was examined by the Department of Criminal Intelligence in order to find out whether it was of a 'seditious character'. But although it was stated that the book "was obviously intended to provoke discontent with the present rather than to give a faithful picture of the past", it was never banned. Cf. NAI, Home Poll- B, Proceedings March 1911, D.C.I.,- "Report for Feb. 1911," p. 14f.

56. Personal communication from Dr. Dharmvir Arya, graduate of the Gurukul Kangri and director of the *Ārya Paropkāriṇi Sabhā*, Ajmer; Ajmer 10-12-1996. The fact, that it has been reprinted thrice (the last time in 1996) also given ample evidence to the fact that it is not regarded as outdated.

57. Specifically all dates given by western historians are shown to be incorrect, thus leading to the conclusion that the Aryan civilisation was the oldest and most developed in the history of mankind.

58. *Bhāratvarṣ kā Itihās (BVKI)*, 1, p. 21-5.

59. According to a view established by Dayanand, the Veda proper was timeless and contained to historical information. The vedic Saṃhirtās, therefore, do not figure in the list of sources.

60. The *Sukraītisāra* is an early medieval text on society and policy in the vein of the famous *Arthaśāstra*. It includes contributions of various authors but is ascribed to the mythical sage Sukra. It

probably was made available to Ramdev through a critical edition by G. Oppert, which was published in Madras in 1882. I am grateful to Pandit K.P. Aithal for this reference.

61. H.B. Sarda, *Hindu Superiority: an Attempt to Determine the Position of the Hindu Race in the Scale of Nations,* Ajmer 1906.
62. *BVKI* 2, p. 256-362.
63. *BVKI* 1, p. 94. This and all the following translations from Hindi are the present author's.
64. *Ibid.*, p. 95f.
65. *Ibid.*, p. 3f.
66. Dharmdatt Vidyālaṃkār, probably a student of Ramdev, wrote a book entitled *Prācīn Bhārat meṃ svarājya,* which was published in 1920. Countless articles published mainly in the *Vedic Magazine* upheld similar views. For a typical example see "The Ancient Glory of a Conquered Race," *The Vedic Magazine & Gurukula Samachar* 10(9), 1917, p. 679-85.
67. *Gurukul Kāṃgṛī kā vṛttānt jismeṃ saṃvat 1966-1967 kā vṛttānt, ādhikārī parīkṣā* etc. Kāṃgṛī 1911, p. 9.
68. E.g. during the *sarasvatī yātrā* 1907 the group visited Delhi where Munshiram told his students that the "fanatical and bigotted Muslim conquerors" had not contributed anything noteworthy in the field of architecture and that the Qutb Minar had not been built by a Muslim but by the Hindu hero Prithviraj Chauhan, *The Vedic Magazine & Gurukula Samachar* 1 (8), 1908, p. 488. Cf. also *The Vedic Magazine & Gurukula Samachar* 1 (6), 1907, p. 370 and *The Vedic Magazine & Gurukula Samachar* 1 (9), 1908, p. 567.
69. *BVKI,* p. 4.
70. M.L. Thakur, "Factors leading to the Split of the Arya Samaj in 1893," *Proceedings of the Punjab History Conference. 18th session 1983,* Patiala 1985, p. 225-31, p. 231.
71. Munśīrām Jijñāsu, "Matṛbhāṣā kā uddhār," in: Bh. Bhāratīya (ed.), *Svāmī Sraddhānand granthāvalī,* vol. 6. Naī Dillī 1987, p. 30-45, p. 34.
72. Govardhan, *Vijñā*npraveśikā—rasāyan was a translation of *Chemistry by* William S. Furneoux; the same author's *Vijñānpraveśikā—Bhautikī* was based on the *Physics Primer by Balfour Stewart.*
73. Cf. for instance *The Vedic Magazine & Gurukula Samachar* 6(8), 1913, p. 654. Even Lord Chelmsford, who visited Kangri in 1916, was impressed by the fact that the science classes in the Gurukul were conducted entirely in Hindi. *The Vedic Magazine & Gurukul Samachar* 10(11), p. 826.
74. Bh. Gupta Ārya bhāṣā pāṭhāvalī, 2 Vols., Kāṃgṛī 1913.
75. *Ibid.*, p. 1f.

76. *Ibid.*, p. 6.
77. Home Dept. Poll.—B, Proceedings May 1912, nos. 14-18, "Weekly Report of the Director of Criminal Intelligence for April 1912," p. 15.
78. The advocates of the institution used a similar metaphor, depiciting the Gurukul as 'laboratory and exhibition' (*prayogśālā aur pradarśini*) of the Arya Samaj. Cf e. g. Indra Viyāvācaspati, Gurukul aur Ārya Samāj'; in: *Sraddhā*, 8 phālguṇ 1977 VS [18-2-1921], p. 3-4, p. 3.
79. *Saddarm Pracārak*, 27-paus 1970 VS [10-11-1914], p. 11.
80. *The Vedic Magazine & Gurukula Samachar* 2 (11/12), 1909, p. 111-13.
81. *The Vedic Magazine & Gurukula Samachar* 13(3), 1920, p.183f.
82. *The Vedic Magazine & Gurukula Samachar* 2(11/12), 1909, p. 111.
83. Home Dept. Poll.—B, Proceedings June 1909 Nos. 108-14, "Weekly Report of the Director of Criminal Intelligence for April 1909," p. 9-11.
84. In 1914 for example Madan Mohan Malaviya presided over the meeting.
85. *The Vedic Magazine & Gurukula Samachar* 10(11), 1917, p. 824-6. These are the main contents of the four resolutions passed by the *sammelan* in 1917 which is by far the best documented. It seems that the resolutions passed in other years were quite similar. Cf. also Home Dept., Poll.-B, June 1911, Nos. 4-8, "Weekly Report of the Director of Criminal Intelligence for May 1911," p. 5.
86. See also R. Siṃhā, *Hindī bhāṣā aur Sāhitya ko ārya samāj kī den*, Lakhnaū 1966, p. 119-23.
87. Government-Hindi.
88. Actually, the editors of the *Gurukula Samachar*, published monthly as an appendix to the widely read *Vedic Magazine*, had chosen two mottos which appeared on the front page of every edition from the end of 1907 *Gurukula Samachar* 1(6), 1907, p. 381.
89. Cf. e.g. K.W. Jones, "The Negative Component of Hindu Consciousness,"*Indo British Review* 1, 1991, p. 57-72, J. Rosselli, "The Self-image of Effeteness: Physical Education and Nationalism in Nineteenth Century Bengal," *Past and Present*, 86, 1980, p. 121-48, and M. Sinha, *Colonial Masculinity. The 'manly Englishman' and the Effeminate Bengali in the Late Nineteenth Century*, Delhi (repr.) 1997, esp. p. 1-24 and I Chowdhury, *The frail Hero and Virile History. Gender and the Politics of Culture in Colonial Bengal.* Delhi et al. 1998.
90. "The Spiritual Aspect of the Gurukula," *The Vedic Magazine & Gurukula Samachar* 6 (10/11) 1913, p. 863-85, p.873.
91. Cf. "A Glimpse of Rishi Dayanand's Revived System of Education, the Gurukula" *The Vedic Magazine & Gurukula Samachar* 2(8), Feb. 1909, p. 1-9.

92. The brahmacharies were often referred to as "soldiers" or "recruits" (cf. for instance *Saddharm Pracārak*, 27. Pauṣ 1970 VS, p. 11) who would leave the institution "better equipped and better armed to meet the foe". *The Vedic Magazine & Gurukula Samachar* 7(4) Oct. 1913, p. 319.

93. The striking similarities—both in ideology and the stress of physical culture—between the various indigenous Boy Scout Organisations that emerged in British India from the 1910ies onwards and the Gurukul are dealt with exhaustively by C.A. Watt, "Ephebic Patriots or Seditious Sevaks? The Boy Scout Movement in Colonial India, 1908-1921," (unpubl. Conference paper), Cambridge 1998.

94. Cf. Satyaketu Vedālaṃkār, Ārya Samāj Kā itihās, 7 Vols., Naī Dillī 1987, vol. 3, p. 185.

85. Cf. For example "Al Hadil", 1-5-1908; *SNNUP* 1908, p. 419f.

96. Cf. Munshiram (ed.), *Gurukul Kangri: Biennial Report 1907-08*, Suppl. I, App. B, p. 61. Apart from the homogenising aspect, the adoption of a school uniform suggests that here also British customs were emulated.

97. D. Gajra, "The Metaphysical Basis of Education", *The Vedic Magazine & Gurukula Samachar* 10(1), 1916, p. 109-25, p. 122f.

98. Cf. Gurukul Kāṃgṛī Viśvavidyālay Haridvār (ed.), *Adhiṣṭhātāoṃ ke karttavya,* Haridvār [2] 1959 [[1]ca 1903], *passim.*

99. Cf. A.J. Parel, (ed.), *M.K. Gandhi, Hind Swaraj and other writings.* Delhi (repr.) 1997, p. liv.

100. For the following see Gandhi's speech "Saccī ṣikṣā," in: Viṣṇudatt Rākeś (ed.), *Dīkṣālok,* p. 36-41.

101. V.L. Sharma, A *Handbook of the Arya Samaj,* Allabad [2] 1912; p. 81.

102. 'Educationist' (pseud): "Physical Education. Its necessity in India," *The Vedic Magazine & Gurukula Samachar* 13(3), 1920, p. 124-8.

103. Munshiram (ed.), *Gurukul Kangri: Biennial Report 1907-08,* p. viif.

104. Indra Vidyāvācaspati, *Amar śahīd,* p. 61f.

105. *The Leader,* 1-4-1918, p. 5 I am indebted to Carey Watt for making me aware of this particular source.

106. Cf. also Jordens, *Swāmī Dayānanda, P. 283ff.*

107. M.C. Sinha, "Gurukula as a System of Education," loc, cit., P. 1079.

108. Balkrishna, *The Gurukula System of Education and its Critics,* Kangri 1911, p. 22.

109. Sinha, "Gurukula as a System," p. 1078.

110. For the former concept cf. H. Fischer-Tiné, 'Kindly Elders of the Hindu Biradri; The Arya Samaj's Struggle for Influence and Hindu

Muslim Relationships 1875-1926,' in: A. Copley (ed.): *Gurus and their Followers. New Religious Reform Movements in Colonial India,* Delhi 2000, p. 107-27, and C. Clémentin-Ojha, "La śuddhi de l'Arya Samaj ou l'invention d'un rituel de (re)conversion à l'Hindouisme," *Archives de Sciences Sociales des Religions* 87 (3) 1994, p. 99-114; for the Arya reinterpretation of *niyog, a* sanctioned temporary sexual relationship of a widow with one or several men with the sole aim of begetting children see Jordens, *Swami Dayanand,* p. 117f and M. Kishwar, "The Daughters of Aryavarta," *Indian Economic and Social History Review* 23(2), 1986, p. 151-86.

111. *The Vedic Magazine & Gurukula Samachar* 7(6), 1913, p. 412.

112. In an article published in the *Vedic Magazine* the concept of *brahmacarya* is linked with pseudo-scientific views in a way that reminds on the racial laws of Nazi-Germany: "[.....] it is necessary, that only fit persons should be allowed to marry and take on themselves the responsible duties that pertain to parenthood. It is very essential that they should be of good stock. For parent-hood of the diseased, the insane, The alcoholic [....] is a crime against the future." Cf. "Eugenics: The Ennoblement of Mankind,"*The Vedic Magazine & Gurukula Samachar* 4(12), 1911, p. 1-15. See also Keshav Dev Shastri, "Sexual Hygiene," *The Vedic Magazine & Gurukula Samachar* 15(4), 1921, p. 192-7 and An Admirer (pseud.), "Swami Dayanand on Conscious Race Culture," *The Vedic Magazine & Gurukula Samachar* 10(11), 1917 p. 827-33. Before drawing unfair conclusions, it has to be taken into account, that the belief in eugenics was so widespread in Europe at the time that it almost was part of general knowledge. Cf. H.C. Harten, "Padagogik und Eugenik im 'rassenhygienischen' Diskurs vor 1933," *Paedagogica Historica* 33(3) 1997, p. 765-800, especially p. 767-84 and M. Thomson. *The Problem of Mental Deficiency. Eugenics, Democracy and Social Policy in Britain c. 1870-1959,* Oxford 1998, especially p. 19-23. For a general discussion of racism in the Indian context see P. Robb, *The Concept of Race in South Asia,* Delhi et al. (Repr.) 1997.

—HARALD FISCHER-TINE

CHAPTER - XI

WORKING CLASS CONSCIOUSNESS IN COLONIAL INDIA

The aim of this paper is to pose some questions regarding class conflict and its social and political manifestations in the late 1920's using, not entirely arbitrarily, an analysis of certain events of 1928-29 as a point of departure.[1] The choice of this period is not arbitrary since, I shall argue in this paper, this period was a nodal point where certain long-term trends coverage towards an intensification of class conflict and much that was latent become explicit in dramatic strike action in Bombay textile industry in 1928-29. The choice of the questions I wish to raise may, however, appear arbitrary since the explication of the entire problematic from which these questions originate is not a part of the present exercise. I shall limit myself to a few questions. The first set of questions relate to technological changes in the cotton textile industry which intensified labour-capital conflict (Section-I). The organisation of institutions promoting class solidarity on both sides, capitalist and working class, and the synergistic process of interaction that tended to crystallise class solidarity on both sides of the battle lines in 1928-29 raise another set of problems (Section II). Finally, we shall turn to the quality of consciousness displayed by the working class in the 1928-29 struggles and try to locate the source of weakness in their movement. (Section III).

The significance of the general strikes of 1928-29 in Bombay was emphasised by R.P. Dutt in *India Today* and the left has continued to regard these years as a watershed. This is partly because the emergence of left leadership in Western Indian labour movement was coincident with these strikes. The *pravda*[2] had hailed the "victorious revolutionary trade union in Bombay", just about the time when the defeat of the Girni Kamgar Union (Red Flag) became an acknowledged fact. Authors at different ends of the left spectrum like Sukomal Sen and V.B.Karnik agree on the significance of the strike in the history of Indian working class movement while deffering on the communist's performance.[3] However, most of the available accounts of the strikes of 1928-29 concentrate almost exclusively on the ideas and activities of the leadership and the findings of the *strike Inquiry Committee*, the only source other than the Meerut depositions of the leaders. (M.D.Morris is exceptional in being interested only in the labour management aspect of the strike experience). Evidently we have to go beyond the mere juxtaposition of extracts from *In Pre Cor,* AITUC resolutions, and memoirs of left leaders to explore the techno-economic changes to which the mill-hands reacted, the alignment of forces capital brought to bear upon the strike, the structuration of working class consciousness etc.

At the beginning a semantic problem may be eliminated. In this paper the term class, e.g., 'the working class', has been used with this limited connotation that certain objective existence conditions provide a commonality of basic interests derived from position in the productive system; the use of the term class here does *not* posit the existence of class consciousness (of the kind that is conjured up by phrases like 'class for itself ') among the constituents of the class. In fact one of the points made here is the relevance of Lukacs's idea of "gradation" in levels of consciousness which has been developed by some sociologists like Giddens into elaborate typologies (class identity-conflict awareness-revolutionary class consciousness) and has left a mark on empirical studies like that of John Foster (labour consciousness-class consciousness). Perhaps this notion in Lukacs is more useful than his more well-known formulation concerning "false consciousness".[4]

I

In the 1920's the Bombay textile industry was in the grips of a major technological transformation. As A.K. Bagchi has pointed out, this was not so much in terms of introduction of new machinery as "better deployment of labour in relation to .machinery".[5] In fact, Bombay had, compared to Ahmedabad, a greater proportion of capital goods of older vintage which made it difficult to adjust to requirements of expanding domestic market (displacement of British manufactures) and to react to the challenge of Japanese competition. How the working class was affected by this response on the part of the Bombay mill-owners, "better deployment of labour", has remained rather obscure.

The millowners, both individually and through the mill-owners' Association, pursued two schemes—known as 'rationalisation' and 'standardisation of wages'. M.D. Morris's is the only study of this problem. But it is difficult to agree with his argument in this matter. "In the minds of the employers the standardisation of wage rates was integrally linked with a rationalisation of work.... Unfortunately for labour force stability, the employers felt forced [under 'economic crisis'] to face both problems at the same time... and no trade union in 1928 had the will or power to enforce acceptance of such combined proposals on the workers, especially when this threatened additional unemployment."[6] This is rather naive in suggesting that employers were willing to separate the issues of rationalisation and wage standardisation but for the fortuitous coincidence of an 'economic crisis'. There is no doubt that these two issues were integrally linked in the millowners' mind precisely because they together provided for reduction in labour costs through intensification of labour without an acknowledged wage cut. The consequences of rationalisation of labour process in terms of labour intensification is not touched upon by Morris. Another problem with his analysis is a suggestion that resistance to rationalisation was irrational on the part of workers. The mill-owners' attempt to change the methods of labour utilization, i.e. "radical reform in the industry, could be carried out only over the violent protests of the increasingly self-conscious work force or with its cooperation"; this cooperation, Morris says, was denied and "in the tumultuous, fear-ridden, and violent atmosphere of the mills, the demands of the Communists especially played on the workers' hostility to the employers."[7] Only an overestimation of workers' irrationality and of the rationality of labour-capital cooperation can lead to such conclusions. The mill-owners had as good reasons for undertaking rationalisation and wage standardisation simultaneously as the workers had for opposing them.

By and large these two schemes meant intensification of labour in general and a fall in what S.A. Dange called "absolute wages". This was effectively concealed by the management. The day to day reports on the proceedings of the Strike Inquiry Committee show that the millowners' representatives—Stones and Saklatvala—were masters or prevarication. For example :

N.M.Joshi : "You stated that if a man did double work he would get 50% increase in wages."

Stones : "Our principle has been definitely stated as: a fairday's wages for a fair day's work."[8]

S.A.Dange made the point that even with wages stable or increasing, there may be less wages for work performed: "There is an absolute increase and a relative increase in these things. There may be a relative increase for all appearances by increasing the work. In that case the increase does not work absolutely."[9] The management took refuge under technical complexities. They also reduced wage rates by delcaring rates for "new sorts" (new types of manufacture) for which there was no standard rate earlier. The answer to these tactics would have to use time and motion studies, to get data on speed of machines, productivity per capita, etc. which were not available to the labour leaders.

It is in the confidential reports of Millowners' Association that one can get the details of changes in labour process induced by technical changes. The BMOA surveyed 74 mills to report to the Director General of Commercial Intelligence the following changes in 1927-29: (a) machinery was rebuilt or rearranged to permit of greater number of spindles being attended to by one operative, and 2 sides of spinning frame by one operatives. (b) An increase in spindles per spinner by 60 to 100 spindles was obtained by lengthening the spinning frames in some mills. (c) Higher speed of winding and warping was introduced. (d) More work was compressed by saving time by various means, e.g. winding of hanks for dyeing avoided by direct dyeing in the cheese or beam, and (e) using universal winding machines which put more weft on the shuttle thus reducing stoppage for weft replacement. (f) Some mills also used high drafting in spinning, eliminating the roving frame and yarn being spun directly from the intermediate frames.[10]

The effects were (a) intensification of labour, without corresponding wage increase, and (b) redundancy and consequent reduction in employment. One recalls Marx's description of the intensification of labour which in England was response of the employers to the shortening of mill working hours in the 1860's. "The denser hour of the ten hours working day contain more labour, i.e. expanded labour power, then the more porous hour of the twelve hours' working day."[11] Machinery and new organisation of work " imposes on the workman increased expenditure of labour power" and this is " effected in two ways: by increasing the speed of machinery, and by giving the workman more machinery to tent".[12] Among the 17 points in the charter of Demands during the strike of 1928 we find several relating to labour intensification due to rationalisation. Point no. 7, demanded that the system of each worker looking after 3 looms or the whole frame (2 sides) should not be introduced without workers' consent. Point 6 related to new rates of piece work, and point 5 to new rates for "new sorts". [13]

However, it was not so much the labour-intensification effect as the threat of redundancy and unemployment that worried the workers. The BMOA reported reduction in employment in 1927-29 to the extent of 10 to 11 thousand as a result of rationalisation.[14] Possibly the rate of redundancy was greater. In 1926-27 the numbers employed was 154, 400 according to the Director General of Commercial Intelligence, and in 1927-28 this fell to 129,300.[15] There is minor discrepancy between these and the figures compiled later :

TABLE : 1 [16]

No. of working Factories, Factory Employment in Textiles Industry in Greater Bombay, 1923-32

Year	Wkg. factories (Textiles)	Textiles Employment in thousands	% to total factory employed
1923	92	152	75.0
1924	92	153	75.2
1925	93	154	74.2
1926	92	155	72.8
1927	91	153	73.0
1928	91	127	70.1
1929	89	127	69.9
1930	89	134	72.7
1931	86	132	73.9
1932	85	147	76.5

It is noticeable that in 1927-28 there was a 17.3% fall in employment. The only means of checking these figures is to compare them with census data. The Census shows a fall of textile factory employment from 1.41 lakhs (1921) to 1.23 lakhs (1931).[17] However 1931 being a full depression year the comparison is of limited value.

One of the features of the strikes of 1928-29 was the very prominent participation of female workers in the agitation including picketing. One explanation of this is provided by the data on female employment (again subject to the above limitation):

TABLE : 2 [18]

No. of Female Workers per 1000 Male Workers in Greater Bombay

Year	No. of female workers
1911	158
1921	187
1931	123

In textile industry specifically, the number of female workers declined from 32,900 (1921) to 17,900(1931) a much sharper decline than that of all-workers in textiles. The census also shows a ratio of dependents to workers growing from 0.66 (1921) to 1.09 (1931).[19]

What impact did the contraction of employment opportunities and the non-employment of women have on the living standards of working class families can be only surmised. There is no working class budget survey in the late 1920's. However, only 6 years before the strike G.Findlay Shirras, Director of Labour Office, had conducted a survey which was reported in the *Labour Gazette.* At that time (1921-22) the government had estimated that "industrial workers consume the maximum of cereals allowed by the Famine Code but less than the diet prescribed in the Bombay Jail Manual".[20] With the exception of salt in all other items, cereals, pulses, meat, oils, etc. the average industrial working class family mambers consumed less than the prisoners in jail. It is true that textile workers were a little better paid than the average industrial worker, but that does not affect this picture very much for 49.5% of the above sample budgets were of textile workers' families.

To sum up, rationalisation meant harder work for the lucky mill-hand and no work for the unlucky ones. In a little known lecture on 1943 D.R. Gadgil deduced the following from the textile industry situation in the late 'twenties and the' thirties: "it may happen that rationalisation, widely adopted, brings about such changes in the market relations between labour and capital that labour as a whole suffers either by an added volume of unemployment or by a reduced share of the product of the industry that it is able to secure for itself."[21]

II

In an earlier paper[22] I have suggested that the battle lines were drawn, the class conflict is intensified, in the 1920's and that it is absurd to study big capital in India divorced from its relationship with labour. I would like to pursue that argument a little farther, for my earlier paper did not do justice to the complexities of labour-capital relationship and the growth of class organisations (in what I shall call a synergistic interactional process).

Nicos Poulantas makes an important point when he argues that classes cannot be defined outside of class struggle. " classes involve in one and same process both class contradictions and class struggle: social classes do not firstly exist as such and only then enter into class struggle. Social classes coincide with class practice, i.e. the class struggle, and are only defined in mutual opposition."[23] (Much that Poulantzas says about advanced capitalist society does not and is not intended to apply to backward or colonial contexts, and we may also disagree with his rather peculiar notion of structural determination of class both at the political ideological and economic levels. But we are concerned here with his methodological point of departure). This methodological point is important because convenience shapes our habits of thinking and we tend to forget that classes are not "pigeon-holes in a static social structure"; it is so much more convenient to burrow into a pigeon-hole of one's own making.[24]

If we do not fail to locate classes in their interactional/ antagonistic context and if we avoid a static conception of classes as ' things', the history of labour is inseparable from that of capital. What we simplify as a polar relationship between labour and capital is, of course, within the political field of forces of a complex pentagonal interaction between organised labour and Indian and foreign capitalist interests, with their apex bodies the ATTUC, FICC, and ACCI on the one hand, and the nationalist leadership at the helm of the congress and the colonial state on the other. (Perhaps one should add that this is just a schematic map of the interaction process and does not imply a monolithic homogeneity at any point in the polygon).

In the late 1920's the organisation of all-national apex organisation of capitalist associations, the FICC (December 1927), and the emergence of a radical leadership in the trade union movement (their self-assertion in the AITUC in the sessions of

Kanpur 1927, Jharia 1928, leading to the split in Nagpur 1929- and above all the growth of the GKU from 1928) accentuated the "transparency" of class confrontation and heightened awareness and solidarity on both sides of the barricades. Here we need not go into the history of the trade union movement in India as a whole and the development of radical ideologies within the movement. This story is available in a number of works.[25]

So far as Bombay textile industry is concerned the Bombay Textile Labour Union (BTLU), founded in 1926 by N.M.Joshi (President) and R.R.Bakhale (General Secretary), and the Girni Kamgar Mahamandal, led by Arjun Atmaram Alve, were the only trade unions in the beginning of 1928. In the first quarter of 1928 their position was threatened by the growth of a third union, Mill Workers' Union (President: S.J.Jhabvala) and the very effective intervention of some members of the Workers' and Peasants' Party in organising the spontaneous surge of resentment of mill hands against the nationalisation scheme, consequent retrenchment, and coincident wage reduction (e.g. for 'new sorts' produced by mills). BTLU and GKM were compelled to recognise the mood of the workers evidenced by demonstrations (April 16, 1928), and the formation of a Strike Committee by the militants. Although the BTLU had the largest number of registered members its opposition to the proposed strike was swept aside by the workers (general strike from April 26). A joint strike Committee was formed (May 2).[26] This consisted of 15 representatives of BTLU (including Joshi, F.J.Ginwala, and Asavale) 11 from the GKM (including Alve, Dange, Mirajkar), and 4 from the MWU (including Jhabvala and Nimbkar).[27] While this Committee was functioning (from May 3), the Girni Kamgar union was founded (22 May) with a small body of 300 members. Communists who have been mentioned above as working in the GKM and MWU founded this union known generally as *Lal Bavta* (Red Flag). It was registered and recognised by the Bombay Mill-owners Association (June 5).[28] This was the the union that was in effective leadership in the 1928 general strike (April 26 to October 6) and exclusive control of the 1929 strike action (April 26 to the fourth week of May when the general strike petered out, though the GKU did not formally call it off till September 19). Between the two strike periods the front rank of GKU leadership was arrested (20 March 1929) for trial at Meerut and a younger leadership, S.V. Deshpande and B.T. Ranadive, too over.[29]

We are not interested in chnonicling the history of the strikes beyond this brief outline. Before we proceed to discuss capitalist reactions to these developments let us brefly summarise the casus belli and the form of union organisation. The 1929 strike was simply against retrenchment combined with victimisation of union activists who had been taken a prominent part in the previous strike. The 1928 strike was directed chiefly against nationalisation and surreptitious wage reduction. The seventeen point Charter of Demands (May 3) can be divided into three parts.[30] Some points related to rationalisation, which we have seen in Section I above. Another set of points (1,2,8 and 12) demanded restoration of wages to the 1925 level, raise for those who received less than Rs. 30 per month, consolidation of H.P.A. (high price allowance) with wages, and 10 hours maximum limit on hours of work. A third set of points related to miscellaneous grievances regarding working conditions (machine cleaning, attendance record, termination of service notice, etc.). The interesting thing to note is that on each issue the charter demanded "consultation with representatives of workers' organisation", "approval of workers through their organisation" etc.[31] This was obviously meant to make a place for the union in the 'government of the factory' so to say—it had a political significance beyond the contents of demand. The charter was framed by the Joint Strike Committee of which the composition has been described above. On this coordinating body were represented the Managing Committees of the trade Unions. The managing committees in turn consisted of representatives of Mill Committees. At each of these three levels actual manual workers were included though their participation in negotiations with the employers was negligible compared to the role of "Advisers" like Joshi or Dange.[32]

A.A. Purcell, M.P., and delegate of the British TUC to the Kanpur session of AITUC, made a very interesting comparison: "the growth of trade unionism in our country has been largely coincident with the growth of capitalism itself. The young Indian movement is, however, faced with the experienced and highly organised movement of the employers in the country".[33] Indian business as a lobby was active even from the 1860's and was a force to reckon with in Bombay's politics from the last quarter of the 19th century; from acting as informal interest groups occasionally uniting to memorialise the government on specific issues in the 1860's, by early 20th century they had begun to organise themselves into permanent bodies of which the most important were the Indian Merchants' Chamber and the Mill-owners' Association.[34] They had vast experience in the game that interest groups can play. But the situation confronting them in 1928-29 presented new problems. Industrial employers had begun to learn to live with trade unions (especially after the passage of the Trade Union Act of 1926) but here was something far more dangerous.

The reaction of the industrial capitalists, and the capitalist class on a whole, was very perceptive. One can broadly distinguish four different strategies supported in various degrees by different sections of big capital. The first and the simplest reaction to the problem of communist leadership in the working class movement was typified by Sir D.R. Tata. The BMOA had expressed its alarm to the Government of India and had gone to Press with quotation from the *Pravda* about the "Bolshevik" inroads.[35] P. Thakurdas had spoken in the Legislative Assembly urging strong action to stem this threat.[36] Sir D.R.Tata however was not satisfied with such action. He was "convinced of the necessity of a strong capitalist organisation to combat this poisonous evil" causing "labour troubles in Bombay and elsewhere". (Jamshedpur was deep in labour trouble). And European and Indian capital, Tata thought, "are at one with us where the red flag is, concerned."[37] A political wing of the capitalists' was needed to protect "the interests of those who have a large stake in the business of the country, faced as they are at present with so many destructive elements, in particular the Red Flag, bent upon creating mischief among the workmen and bent upon violence against the capitalists."[38] To these culminations the reaction of his friends Sir P. Thakurdas and G.D. Birla were rather cold. Communism, Birla wrote, "finds a fertile soil only in poverty and discontent. Most of the capitalists ignore the fact that they themselves are responsible for breeding communism, and I have not the least doubt in my mind that a purely capitalist organisation is the last body to put up an effective fight against communism".[39]

What then was the alternative? This is spelt out by Birla in several letters: "what we capitalists can do" is to "cooperate with those who through constitutional means want to change the government for a national one".[40] (Later, when there were socialists within the Congress, Biral wrote: "Vallabbhai, Rajaji and Rajendra Babu are all fighting communism and socialism. It is therefore necessary that some of us who represent healthy capitalism should help Gandhiji as far as possible and work with a common object."[41] Birla believed that Gandhi would not stand for socialism in the Congress.) It was about this time that Thakurdas declared as the President of the Federation of Indian Chamber of Commerce: "Indian commerce and industry are intimately associated with, and are, indeed an integral part of the national movement—growing with its growth and strengthening with its strength....."[42]

A third line of attack stemmed from the above strategy: the propagation of labour-capital cooperation as a national duty. Thus Tairsee, President of the Indian Merchants' Chamber (Bombay) de;ored "appeals to class warfare" and advocated "rational and national lines" of cooperation between labour and capital.[43] Earlier the President of the Indian Chamber of Commerce (Calcutta) had similarly appealed to labour not to be misled by those who were "accentuating the cleavage between Indian capital and labour."[44] The idea being put forward was that future prospects of India depended on industry, therefore labour must not damage these prospects by refusing cooperation. Ahmedabad provided a ready model for such cooperation.

A fourth line of action was to pressure the government for legislation and administrative action against the "Bolshevik" threat in the labour movement. Thus the President of the Maharashtriya Vyapari Parishad urged the government to used extraordinary powers to suppress "Bolshevick influence" which was "undermining Indian society".[45] Thakurdas, during the mill strike of 1928, privately saw the Police Commissioner to ask him "why he would not remove Dange and Nimbkar by executive order and thus stop further poisoning of the mill hands' minds in Bombay".[46] He also lobbied Sir George Rainy with the same purpose and promised to organise political support for such action in the Legislative Assembly.[47] Sir P.C. Sethna was equally active in obtaining government aid to "check the activities of the communist strike leaders"; he was one of the promoters of the Trade Disputes Bill, 1928, to curb union activities.[48] The Mill-owners' Association put strong pressure on the Government of Bombay to enact a Criminal Intimidation law to make picketing by strikers cognizable offence. The Viceroy refused to exercise his special powers to make an ordinance, but the Bombay Legislative Council passed it promptly in a session specially convened earlier than it was due.[49]

Actually the Government's actions, motivated in part by reasons of their own, rendered signal service to the industrialists in a number of ways. The Trade Dsiputes Act of 1928 and the arrest of the Meerut accused in March 1929 are prominent instances. But it was the second and third lines of attack on the radical labour movement which appreared to business leaders to be more suited to their needs at that particular juncture in 1928-29. About this time the Currency Question exercised the businessmen and the tariff question brought them into direct clash not only with the foreign capitalists' ASCI, but directly with the government (which had recently rejected the Tariff Board's recommendations in favour of Indian cotton textlile interests).[50] Monetary stringency was acutely felt by Bombay mill owners. Mody, President of BMOA, estimated that "the industry as a whole had deficit amounting to Rs. 2.07 crores at the ead of 1929 without taking into consideration a contingent liability of Rs. 1.18 crores and the fact that practically no depreciation could be allocated during the year."[51] There was a "serious lack of borrowing power" and in many mills all liquid assets had been pledged. Under these circumstances the Govt. of India's currency and tariff policies were bound to bring Bombay businessmen closer to the nationalist leadership. Even the loyal Sir P.C. Sethna suspected that "our British friends are not sorry that....Indian capitalists should suffer".[52] He went so far as to declare himself as "half a Swarajist"![53] It was the Swarajists who attracted most trust from businessmen at Bombay till about 1928.[54] Financing Political parties with doles from time to time was not uncommon. Bombay had always been a source of Congress funds.[55] Motilal Nehru had live contacts in Bombay and at least in 1928 there is evidence of contribution sought from Bombay businessmen, especially Thakurdas.[56] Soon after this the revival of the boycott programme would forge further links between the nationalist leadership and the cotton millowners.

One of the dividends of good ralations with the "moderate" national leaders (as distinct from suspect radicals like Bose and J. Nehru) was the containment of radicalism in the labour movement and a schism within which was dramatised in the split at the AITUC Nagpur session, 1929. In Bombay in 1928, to the credit of the Joint Strike Committee, unity was, for purposes of strike action, sustained (though not in the long run). The Joint Strike Committee wrote to the Secretary, Mill-owners' Association: "In regard to your query as to which of the members of the Committee are exstremists and which moderates, we have to inform you that our Committee does not recognise any distinction such as moderate and extremists among its members so far as the prosecution of the demands sent to you is concerned."[57] That was a remarkable reply to an attempt to divide them. Incidentally, the avoidence of intervention by top level nationalist leaders during the industrial war of 1928-29 in Bombay was also remarkable.[58]

The outcome of this industrial war was complete fuilure of the workers' movement to gain the objective in their Charter of Demands. Negotiations between the subcommittee of BMOA and the Joint Strike Committee ended in stalemate, the 1928 strike Inquiry Commission's report yielded no gains to workers, retrenchment continued throughout 1929 and victimisation along with it. The Girni Kamgar Union was reduced in membership strength from 65000 (March 1929) to a few hundreds by the end of the year. Could this be the end? Sir Harry Haig wrote in a memo in the Home Department in 1929: "It appears to me that the suppression of communists as such will not provide anything like a permanent remedy for the trouble between labour and capital in the Bombay mill industry, and no legislation can prevent discontented workmen from following extremist leaders."[59]

III

We have used the term 'class' here in a limited sense defined in the beginning of this paper—limited in that it does not postulate class consciousness. This is because even the most cursory readings in labour history makes one wary of generalisations concerning working class consciousness. Further, from the long view as opposed to the short-run perspective, if 'class' in the process of becoming is the object of study, to attribute to it consciousness by the very act of definition is literally preposterous. While it is possible to defend the definition employed here, one cannot defer as assessment of the quality of consciousness of the working class at this particular point of time. Given the severe limitations on our present knowledge, we have to attempt some very tentative answers to this crucial question.

To begin with one may contrast statements of two observers, both in the leadership of the strike movements of this period. K.N. Joglekar speaks very confidently of the dawning of consciousness: "it was through the experiences of the strike that the workers realized the importance and significance of their class organization...." S.V. Ghate, on the other hand, sounds a more cautious note. He recounts how a G.K.U. President repudiated communism within a year ("Ghate came to me and asked me to sign a form and I signed that") and yet Ghate maintains that "***some*** of the ***leaders*** did understand what communism stood for." One statement by him is worth quoting in extenso: "It is some elemental consciousness that comes", said Ghate of the workers in general. "All these years they had been suppressed. They did not know what they could and what they could not do. Now suddenly there was the union which uphold them..... All the suppressed anger against the haves came up, but we were genuinely not interested in that, gonuinely not interested. We [i.e. Ghate, Joglekar, Mirajkar, Nimbkar and Dange] were interested only in the union becoming strong so that later on we could organise the workers".

In the present state of research it is impossible to resolve, on the basis of grass-root level documentation, the discrepancy between the above views. One can only make certain inferences from the behaviours of workers acting an masse. First, if discipline and loyalty to the class organisation is an index of motivation and conscious deliberation, the textile workers in 1928-29 score very highly. For instance Sir Harry Haig of the Home Department (G.O.I.) noted that on April 26, 1929, exactly at 12 noon, as announced by the G.K.U., 75,000 workers in different mills downed tools and left their place of work. Haig and Kelly, the Police Commissioner (Bombay), cited this incident to underline the point that there was disciplined and voluntary participation. This view was contrary to that of the mill-owners who ascribed the successful general strike to "intimidation". The Bombay Police Department and Haig advised the Viceroy that "mill-owners were exaggerating extent and effect of intimidation". In this connection one should also bear in mind the tenacity of striking workers in 1928: they sustained a general strike for 6 months costing them about Rs. 25,000,000 in wages.

On the other hand, when the movement was on the down-swing discipline and commitment disintegrated rapidly. The G.K.U. had about 300 members in May 1928, 54,000 in December 1928, 65,000 in March 1929 and a few hundreds at the end of 1929. Membership had increased astronomically when the movement was on the upswing and the defeat of the April-May 1929 strike led to desertion of the ranks on a mass scale and in an incredibly short time. It also seems that the period between the strikes of April–October 1928 and April-May 1929 was a period of trial for the leadership, both BTLU and GKU, for they were unable to check wild cat strikes spontaneously generated without reference to factory committees or the trade unions. Mr. Saklatvala speaking on behalf of the BMOA tauntingly asked the trade union leaders, Joshi, Dange, Asavale etc.: "If you are leaders you should have some influence?", and Asavale, Vice-President, BTLU, replied: "workers themselves do not listen". Likewise in the G.K.U., Ghate testified later, the union was unable to stem the rising tide of lightning strikes which were purposeless and inimical to organised movement. Ghate said that workers, anxious for action, did not give the GKU time to organise them in those days before the April 1929 general strike. In may 1929 when the general strike began to fail all the weaknesses came to the surface. The G.K.U. leaflets calling for "disciplined unity" (April 25), urging "peaceful means" (i.e. picketing and not intimidation which became common when the strike began to disintegrate), warnings agianst "communal bitterness" (May 6), call to "fight to the end" (May 7), advice to strikers to leave for their village home rather than join work (May 17), promise of relief to the hungry strikers (May 24),—even in these drastically abbreviated headlines, tell their own story. Disunity under impending defeat, use of intimidation when loyalty faltered, readiness to be duped into communal violence fomented by mill-owners, and a landslide towards capitulation under economic duress—this was the state of the union when the 1929 strike began to falter and fail.

Two explanations of the failure of the great strikes of 1928-29 have been suggested. First, that the workers were pauperised by the 6 month long strike in 1928 and that their staying power was very limited in early 1929. Secondly, that the leadership failed the workers in 1929 after the arrest of front rank leaders (Meerut trials), for the new leaders like B.T. Randive and S.V. Deshpande were inexperienced, too much influenced by dictates from Moscow, and too prone to launch on the "criminal adventure" of general strike. The first explanation is obviously true and one may add that the bargaining position of workers was poor in the late 1920's under the threat of economic crisis and unemployment. The second explanation, offered by Karnik, is debatable. But neither of these explanations were germane to the present issue in that these exogenous factors are unrelated to the constraints emanating within the working class at this juncture. We shall examine two other hypotheses. First, if the numbers of relatively recent entrants into industrial employment is large, their presence may dilute industrial workers' commitment and consciousness which go into the making of their class organisation. Second, traditional schisms, religious or ethnic, in a heterogeneous milieu may offer obstacles to the formation of classes as coherent units and occlude working class outlook.

To start with one should note that the left leadership was not wanting in efforts to "raise the consciousness"of the workers. The strikes were certainly periods of intense political education. According to one leader, 800 meetings were held at the mill gates, workers' ***chawls*** etc. in 6 months during the 1928 strike. The available police reporters' summaries indicate a strong political content with frequent references to the proletarian revolution in Russia. The G.K.U. pamphlets referred to earlier also contained a strong revolutionary message. How active the mill-hands were in the Factory level and Managing Committees we do not know—but the B.T.L.U. and the left unions put 17 representatives of Managing Committees on the Joint Strike Committee (out of a total of 30 members). Thus a second rank leadership was sought to be developed from among the workers. The strike committee members included weavers, spinners, fitters, etc. so identified by occupation in the records. At the same time, it is disquieting how little was the participation of these workers members in the deliberations in high level meetings of which some preceedings are available. The mill hands allowed the members identified as "Advisers" to be the spokesmen—R.S. Asavale (MLC), N.M. Joshi (MLA), S.S. Mirajkar, S.A. Dange, R.S. Nimbkar (Advisers) etc. Moreover, the history of the leftist union was one of unionisation through strike action. To that form of action the workers' commitment was strong, but did their commitment extend any further? Perhaps there was a disjunction between the short term objectives, sustained by what Lenin calls "trade union consciousness", and the long term political programme, ingrafted by the leadership.

Let us turn to the two hypotheses mentioned earlier. The first appears at first sight easy to eliminate. For it is well-known that M.D. Morris has taken great pains to prove that industrially committed labour force had come into existence in Bombay long before the 1920's. In particular he hs argued that there is a "very clear trend of increasing length of service" in Bombay textile industry. However, this trend is not so very clear for the pre-1928 period. Data are available for only one year (1890) and that too of a dubious sample (26 mill-hands, witnesses before the Factory Commission). The estimate for 1927-28 is, however, technically sound and Morris deduces from it that 37.5% had served in the industry for less than 5 years and 23.4% for 5-9 years. However, if one looks into Morris's data closely one finds that not only did the Labour Directorate suggest that their estimate tended to over-estimate length of service, but also that there are available figures adjusted to exclude nonemployment in the industry. These adjusted figures show that in 1927-28 46.5% of the sample had been in the industry for less than 5 years and 24.3% for 5-9 years. Therefore it seem that Morris, in arguing against the labour instability thesis, has underestimated the proportion of new entrants in the industry with less than 5 years industrial experience.

As R.K. Newman has pointed out, the last census before the strike put the member of Bombay-born among mill-hands at about 4,000 out of 146,000 employed daily (1921). Even if one accept Morris's upward revision of this ratio to 18.9%, this is a small proportion. During 1928 the staying power of the strikers might have been augmented with resources derived from their rural links. There is, however, no evidence for this. But in 1929 there was undoubtedly a large-scale migration back to their village homes. The Press reported on trains overflowing and special steamers plying and 20,000 were reported to have left. Incidentally, the Government felt "apprehensive of the effect of the return to villages in large numbers of mill-hands infected with these subversive ideas."

To sum up this argument, the number of new entrants in the testile industry was substantial (46.5% with less than 5 years industrial experience) and the rural links of many of them were alive. This had a bearing on their effective organisation and consciousness. Perhaps, from the 1930's as the numbers of new entrants diminished and proportion of workers with long industrial work experience increased, their "organisability" as a class increased.

Our second hypothesis was that traditional divisions became blocks in the way of consolidation of classes as cohesive units. This has relevance to the fact that involvement in communal riots weakend workers' solidarity in Bombay at two crucial junctures:

in February 1929 when preparations for the General strike were afoot and April-May 1929 when the General Strike was on. The *Police Report* (1929) on the second riot and the *Bombay Riot Enquiry Commission Report* (1929) on both the riots, make it abundantly clear that the riots originated in the mill area in the *chawls.* This version was also supported by Press reports. The left trade union leader Ghate believed that the first riot was "provoked by the workers themselves".

A diversion into the causes of the riot and causes of workers' involvement in the riots may be instructive. At first sight the communal riots appear to be reenactment of the familiar festival of violence Indian has seen so often. Widespread rumour about Musalmans (Pathans) kindnapping Hindu children was the immediate cause of the first riot (149 persons killed), and Muslim objection to music and Hindu *palkhi* precession in the neighbourhood of a mosque was the immediate provocation for the second riot (35 persons killed). Scribblers of pamphlets gave, as usual, a helping hand. While the Muslim scribbler (language Gujarati) would ask "will Mosques have to be closed up?", the Hindu scribbler (language Marathi) would exhort the cereligionists to join the Hindu Sanrakshak Mandal to "get protection" and to give protection to Hindu temples. A political leader—it happened to be a Muslim leader, Shaukat Ali—would state to the Press his resolve "to organise the Mohommedans for purpose of self-defence"—and withdraw the statement after its publication has done the intended damage. The "prominent citizens" would pin the blame on the "inflammatory speeches"of left radicals (GKU Leaders' speeches during 1928 strike) which "weakened respect for law and order". And the Government Enquiry Committee presided over by a British civil servant aided, predictably, by one Hindu and one Muslim gentleman, would concur with this view that communists were to blame for the communal outbreak. It was all dreadfully familiar, except for that last bit of irony.

One closer examination the detailed evidence reveals some interesting facts. In 1929 many among the Muslim workers were persuaded to act as strike breakers and the consequent striker vs. non-striker conflict easily got transformed into a communal riot. Black-legs were used on a large scale first in December 1928 to break the strike in the foreign owned oil installations at Sewri (Burmah Shell Co.). These black-legs were Pathans and clashes with them led to attacks on Pathans watchmen etc. in cotton mills, and eventually to "a regular Pathan-hunt by the mill hands" in the mill area and to generalised Hindu-Muslim riot. It is true that the *chawl* population took the most active part in the riot, but this was at least in part the result of manipulation by their employers. A Muslim correspondent wrote in the *Bombay Chronicle*: "The Musalman section of the mill workers have been won over by the owners with tempting wages (temporary of course) and lorries for their safe conveyance to and from mills, etc. But what will be the psychological effect produced in the mass mind of the vast number of illiterate Hindu workers?".

That effect was of course exactly suited to the designs of mill-owners. It is interesting to note G.D. Birla's forthright comments: "I noticed in the papers that Mohammadan strikers are coming back to work while Hindus are keeping out. One likes to see the strike ended, but I am a bit upset by the way in which communal tension has been utilised by the Millowners for ending the strike." Repeatedly Birla condemned this "exploitation of the communal situation" by Bombay mill-owners. The condemnation was not worth very much since it was in confidence to Thakurdas: Birla had, of course, no stake to lose. However, that does not diminish the value of his assessement of the situation. Incidentally, in the closed world of Bombay business magnets there might have been also strong reaction to this manipulation of communalism from a pro-Hindu lobby. P. Thakurdas writing to Tairsee, President of Indian Merchants' Chamber, urges that "Sane practical patriotic Hindus.....not be carried away by any religious over-zeal." The industrialists were not likely to be carried away by such zeal in their steady persuit of means of breaking the strike of 1929. The extablishment of military pickets in working class areas during the riots were particularly opportune. The army pickets were kept even after the termination of riots. The Police Report ovserved that "the withdrawal [of army] was carried out by slow degrees owing to the state of high nervous tension....and also becuase there was the likelihood of industrial disturbances owing to the general mill strike, and the decision of the millowners to withhold the pay of strikers on pay day, the 15th May." Thus did the government combine the duty of suppressing communalism and communism at one stroke.

Another economic element in this complex situation was that the Pathans were identified in the mill hands' mind as money-lenders. The survey of working class family budgets in 1921-22 showed that 47% of workers' families were in debt; indebtedness extended "ordinarily to the equivalent of two and half a months' earning." The usual rate of interest was 75% per annum and in some cases it was 150% or more. The Riots Inquiry Committee noted that Pathan money-lenders'homes and records were particular objects of attacks. According to Ghate the resentment of the indebted against *Kabuliwallas* was the main cause of the first riot of 1929.

To sum up, The mill hands' weaknesses, their readiness to fall under the influence of communal propaganda, was exploited by the Indian mill-owners. The community oriented institutions like the *Akhadas*, the *Shuddhi* movement, the *tanzimat* movement etc. provided a cultural milieu laden with latent communal tension. The leftist trade union leadership was unable to counteract this, although in at least one leaflet the GKU warned workers against the communal riots the mill-owners were provoking. Kumari Jayawardana has shown that in Ceylon "one of the direct consequences of the economic depression was an increase in communal tension among the working class" and strike breaking by imported Indian blacklogs from 1929. No where has it been easy to erase communalism from the consciousness of the workers.

We know too little about the development of working class consciousness in India to employ sophisticated typelogies (e.g. Giddens') concerning varying levels of consciousness. However, the recognition of such varying levels is in itself a useful check against romanticisation. At the same time, the analysis of constraints on the growth of class consciousness in colonial India has to proceed on new lines. The constraints pointed out by J. Foster in his historical study of decline of revolutionary class consciousness in Britain, or the process of decomposition of labour and statification that followers of Dahrendorf have analysed, belong to a different context, that of more advanced capitalist societies. For one thing, a fundamental difference is that capitalist relations not having been sufficiently generalised in colonial society, the multi-structural character of the economy in colonial India imparts a special complexity to the class structure, and hence an "opaqueness" to perception of classes. Secondly, more particularly about industrial capital: it becomes the standard bearer of "national development" which affords it some advantages in the struggle of 'national capital' versus working class. Here the role of intelligentsia, I have suggested elsewhere, was crucial in promoting an ideology subordinating inter-class conflicts to a "supra-class" contradiction between "national interests"and imperialism. Thirdly, stratification within the working class, wage differentiation, and social distancing between skilled/high wage manual/low wage labour which affects class cohesion in advanced capitalism has hardly begun in colonial India. For example, immediately before the strike of 1928 there was a survey of wages. This indicated wide gap between "coolio"wages (Rs. 24.4 per month) and average monthly earnings of all workers (Rs. 37.6 P.M.); but the mode of earnings distribution for all workers (Rs. 25 P.M.) was almost equal to unskilled workers' average, and the median of earnings distribution (Rs. 30.8) for all workers was only a quarter higher than unskilled wages. Fourthly and finally, the carryover of communal and other divisive tendencies occlude class consciousness in colonial India, blocking the cohesion of a class, though this may not always come in the way of collective action in the political arena. These are some of the reasons why we have to look at the growth of working class and its consciousness in a colonial society in a new perspective different from that developed in the context of advanced capitalist western societies.

REFERENCES

1. The following abbreviations have been used: N.M.J. (N.M. Joshi Papers, NMML); AITUC (Paper of All India Trade Union Congress, NMML); I.L. (Industry & Labour Dept.) Home Poll. (Home Dept., Political Branch, Govt. of India, NAI); Comm. (Commerce Dept., GOI, NAI); P.T. (P. Thakurdas Papers, NMML) PCS (P.C. Sethna Papers) S.V. Ghate (Interview Transcript, NMML); AICC (NMML); BMOA (Mill-owners' Association of Bombay); FICC (Federation Indian Chamber of Commerce); IMCC (Indian Merchants' Chamber of Commerce, Bombay).
2. *Pravda*, 22 June 1929, Engl. Tr. in P.T., 42 (V).
3. Sukomal Son *Working Class of India* (Calcutta, 1977) pp. 259-265. V.B. Karnik *Strikes in India* (Bombay, 1967) Ch. VII.
4. Georg Lukacs *History and Class Consciousness* (London, 1971), p. 79 and p. 46 ff. Anthony Giddens *The Class Structure of the Advanced Societies* (London, 1977), p. 112 and chapter 6. John Foster *Class Struggle and the Industrial Revolution* (London. 1974).
5. A.K. Bagchi *Private Investment in India* 1900-39 (Cambridge, 1972) p. 247 ff.
6. M.D. Morris *The Emergence of on Industrial Labour force in India* (Bombay, 1965) p. 171.

7. Morris *op. cit.* p. 186.
8. N.M. Joshi papers, File No. 42 Pregs of Jt. Strike Enquiry Comm., 14-16 Nov. 1928.
9. *Ibid.*, pg. c-8.
10. Commerce Dept. (GOI) Sept. 1930 (B) no 1946-C-serial 1-4, 4 Mody, BMOA, to G. Rainy, Commerce Member, GOI, 14 Jan., 1930.
11. K. Marx *Capital* Vol. I (Moscow, 1953) p. 410.
12. *Ibid.*, p. 412; cf. chapter XV and XVIII.
13. N.M. Joshi Papers, File no. 45, letter from Joint Secys, Joint Mill Strike Committee, to Secretary, Mill-owners' Association, 3 May 1928.
14. Comm (GOI) Sept. 1930 (B) 1940-C-SI. 1-4, Mody to Rainy. 14 Jan. 1930.
15. Comm. (GOI) Set. 1930 (B) 1946-C, Note by DGCIS with BMOA Report updating Indian Tariff Board statistical table I, Appendix II.
16. Abstracted from Reports under Factories Act 1923-1933, D.T. Lakdawala *Work, Wages and Wellbeing in an Indian Metropolis: Economic Survey of Bombay City*, pp. 622-24.
17. *Ibid.*, p. 52 According to Census Reports employment in textile industry was 1,20,499 (1911), 1,40,597, 1,23,539 (1931) which was 64.5%, 63.3% and 67.6% respectively of total employment in all industries. These do not exactly tally with Factory Report date.
18. *Ibid.*, table II-36.
19. *Ibid.*, table II-41.
20. G. Findlay Shirras *Report on an Enquiry into Working Class Budgets in Bombay* (Labour Office, Bombay Govt., 1923), p. 21.
21. D.R. Gadgil *Regulation of Wages and other problems of Industrial Labour in India* (Poona, 1943), p. 62. He was at the time of writing a member of Bombay Textile Labour Enquiry Committee.
22. S. Bhattacharya, 'Cotton Mills and Spinning Wheels. Swadeshi and the Indian Capitalist Class, 1920-22', *Economic and Political Weekly* (Bombay), 14 November 1976.
23. N. Poulantzas *Classes in Contemporary Capitalism* (London, 1975), p. 14.
24. Erik Olin Wright 'Class Boundaries in Advanced Capitalist Societies' *New Left Review*, 98, (1976) p.5.
25. Sokomal Sen *Working Calss of India* (Calcutta, 1977): K. Panikkar *An Outline History of the AITUC* (New Delhi, 1959); S.D. Punekar *Trade Unions in India* (Bombay, 1948); J.S. Mathur *Indian Working Class Movements* (Allahabad, 1964); and *Indian Trade Unions:* A Survey (Bombay, 1978).
26. NMJ Papers, File No. 45, letter cited in f.n. 13 above and an unsigned undated loose leaf which appear to be the draft of

agreement to form the Jt. Committee; the Committee here was composed differently from the one actually set up.

27. NMJ Papers, File no. 45, Jt. Secys. Jt. Mill Strike Comm., to Secy. BMOA, 6 May 1928.
28. NMJ Papers, File no. 45, J.P. Wadia, Actg. Secy, BMOA, to Secy., BTLY, 5 June 1928.
29. The AITUC later condemned the arrests in a formal resolution moved by V.V. Giri and J. Nehru in the chair deplored the "offensive against the labour movement". AITUC Papers, File no. 1, Minutes of Executive Council Meeting, Bombay, April 27-28, 1929. Also see AITUC. File no. 1, letters from All-China Labour Federation to AITUC, 2 March 1927.
30. NMJ, File no. 45, Jt. Secy. JMSC, to Secy, BMOA, 3 May 1928.
31. *Lec. Cit.* paragraphs 2, 3, 5, 7.
32. NMJ, File no. 42, Progs of Strike Enquiry Committee; and file no. 45 containing records of negotiation between subcommittees of BMOA and Jt. Strike Committee; File no. 54, BTLU Statement to Court of Inquiry (1929) by R.R. Bakhale, 15 July 1929.
33. A.A. Purcell's speech reported in *Annual Register* Vol. II, 1927, quoted in S. Sen *op. cit.*, p. 282 (I have not been able to check the source).
34. cf. C. Debbin *Urban Leadership in Western India* (Oxford, 1972); A.D.D. Gorden (Delhi, 1978) *Businessmen and Politics.*
35. *Bombay Chronicle,* 18 May 1929; *Daily Mail,* 2 July 1929.
36. P. Thakurdas Papers, 42 (V), P.T. to M. Mazumdar, Secy. To D.R. Tata, 24 July 1929.
37. P.T. 42, (V), N. Mazumdar (Secy. to Tata) to PT, 3 July 1929.
38. P.T. 42 (II) Mazumdar for Tata P.T., 22 May, 1929.
39. P.T. 42 (V) G.D. Birla to P. Thakurdas, 30 July 1929.
40. *Loc. cit.*
41. P.T. 42 (VI), G.D. Birla to P. Thakurdas, 3 Aug. 1934.
42. Quoted in Bhattacharya *op. cit.*
43. *Indian Daily Mail,* 28 April 1929.
44. *Report of Indian Chamber of Commerce* (Calcutta, 1926) p. 4.
45. P.T. 42 (III), *Bombay Samachar,* 5 Dec. 1928.
46. P.T. 42 (II), P. Thakurdas to N. Mazumdar (Secy. to Tata) 7 June 1929.
47. *Loc. cit.*
48. P.C. Sethna Papers, (uncatalogued), Sethna to Srinivas, 13 Aug. 1928.
49. Home Poll. 303/1929 & K.W., especially the Note by H.G. Haig, 4.6.29.
50. For a review of the over-all scene Bipan Chandra 'Indian Capitalist Class and British Imperialism', R.S. Sharma (ed.) *Indian society: Historical Probings* (Delhi 1977) and for a detailed study of later

years Sumit Sarkar 'The Logic of Gandhian Nationalism' *Indian Historical Review* July 1976, Vol. III 1 no. 1.

51. Commerce Dept. (GOI) Sept. 1930, no. 1946-C, Secy. BMOA, to Secy, Commerce Dept. 7 Jan. 1930.
52. P.C.S. Papers, Sethna to Srinivas, 13 Aug. 1928.
53. P.C.S. Papers, Sethna to Lindsan, 4 May 1928.
54. A.D.D. Gordon *Businessmen and Politics* (Delhi, 1978).
55. See e.g. AICC Papers, no. 5/1924, 28/1924, J. Nehru, Kitchlow and G.B. Deshpande's reports on Congress Funds. Bombay business had contributed substantially to Tilak Swaraj Fund of Bhattacharya *op. cit.*
56. P.T. File no. 71, P.T. to Motilal Nehru, 8 Oct. 1928; M. Nehru to P.T., 29 Sept. 1928; P.T. File no. 42 (II), G.D. Birla to P.T. 26 April 1929.
57. N.M. Joshi Papers, File no. 45., Jt. Secy, JMSC, to Secy. BMOA, 6 May 1928.
58. This might have been one of the reasons why textile labour was completely apathetic to the Civil Disabedience movement; see Ravinder Kumar: 'From Swaraj to Purna Swaraj : 1920-32' D.A. Low (Ed.) *Congress and the Raj : Facets of the Indian Struggle 1917-47.*
57. Home Poll. 303/1929, Confidential Note by H.G. Haig, 4.6.29.
60. *Meerut Conspiracy Case Records,* Defence Statement of K.N. Joglekar, 3 (5).
61. S.V. Ghate, Interview with, Transcript of, July 9, 1970, in NMML Oral History Transcript, Accossion no. 326, hereafter referred as SVG., p. 47.
62. SVG. Transcript. p. 60.
63. Home Poll. 303/1929.
64. *Ibid.*, Telegram from Home GOI to Viceroy.
65. NMJ, File no. 42, Preceeding of Enquiry Committee, 16 Nov. 1928.
66. SVG Transcript, pp. 52-53.
67. In the absence of the papers of GKU the leaflets reported by the Press are used here. References are to *Bombay Chronicle* 26 April, 7, 8, 18, 25 May, 1929.
68. S. Sen *op. cit.*, pp. 263-265; V.B. Karnik *op. cit.* (1978) p. 74.
69. SVG Transscript. p. 43.
70. Home Poll 10/100 1930 Report of Percival Committee Appendix, Summary of Speeches.
71. NMJ, 45, Secy. JSC to Secy. BMOA, 6 May 1928.
72. M.D. Morris *op. cit.* p. 89.
73. R.K. Newman 'Social Factors in the Recruitment of Bombay Millhands', KN Chaudhuri & C.J. Dewey *Economy and Society* (Oxford, 1979).

74. Bombay Chronicle 18, 19 May, 1929 *Times of India* 23 May 1929.
75. Home Poll. 303/1929, Note by H. Haig, 11.6.29.
76. SVG Transcripts, p. 57.
77. *Ibid.*, Report of the Bombay Riots Enquiry Committee 1929, Chapter I.
78. Home Poll. 10/10/1930 Police Report on Bombay Riot of April-May 1929.
79. *Ibid.*, Police Report.
80. *Ibid.*, Enquiry Committee Report p. 15
81. *Ibid.*, Chapter I.
82. *Ibid.*, Home Dept. (Bombay) to Home Dept. (GOI), Cable dt. 4.5.29
83. Home Poll. 10/10 1929 Enquiry Committee Report, Chapter III.
84. *Bombay Chronicle,* 13 May 1929, S. Murtaza's letter to editor.
85. P.T., 42 (II), G.D. Birla to Thakurdas, 19 June 1929.
86. P.T. 81 (II) G.D. Birla to Thakurdas, 10 May 1929.
87. P.T. 81 (I), P. Thakurdas to L.R. Tairsco, 23 Feb. 1929.
88. Home Poll. 10/10/1929 Police Report.
89. G. Findlay Shirras *Op. cit.* p. 33.
90. SVG Transcript. p. 53.
91. Home Poll 10/10/1929 Riot Enquiry Committee Report p. 18.
92. V.K. Jayawadana *The Rise of the Labour Movement in Ceylon* (Duke University, 1972).
93. D. Mazumdar 'Labour supply in early industrialisation : the case of Bombay textile industry' *Economic History Review,* Aug. 1973, p. 482.

—PROF. S. BHATTACHARYA

CHAPTER - XII

COLONIALISM AND NATIONALISTS

First detailed and coherent critique of colonialism in its various aspects was made by the early Indian nationalists during 1870-1905. In the inter-war period, first the Commintern and its journals and then several scholars around the journals *Far Eastern Quarterly* (New York) and *Amerisia* (New York) and the Institute of Pacific Affairs in New York, such as Owen Lettimore, Keith Mitchell and Joseph Barnes made important contributions in the study of specific areas. Leland Jenks promoted, at Yale, the study of U.S.imperialism in different areas of Latin America. Leonard Wolf provided insights into the working of colonialism in Africa. A major non-Marxist approach came from J.S.Furnival. At popular plans, Kumar Ghoshal's work deserves mention. In India, nationalist economists- K.T. Shah, C.N. Vakil, Bal Krishna, Wadia and Merchant among others, continued to provide empirical and theoretical support to the early nationalist approach. But the most significant and structured contribution came from R.Palm Dutt in his *India Today* and then by A.R. Desai in his *Social Background of Indian Nationalism*.

Surprising omission in this respect was the complete ignoring and even suppression of the subject in the universities of the chief metropolitan countries of the day, i.e., Britain and France. (An omission which is even more glaring today, except that, which a small minority of Marxist scholars have made significant contributions, the dominant academics in their universities have advanced from neglect to attack on the Marxist analysis of colonialism and to a defence of the colonial record).

As the anti-imperialist movements moved towards success in large parts of the world and advanced towards intense struggle in other parts, the academics outside the Socialist countries (including India) remained surprisingly quiet on the subject during the first two decades after 1945, the lone exceptions being a short article by B.N. Ganguli in 1958 and another by Arun Bose in the early 1960s. (Clifford Gurtz's work on *Agricultural involution in Indonesia* and Mohammed Husain's on Egypt also deserve notice). However, tangential elaborations of aspects of colonialism were made by the early dependency theorists like Prelisch. The socialist bloc academics did, however, continue to write about colonialism in the earlier manner of the Commintern.

In the Western capitalist countries—and not only in the USA—McCarthy's witch-hunting campaign prevented the development of the earlier US tradition of the study of colonialism. He made the use of the term 'colonialism' one of the litmus tests for 'ferreting out''Communist' intellectuals in the universities and research institutes. One result was the driving out from their jobs of scholars like Owen Lettimore, Daniel Thorner and Lawrence Rosinger, and the virtual closing down of the Institute of Pacific Affairs—it was found to migrate to Canada in an attenuated form.

The Cuban Revolution, the Algerian and Vietnamese national liberation wars, the struggle for freedom of the peoples under Portuguese domination, and powerful stirrings in Brazil, Chile, Argentina and other Latin American countries, finally led after 1965 to an explosion of well researched academic writings on the subject of colonialism. The first to make a massive breakthrough was A. Gunder Frank, who was soon followed by the centrist and left-wing dependency economists and historians from Latin America C. Furtado, Theodore D.M. Santos and others. A seminal contribution had been made in 1957 by Paul Baron who, in his *Political Economy of Growth*, restored the concept of social surplus in relation to colonial underdevelopment to the centre of the subject. Gunder Frank was followed in quick succession by Samir Amin, and then by other world systems analysts led by Immanuel Wallerstein. An important, though highly controversial, contribution on the very important aspect of Unequal Exchange came from Arghiri Emmanuel. One scholar who has, along with Gunder Frank and Samir Amin, continued over the years to contribute in a basic manner to the subject is Hamza Alavi. More recently, A.K. Bagchi has made a major contribution,though his work is, in the main, devoted to the underdevelopment and economic backwardness of the Third World, which spans both the colonial and the post-colonial periods. Mention may also be made of articles on the subject by Javius Banaji and Bipan Chandra. And, of course, since the early 1970s there is a spate of excellent writing on colonialism in individual countries and on its specific aspects.

The cultural aspects of colonialism have been discussed by A. Cabral, Franz Fenon, Rudolfo Constantino and Edward Said. This field is also being yearly enriched.

The study of the colonial state and colonial political institutions and their relation to colonial economic and state structure and to the metropolitan state structure, political system and political institutions is yet awaited as also a serious study of colonial ideology (To my knowledge, the only discussion of the former, though very brief and synoptic, is in my article "Colonialism, Stages of Colonialism and Colonial State" and the address on the "Long-Term Dynamics of the Indian National Congress").

I

I would today be discussing some important aspects of colonialism when viewed as a structure. I will start by pointing out some important aspects that I will not be dealing with. I will not take up in detail the impact of colonialism. I will not at all take up the reverse impact of colonialism in the economic development of the metropolis which was rather massive during the 18th and 19th centuries. I will also not be able to discuss the political, administrative, cultural and social aspects of colonialism nor the ideological justification and legitimation of colonial domination earlier or today by imperialist statesmen, administrators and academics. Thus I will not be able to make a critical examination of the spate of economic historians, who deny the role of colonialism in the underdevelopment of the colonies and whose recent most compilations on the *New Cambridge History of Europe* and the *Cambridge Economic History of India*, Vol. II. (Those interested in a critique of the latter may see the *Social Scientist*, Nos. 139 and 140).

I would like to make only one point in this respect. Theories of colonialism and history of looking at colonialism were themselves part of the process of colonialism. They played and continue to play an important role in the structuring and the effects to maintain colonialism—and they have to be studied as part of the study of colonialism. Theories of imperialism and colonialism evolved in the course of the development of colonial economy, polity and society and were in themselves *important elements of colonialism* as also of the anti-colonial struggle. Moreover, men and women act through ideas; the phenomenon of colonialism was and is not automatically evident either to the colonisers or to the colonised; it was and is *grasped* by the participants through these theories. Therefore, these theories become important elements in the determination of colonial structure as also the struggle against colonialism. And since imperialism and colonialism are still with us in the world though sometimes as mere psychological hang-up or ideological effects of colonialism—these theories continue to play an important role. For the same reason, as M. Barret Brown has put it, the nature of these theories has determined whether they would "be a tool of apologetics" of colonialism, or of "scientific enquiry".

I believe that significant commonness as also differences exist between colonialism and semi-colonialism (as in pre-1949 China or Latin America). I will treat the two as the same, except in two basic aspects, i.e., nature of state and the role of class struggle, which will be separately brought out.

Also, recognizing that specific features of colonialism in individual countries are crucially related to the nature of the specific pre-colonial country or society as also its size, geography and geographical location, I have resisted the temptation to deal with the subject.

What I hope to deal with today are the colonial structure, including the colonial state, the stages of colonialism, colonial classes and class struggles, and the inner contradictions of colonialism.

II

It is clear that colonial societies contain a large number of modes of production, relations of production, and forms of exploitation. One view, represented by a large number of sociologists, political scientists and economists is that colonial society was a traditional society and that colonialism retained basically or largely old relations and modes of production. Others have seen colonialism as a transitional society which would have, on its own, without being sheltered, gradually developed into a modern or capitalist society. Still others believe colonial societies to be dualistic in which the modern capitalist sector coexists side by side with traditional pre-capitalist sector. The two sectors are held in a relatively static balance because the modern impulse was too weak to shift the weight of tradition in a basic manner, while the traditional forces were not strong enough to overthrow the modern sector which was backed by the strength of the colonial power.

Many Marxists and other radical writers have tended to follow a more anti-colonial version of the duality model which may be described as the "partial modernity" or "arrested growth" model according to which imperialism partially modernized the colony but failed to carry out the task fully. Thus, the restrictive, inhibitive or feudal or semi-feudal features of colonial economy are seen to be the remnants of the past which imperialism failed to, or did not desire to, uproot. For example, these writers accuse colonialism of 'preserving' feudal exploitation and of 'deforming the evolution of Indian feudalism'. A recent Marxist writer has criticised colonialism for "preservation in many instances of precapitalist relations and classes in the interests of metropolitan capital"; and again that colonialism "did not require the destruction of existing pre-capitalist formations".

There is, of course, nothing theoretically wrong with the notion that pre-capitalist modes and relations of production continue to exist in a colonial society. But, in historical fact, colonialism does not in most cases preserve the pre-colonial modes of production, etc.; it transforms and restructures them to make them integral parts of a new colonial structure. Transformed by colonialism these modes, etc., are no longer pre-colonial or pre-capitalist. In fact, in many cases, what appear to be traditional elements or remnants of the pre-capitalist modes are often creations of the colonial period. Many writers accept the notion of remnants or preservation of pre-capitalist or pre-colonial formations because of their failure to conceive a colonial economy which is neither capitalist as in Britain nor pre capitalist. They assume that those features of colonial economy which are not capitalist must be pre-capitalist and pre-colonial. The remnants become the residual elements of historical development, with capitalism accused of not removing them or of preserving them in its own interests.

The development of agrarian relations in the colonies—for example, India, Indonesia, Egypt, Latin America—provides an interesting example of this. For example, the semi-feudal structure of agrarian relations in colonial India was not a carry over or perpetuation from the Mughal period. It was the result of two serious and massive efforts to transform pre-colonial agriculture into capitalist agriculture. But since this was done under colonial conditions, the result was a semi-feudal semi-colonial agriculture dominated by the colonial state, world capitalist market, landlords, merchants and moneylenders and having many capitalist features: bourgeois property relations, commercialization and elements of capitalist agriculture. This effort to change pre-colonial agriculture into capitalist agriculture and the coming into being of a different agrarian structure was perceived quite early and clearly by Karl Marx who wrote in *Das Capital,* Volume III : "If any nation's history, then the history of the English in India is a string of futile and really absurd (in practice infamous) economic experiments. In Bengal they created a caricature of large-scale English landed estates; in south-eastern India a caricature of small parcelled property; in the north-west they did all they could to transform the Indian economic community—with common ownership of the soil into a caricature of self".

We can thus say that the colonies underwent a fundamental transformation under colonialism which led to their becoming structured colonial societies. Moreover, colonialism did make the colony an integral part of the world capitalist system. But did this integration lead to the developement of a capitalist economy and structure? Let us take the example of India.

During the 19th century, the colonial transformation of the colonies, especially of India, was carried out under the slogan of making them capitalist, and the task, it was said, was getting accomplished-elements of capitalist development in agriculture, trade and industry were pointed out. This view has been the staple of imperialist writers since the days of John Strachy. It is very much in vogue even today. The manifest deficiencies of capitalist development in the colonies are then ascribed to the poverty of the initial conditions from which colonialism had to initiate the task and to the density of their social,economic, geographical, demographic, and cultural conditions which capitalism found difficult to penetrate and overcome, except very slowly. Among some Marxists, this notion tends to find acceptance because of the classical economists' view which Marx and Engels and early Indian intellectuals such as Raja Rammohan Roy tended to accept that the colonising capitalist society would reproduce its capitalist character in the colony. As Marx and Engels put it in the *Communist Manifesto,* capitalism, being a world system, "compels all nations, on pain of extinction, to adopt the bourgeois mode of production,... to become bourgeois themselves. In one word, it creates a world after its own image". In other words, despite 'blood, sweat and tears' and 'swinishness', a colony would be transformed into an image of the metropolitan country, that is, into a full-fledged industrial, capitalist society.

It is, however, to be noted that Marx was only seeing the potential; he neither studied the colonial reality in depth nor had the contradictions of societies dominated by industrial capitalist metropoles come to the surface as yet. Marx was quite right in pointing to the universal character of capitalism, to the fact that it would not-indeed could not-, because of its very character, remain confined to a single country or region. It must engulf, penetrate and transform the entire world. It was, in other words, a world system. What Marx failed to see was that, while capitalism is a single world system and colonies become its basic constituents, *colonies do not become capitalist in the same way as the metropoles do.* Capitalism is a world system but it has one face in the metropolis and another in the colony. Nor is it that imperialism does not attempt to transform and develop the colonies in a capitalist direction and around the capitalist principle of extended reproduction. It does, as Marx saw clearly. But because it does so under colonial conditions, it neither makes them into a spit image of itself nor does it succeed in developing them. It under-develops them and transforms them into colonial societies. We may suggest that imperialism introduces capitalism, capitalist production and property relations in the colonies but not capitalist development. It uproots and transforms the old economy and social formation and structures, but the new colonial economy and social formation were not more conducive to development. They were quite regressive. The colony was integrated into world capitalism without enjoying any of the basic benefits of capitalist developement and, in particular, without taking part in the industrial revolution. Colonialism did mean the introduction of capitalist relations of production or capitalist structure into trade, industry, agriculture and banking, and bourgeois state structure, legal and property relations, but not the development of capitalist production or of "productive powers "(Marx).

After all, capitalist mode of production involves not only capitalist relations of production but also the development of productive forces in agriculture and industry. There is no capitalist development when the social forces of production are not developed and constantly revolutionized. This is where lies the superiority, or even definition, of capitalism over all previous modes of production. Thus, capitalism means above all the development of productive forces. In the colonies there was no constant revolutionization of the forces of production. While there was no breakthrough in industry, in agriculture there was in most colonies, except where foreign-controlled plantation system was introduced, constant growth of semi-feudalism and stagnation in productivity. Colonialism was thus not like capitalism an advanced stage of social development. It was an image of metropolitan capitalism, but it was its negative image, its opposite side, its non-development side. We may put the crucial difference between capitalism and colonialism in another manner. "Capitalism develops and cannot help but develop social productive forces and is overthrown as a result of the development of the contradiction generated by this development between relations of production and the forces of production. Colonialism, on the other hand, has to be overthrown because it does not develop but represses productive forces. Its inner contradictions result not from development of productive forces but from the lack of their development". If social change under capitalism results from the contradiction between production relations and productive forces, under colonialism it results from the contradiction between colonial relations and all productive forces including those of capitalism.

III

A powerful case for seeing colonialism as a distinct mode of production has been made over the years by Hamza Alavi. He describes colonialism as "colonial cepitalism", that is, "a capitalist mode of production that has a specifically colonial structure", the two specific features of colonialism as a mode of production being "the internal disarticulation of the present economy and its external integration" and the realization of " the extended reproduction of capital" not "within the colony" but "only via the metropolis".

In our view, colonialism does not represent or constitute a mode of production; it is a social formation in which several modes of production and relations of production and forms of exploitation exist, including the capitalist mode of production etc. There is coexistence, though not necessarily peaceful or non-antagonistic, of feudalism, semi-feudalism, slavery, bondage, petty commodity production, merchant and usury exploitation, and agrarian, industrial and finance capitalism. These different modes have different mixes in different colonies and at different times and stages of colonialism. And, of course, all the different modes of production are subordinated to the metropolitan capital.

Colonialism, in the long course of its history since the 17th century, does not represent a mode of production, *its basic feature is the appropriation of the social surplus produced in the colony by varied modes of production.*

Colonial appropriation of surplus is not *crucially* linked to the metropolitan bourgeoisie's *ownership of the means of production* or to the form of appropriation of surplus at the point of production, or to the *level of the development of productive forces*, except very partially during the third or finance imperialist stage of colonialism. In this respect, colonialism differs in a basic manner from capitalism in which surplus is appropriated by means of ownership or control over the means and conditions of production. It is to be noted that in its long history in India, for example, colonialism did not introduce new relations of exploitation or modes of production of social surplus.

Many recent writers tend to rightly reject the concept of colonial mode of production, but believing that there has to be a dominant mode of production in an economy opt for the characterization of colonialism as the capitalist mode of production, just as others do for the feudal or semifeudal mode.

IV

Colonialism is best seen as a totality or a unified structure. "All the changes and the newly formed institutions and structures, forming a network, mutually interconnected and reinforcing each other, subserved and brought into being the colonial structure". To see colonialism as a structure is also to realize that it will go on reproducing itself till it is shattered.

Despite attempts by a long series of writers from the 1920s, we are not yet in a position to fully understand the colonial structure in the manner in which capitalism was illuminated by Marx. What I wrote in 1976 still holds: "The intellectual resources do not yet exist to understand this (colonial) structure fully and to trace the multifarious channels and ties—the views and arteries—through which this structure is articulated ".

A great deal has been written in recent years about some of the basic features or structural specificities of colonialism. I however feel that little progress has perhaps been made in this respect from the days of Naoroji, Ranade, and Dutt. These features are perhaps now better conceptualized, formulated and defined and given better nomenclatures; but no basic advance has perhaps been made. There is at present no real theory of colonial structure. Perhaps no more than these features can be formulated; and for concrete colonial formulations we have to study colonial interests, policies, forms of surplus extraction and modes of production, state and its institutions, culture and society, ideas and ideologies as functioning within the parameters of colonial structure, which is itself to be defined by their interrelationships as a whole.

What are the basic features of the colonial structure? What are those features of the colonial situation which prevented the realization of the expectations of the classical economists, Marx and Engels, and proto-nationalists such as Rammohan Roy and early Dadabhai Naoroji that the path of capitalist development would be opened up in a country occupied and ruled by the most advanced capitalist country of the world? I may briefly describe the four basic features of the colonial structure as described by the 19th century Indian nationalists as well as the more recent writers.

(i) The first basic feature is the complete but complex integration and enmeshing of the colony with the world capitalist system in a *subordinate* or *subservient* position. Subordination means that the basic issues of the colony's economy and society are not determined by its own needs or the needs and interests of its dominant social classes but by the needs and interests of the metropolitan economy and its capitalist class. It is important to note that subordination of the colony's economy and society is the crucial or determining aspect, and not mere linkage with or integration with world capitalism or the world market. The latter, i.e., linkage and integration with the world market, is true even of independent capitalist economies; nor does such linkage automatically lead to colonialism or semi-colonialism. (This aspect is often missed, leading to newly independent capitalist countries being branded as neo-colonies. This also leads to failure to theorize the difference between Manchu China after 1840 and Japan after 1868. One of the many sources of this error is the failure to take into account the role of the state, for example weak or strong, dependent or independent.)

(ii) The second feature of colonialism is encompassed by twin notions of unequal exchange (Aghiri Emmanuel) and internal disarticulation of the colonial economy and the articulation of its different disarticulated parts through the world market and imperialist hegemony with the metropolitan economy (S. Amin and Hamza Alavi). For example, the colony's agriculture does not directly relate to the colony's industrial sector; it does not articulate internally. Rather it articulates with the world capitalist market and is linked to the metropolitan market which buys its products and whose industrial products are imported into the colony and sold in the rural market thus closing the circuit of commodity circulation. The colony thus experiences "a disarticulated generalized commodity production".

Marx and Engels and early Indian nationalists brought out the same features by pointing to a specifically colonial structure of production whereby the colony specialized in the production of raw materials and the metropolis in manufactured goods, by pointing to the role of railways as subserving the interests not of the Indian industry and trade but the needs of British production, by pointing out that colonialism led to a particular international division of labour by which the metropolis produced high technology, high productivity, high wage goods while the colony produced low technology, low productivity, low wage goods, thus making international trade an instrument of exploitation and underdevelopment, and by criticizing the fact that iron and steel and other capital goods industries were confined to the metropolis.

(iii) The third feature of colonialism is that of the drain of wealth or the unilateral transfer of social surplus to the metropolis through unrequited exports. This aspect was the heart of early nationalists' critique of colonialism and their explanation of the economic underdevelopment and poverty of India, and of Marx's rethinking on the role of colonialism in India. In the 1950s, Paul Baran once again brought the question of the utilization of social surplus to the centre of the stage in the discussion of colonial underdevelopment. Early Indian nationalists as also recent writers also point to the fact that a great deal of the colonial state expenditure on the colonial army and the civil services in the colony represented a similar external drain of surplus.

This aspect has been recently rephrased as the pattern of accumulation of capital on a world scale so that surplus is produced in the colony but accumulated not in the colony but abroad, or that "a substantial part of the surplus generated" in the colony "enters into expanded reproduction not directly within the colonial economy but rather at the imperialist centre". Consequently, "the attendant rise in the organic composition of capital" also occurs in the metropolis. Thus "the colonial form was a deformed extended reproduction".

(iv) The fourth basic feature of colonialism is foreign political domination or the existence and role of the colonial state which plays a crucial role in the colonial structure. While this feature was recognized by most of the 19th century Indian nationalists only after bitter political experience and was given full place in their analysis by the Marxists, its fuller historical role still awaits analysis. In fact, there is an urgent need for a theory of the colonial state and for a historical study of the nature of the colonial state and its relation to colonial society. Such a study would not only enable us to study colonialism better but would also help us analyse and understand post-colonial states and societies better. Here I would like to make a preliminary remark on the subject.

V

Colonial state is a basic part of colonial structure; at the same time, subordination of the colony to the metropolis and other features of the colonial structure are evolved and enforced through the colonial state. The parameters of the colonial structure are constructed through, and determined and maintained by, the colonial state.

The colonial state differs from the capitalist state in important aspects. It does not 'reflect' economic power but creates and enforces it. It is not a superstructure erected on the economic base; it helps create the economic base; it is a part of the economic base of colonialism. It not only enables the ruling classes to extract surplus, it itself is a major channel for surplus appropriation.

Under capitalism, the ruling class is that which, to quote Ralph Miliband, "owns and controls the means of production and which is able, by virtue of the economic power thus conferred upon it, to use the state as its instrument for the domination to society". Reverse is the case under colonialism. It is because of its control over the colonial state that the metropolitan class is able to control, subordinate and exploit the colonial society. In other words, the metropolitan ruling class does not control state power in the colony and its social surplus mainly because of its ownership of the means of production in the colony. It controls the social surplus of the colony and is able to subordinate its producers because it controls the state power there. The metropolitan capitalist class may not own the means of production in the colony to a significant extent as it did not, for example, in India to any significant extent and not even then predominantly.

Furthermore, while the capitalist state is the instrument for enforcing the rule and domination of one class over another, colonial state is the organized power of the metropolitan ruling class for *dominating the entire colonial society.* Also, while in the metropolis the state is a relation between classes, in the colony it is a relation between the foreign ruling class and the colonial people as a whole. This virtually amounts to a truism but it still has to be stressed because nearly all historians and other social scientists of the imperialist school ignore or obscure this aspect and its *implications.*

The colonial state, thus, does not represent any of the indigenous social classes of the colony. It subordinates all of them to the metropolitan capitalist class. It dominates all of them. None of the indigenous upper classes shares state power in the colony, *none of them is a part of the ruling class.* They are not even its subordinate or junior partners. The metropolitan ruling class may share the social surplus in the colony with the indigenous upper classes, but it does not share power with them. Not even princes, regents, landlords and compradores have a share in colonial state power. It is, of course, true that the economic class position of the landlords and capitalists in the colony is "articulated through, and by, the colonial state". But they are not part of the ruling class. Their interests are freely sacrificed to the interests of the metropolitan bourgeoisie. This also enables the colonial state to introduce certain reforms at the cost of the indigenous upper classes such as factory legislation, tenancy and anti-usury legislation, support to minority communalism, and so on. (This explains the paradox of the ease with which Irish landlords talk of tenant interests when they administer India or the Lancashire spokespersons urge labour legislation in India or the anti-semites become champions of minority rights). The colonial state is thus able, for a certain period and in certain situations, to play the landlords and tenants and capitalists and workers and higher and lower castes and all sorts of majorities against minorities against each other. On the other hand, this also means that even the uppermost classes and strata of colonial sociaty are capable of turning against colonialism. Thus the anticolonial struggle could be led even by big landlords as in Poland or Egypt. This also explains the attraction of the elite theory to imperialist administrators and ideologues since the end of the 19th century and till today, for it obfuscates the reality of colonialism and the colonial ruling class by equating the indigenous elite of colonial society with the colonial ruling class, suggesting that both were oppressors of the colonial people in the same manner or in a manner that made no political difference to the anti-colonial struggle. It was with this elite theory that imperialist administrators and intellectuals tried to question the legitimacy of the actual anti-imperialist movement—a task which continues to be undertaken till this day sometimes with radical stance and terminology. To avoid or see through this obfuscation it is necessary to use the concepts of ruling classes and exploiting classes, on the one hand, and the nature of the colonial state and its ruling class or classes, on the other hand.

It is also to be noted that a crucial difference between colonial and semi-colonial societies lies in this very aspect. Firstly, large sections of the ruling classes in semi-colonial societies bear a determinate relation to the means of production; *they appropriate* social *surplus because of the position they occupy in the mode of production.* Secondly, the indigenous upper classes or some of them—landlords, compradores and even sections of the national bourgeoisie-*are part of the class coalition that constitutes* the ruling class. That is, they share in state power, sometimes even as senior partners. Arun Bose has put this aspect quite aptly: "The 'class nature' of a colonial state is determined by the dominant class of the conquering, dominating country. But the class nature of the semi-colonial state is determined by the class nature of the politically dominant class in the semi-colony".

The colonial state differs in this respect from the most authoritarian of pre-colonial states. In the latter case, the state however oppressive, is an organic part of the indigenous society; it is not an instrument for the enforcement of subordination of society to a foreign society or ruling class or for the export of social surplus. (Interestingly, this was the ground on which Dadabhai Naoroji and other nationalists differentiated between the British Indian colonial state and the Mughal state).

Lastly, it is to be noted that the colonial state is basically a bourgeois state. Consequently, it does in several of its stages introduce bourgeois law and legal institutions as also bourgeois property relations, the rule of law and bureaucratic administration. It can, therefore, as is the case with metropolitan bourgeois state, be authoritarian or even fascistic as in many of the colonies in Africa and South-east Asia or it can be semi-authoritarian and demi-democratic as in India. (It can, of course, be never fully democratic). It can also to a certain extent create a constitutional space for itself. It can rule by the bayonet or can assume a semi-hegemonic character, depending on the character of the colonial society, its size, history, etc. as also the character of the colonizing society and its polity. But the bourgeois character of the state and its superiority in certain aspects to some of the pre-colonial or even some of the post-colonial states does not change its basically colonial and therefore negative character.

VI

Seeing colonialism as a structure, which includes the colonial state, alone enables us to fully understand class structure, class alignments, class contradictions and class struggles in the colony and their relation to colonialism. It also enables us to define as also study the politics and political roles of different classes and strata in the colonial situation.

Herein also comes the importance of not seeing colonialism as having, or being, a mode of production in the colony. For if it was so, the principal contradiction would lie between or among the classes involved in the mode of production. This will either mean that the principal contradiction would like among the indigenous classes with the colonial state being opposed only because of its support to the indigenous exploiting classes, or, if the metropolitan bourgeoisie was present as capitalists or owners and controllers of means of production in the colony, the primary contradiction will lie only between the indigenous working class and the metropolitan bourgeoisie, unless the latter also functioned as capitalists and landlords in the villages. On the other hand, the concept of several modes of production in the colony would enable us to identify and analyse the indigenous classes and strata and their mutual relations and class antagonisms and to see in which manner and to what extent are their mutual relations over-determined by colonialism. The concept of the colonial mode of production would enable us to do neither. After all, a major significance of the concept of the mode of production is that it enables us to identify the roles of major classes in society as also its primary contradiction at any stage.

Furthermore, the notion of colonial mode of production or dominant mode of production under colonialism would pose its problem of principal contradiction in the form of some type of class struggle and politics based on it. On the other hand, our manner of viewing colonial structure makes the primary contradiction a societal one. If colonialism subordinates the entire colonial society to an alien ruling class, if no indigenous class is part of the ruling class or a partner in the state, then struggle against colonialism assumes not the form of a class struggle but that of a national liberation struggle, that is, struggle of the entire nation or a popular or people's struggle. It is very different from any of the paradigms of class struggle.

Moreover, the struggle assumes *a political form from the beginning*; it is from the beginning a struggle against the colonial state which is the core, the base of the colonial social formation and in which none of the indigenous classes participates. The political struggle is at no stage *mediated* by economic class struggles. In fact, often economistic class struggle against the ruling class, that is, the British capitalist class, is not possible. For example, except in the case of a few modern industries and plantations, Indian workers and peasants were exploited by Indian landlords, moneylenders, merchants and capitalists. They had to fight the British ruling class not as a class enemy but as a societal enemy, i.e., enemy of the Indian people and social development. The internal class struggles are waged in a colony, and have to be waged, but as part of the struggle to settle issues and contradictions rising in the multiple modes of production. They are not and do not become basic building blocs or initiators of the anti-colonial struggle. That is why classes do not join the national movement through class organizations but as 'people'. National liberation struggle is a people's struggle and not a coalition of classes or class organizations. This is not only true of India, Indonesia or Egypt, but even of Vietnam and China during the phase of anti-Japanese struggle. For example, the Chinese Communist Party or the People's Liberation Army was not a coalition of classes-workers, peasants, petty bourgeoisie and national bourgeoisie—nor did it enter into coalition with class organizations of the peasants, etc., but a proletarian party leading the Chinese people and acting on behalf of all of them against imperialism. The national, anti-colonial struggle is from the beginning waged as a political struggle which incorporates economic and social demands of different sections of society not as elements of class struggle but as issues through which the people come to understand the basis of their participation in the anit-colonial struggle and the vision of the future independent society.

The primary contradiction vis a vis colonialism also then helps situate the status of the internal class struggles within the colonial formation. This analysis not only makes the contradiction between workers and capitalists secondary, but also goes against the notion that anti-feudal struggle is expression of a primary contradiction in colonial society and enjoys the same status as the anti-colonial struggle. *Herein lies a major difference between the political struggle in a colony and a semi-colony.* In a semi-colony, feudal or semi-feudal mode of production and contradiction arising there of may be primary. In a semi-colony, indigenous exploiting classes wield state power, someties as senior partners to colonial powers. Here even a struggle against colonialism, if it is to take a political form, must come up against the state and therefore the ruling classes who are often feudal landlords and compradores. Moreover, class struggle arising out of the dominant mode of production—often feudalism or semi-feudalism—may have a primacy except when colonialism threatens to transform a semi-colony into a colony. This not only explains the differences in the nature of political struggle and class alignment between a colony and a semi-colony, for example, between India and China, but also explains differences in the political struggle in a semi-colony at different times. Thus, in China, anti-feudal struggle assumed primacy even while colonialism was attacked during 1927-33 and 1946-49 when the chief target was the semi-feudal, semi-colonial state and the semi-feudal class which dominated it. But anti-feudal struggle was put in a secondary position—in fact subordinated to the primary contradiction and struggle against colonialism, put in cold storage for the period of the ani-Japanese war, and different sections of the feudal class were allied with or neutralized with only collaborators being attacked. Thus when it appeared that colonialism would overwhelm semi-feudalism semi-colonialism and the struggle was against the intruding colonial state, the Chinese Communist Party refused to give equal place or even much of a place to the anti-feudal struggle. But once, after 1946, the colonial state was no longer the main enemy and arms had to be turned against the internal semi-feudal semi-colonial state, the semi-feudal landlords were once again made the target of present mobilization.

VII

It is to be noted that colonialism goes through several stages during which the fact of subordination is constant but the forms or patterns of subordination undergo changes over time according to changes in the historical development of capitalism as a world system, the place of the individual metropolis within this system and the development of colonialism in the colony itself. Similarly while the appropriation of the colony's surplus by the metropolis is a constant feature, the forms of this appropriation undergo changes from one stage to another. Stages of colonialism are thus basically differentiated by these two features—patterns of subordination and surplus appropriation.

I may also like to point out that Marx was the first to notice this fact, though by the very nature of things he conceptualized only two stages; those of monopoly trade and direct appropriation of surplus, and of free trade or unequal exchange. Basing himself on Lenin, R. Palme Dutt added a third stage, that of finance imperialism. Unfortunately, later writers have tended to ignore wholly or partially this distinction. thus, Samir Amin and many others theorise as if only the third stage constituted colonialism (Lenin who emphasized the third stage never ignored the first two).

VIII

As a structure or social formation, colonialism is from the beginning ravin with inner contradictions whose character changes from stage to stage. The colonial state evolves its policies in part as the effort to resolve these inner contradictions at each stage of colonialism. It may be said that colonialism and the colonial state and its policies are best illuminated through a study of the numerous inner contradictions of colonialism. Even a historiographic point may be made here. Any system or structure 'opens' itself to scientific study only when its inner contradictions emerge or can be discerned. It was the surfacing of the real life class contradictions of capitalism in the 1840s and 1850s that enabled Marx to scientifically study capitalism. The inner contradictions of the first-stage colonialism in India surfaced by the end of 1760s. This enabled both Adam Smith and Karl Marx to understand its basic features. On the other hand, the inner contradictions of the second-stage colonialism-'free trade' colonialism—had not surfaced in India by the 1850s when Marx wrote on India. He could therefore not fully grasp its character or impact except for the impact on handicrafts and agriculture. He did so later in the case of Ireland and very sporadically in case of India. What enabled early Indian nationalists to grasp the basic features of colonialism was the fact that from 1870 onwards they came face to face with the inner contradictions of colonialism.

This aspect of colonialism may be illustrated by bringing out some of the contradictions from which colonialism in India suffered. The following were some of the contradictions during the first stage of colonialism (the list is purely illustrative):

(i) Plundering form of exploitaion v/s reproduction of the conditions of exploitation.
(ii) Exploitation of Bengal v/s reproduction of Bengal's economy.
(iii) Gains by the East India Company's servants v/s gains by the Company.
(iv) Exploitaion of India in the interests of the company and its allied interests v/s exploitation of India in the interests of the developing industrial national economy and the rising industrial bourgeoisie.
(v) The company's dividends and solvency v/s territorial expansion in india, promising future gain, and defence of the existing empire.
(vi) Short-term exploitation v/s long-term exploitation—that is don't kill the goose that lays the golden aggs.

(parenthetically, I might point out that the attempts to resolve these contradictions figure in imperialist historiography and our question papers as reforms of this or that Governor-General).

During the second and third stages of colonialism, it was necessary to modernize and transform India in basic aspects so that its economy could become reproductive on an extended scale and subserve industrial and later finance capital of Britain. This is known as the need to develop India. This came up against the financial constraint. The revenues of India were growing rigid in a stagnant economy. This contradiction made the entire developmental effort limited and petty. It made the colony less useful than desired. It also made Indian people discontented, further limiting the possibilities of taxing the peasantry and other sections of Indian society.

(ii) Similar was the contradiction between civil and military expenditure and developmental expenditure, that is, between the need to develop India and the need for imperial control.

(iii) There was the need to develop agriculture. The peasant had to be helped to save so that he could become a buyer of British goods, invest in agriculture, produce the needed raw materials and in general develop agriculture on an extended scale. There was the counter need to make him pay for the defence and expansion of the empire, for its administration and for its development, and in general for the peasant to provide the social surplus for export. In other words was the peasant to be the mainstay of the colonial state or the base of a reproductive colony? the end result was that all the schemes for capitalist development of agriculture led to its feudalization; and more the British officials abused the money-lender, more both the Government and the peasant depended on him for revenue payment and the peasant for even physical survival.

(iv) There was the contradiction between deindustrialization and pressure on land and development of agriculture, leading to rack-renting and feudalization.

(v) There was the contradiction of balance of payments. Should Indian export surpluses be used for expanding market for British goods or for remitting home profits, etc.

(vi) There was the crucial contradiction between the need for economic development or making India a reproductive colony and the objective consequences of colonialism producing the opposite result. This in turn led to the basic contradiction between colonialism and the Indian people leading to the struggle for national liberation.

(vii) Similarly, even the limited transformation needed to make India a 'useful' colony led to the rise of sociai forces which began to oppose colonialism and organize struggle against it.

—PROF. BIPAN CHANDRA

APPENDIX - I

LIST OF PERSONS KILLED IN THE JALLIANWALA BAGH ON 13TH APRIL, 1919*

Sr. No.	Name and parentage	Caste	Age	Residence
1.	Gagan Nath s/o Ram Dass	Khatri	25	Amritsar City
2.	Mohan Lal s/o Behna Mal	"	48	"
3.	Shib Diyal s/o Solukhan Mal	Kamboh	50	"
4.	Veshno Dass s/o Damodar Dass	Khatri	55	"
5.	Hardiyal s/o Atara Mal	Kamboh	45	"
6.	Ram Das s/o Ganga Das	"	21	"
7.	Hira Nand s/o Chambha Mal	Khatri	50	"
8.	Bhula s/o Mathra Das	Rajput	20	"
9.	Bishan Das s/o Dhanpat Ram	Khatri	32	"
10.	Ganesh Singh s/o Kalu Mal	Arora	42	"
11.	Tirlok Das s/o Harjas Mal	Khatri	25	"
12.	Thakur s/o Prabh Diyal	Kaist	25	"
13.	Giyan Chand s/o Kirpa Ram	Kamboh	15	"

* File—Pb. Govt. Home-Military-Part B —1921—No. 139.

Sr. No.	Name and parentage	Caste	Age	Residence
14.	Harnama s/o Viroo	Barber	30	Amritsar City
15.	Mohan Lal s/o Diya Ram	Khatri	42	"
16.	Hakum Chand s/o Pheru Mal	"	33	"
17.	Nihal Chand s/o Tek Chand	" "	30	"
18.	Thakur Das s/o Malava Mal	"	35	"
19.	Hari Ram s/o Asa Nand	"	32	"
20.	Charn Das s/o Balak Ram	"	36	"
21.	Ram Lubhaya s/o Chaju Ram	"	17	"
22.	Ram Chand s/o Locha Ram	Arora	29	"
23.	Govind Ram s/o Sita Ram	Khatri	35	"
24.	Kan Chand s/o Hem Raj	Brahman	28	"
25.	Nikka s/o Koohi	Mehra	26	"
26.	Ram Dass s/o Jamet Singh	Zargar	28	"
27.	Rakha Mal s/o Gujar Mal	Khatri	36	"
28.	Durga Das s/o Kanshi Ram	"	23	"
29.	Wasu Mal s/o Narsing Das	"	42	"
30.	Giyan Chand s/o Mansa Ram	"	26	"
31.	Mulak Raj s/o Jai Har Nand	"	23	"
32.	Khushi Ram s/o Nikka Mal	Brahmin	28	"

Sr. No.	Name and parentage	Caste	Age	Residence
33.	Chuni Lal s/o Budha Mal	Barber	29	Amritsar City
34.	Devi Chand s/o Hari Ram	Khatri	30	”
35.	Roora s/o Ganga Ram	”	42	”
36.	Kishan Chand s/o Amir Chand	”	38	”
37.	Jai Narain s/o Bhagat Ram	”	32	”
38.	Hira Nand s/o Maharaj Mal	Arora	45	”
39.	Muni Lal s/o Kaniya Lal	Khatri	40	”
40.	Panna Lal s/o Ram Rakha	”	18	”
41.	Tara Chand s/o Bahadur Mal	”	63	”
42.	Thakur Das s/o Dina Nath	”	35	”
43.	Palla s/o Megh Nath	”	20	”
44.	Ram Gopal s/o Sain Das	”	32	”
45.	Moti Ram s/o Mela Ram	”	42	”
46.	Ram Nath s/o Phagu Mal	”	35	”
47.	Chet Ram s/o Narsing Das	”	29	”
48.	Parma Nand s/o Maghi Mal	”	50	”
49.	Vaso Mal s/o Sidhi Mal	”	45	”
50.	Mansa Ram s/o Narsing Das	”	25	”
51.	Sohn Lal s/o Vas Mall	”	9	”

Sr. No.	Name and parentage	Caste	Age	Residence
52.	Nur Mohd. s/o Buta	Rain	60	Amritsar City
53.	Ahmad Din s/o Dara Khan	Rajput	16	"
54.	Nathu s/o Jawahar	Dhobi	80	"
55 to 58 names not known.				
59.	Mohd. Sharif s/o Mohd. Ramzan	Mason	12	"
60.	Mohd. Ramzan s/o Rahim Bat	Kashmiri	24	"
61.	Barkat Ali s/o Alahi Bux	Tarkhan	32	"
62.	Umar Baksh s/o Ida	Kashmiri	60	"
63.	Gulam Mustafa s/o Jumma	"	20	"
64.	Abdul Khaliq s/o Rahim Khan	"	60	"
65.	Mohd. Ibrahim s/o Sikandar Ali	Shiekh	24	"
66.	Imam Din s/o Murad Bux	Lohar	50	"
67.	Shams Din s/o Sikandar Ali	Sheikh	24	"
68.	Mohd. Ismail s/o Miran Bux	Rajput	35	"
69.	Mohd. Sadiq s/o Murad Bux	Sheikh	25	"
70.	Hafiz s/o Ali Mohd.	"	35	"
71.	Khuda Bux s/o Vasao Shah	Fakir	40	"
72.	Mohd. Bux	Mason	36	"
73.	Name not known			
74.	Nathu s/o Gulab	Kamboh	8	"

Sr. No.	Name and parentage	Caste	Age	Residence
75.	Karim	Chaukidar	40	Amritsar City
76.	Miraj Din s/o Ladha	Kharasi	20	"
77.	Waris s/o Chirag Din	Arain	30	"
78.	Miran Bux s/o Nikka	Kashmiri	30	"
79.	Palla s/o Gurditta	Sweeper	40	"
80.	Mahi s/o Lahna	Jat	35	"
81.	Rahmat s/o Nawab Din	Sheikh	21	"
82.	Mohd. Din	Zargar	20	"
83.	Girdhari Lal s/o Ganga Bishan	Brahmin	20	"
84.	Bal Makund s/o Mangal Chand Nohria	Nohria	25	"
85.	Nur Mohd. s/o Jhandu	Teli	30	"
86.	Khair Din s/o Mangtu	"	30	"
87.	Mahbub Shah s/o Ahmed Shah	Sayyid	30	"
88.	Feroz s/o Sher Mohd.	Zargar	25	"
89.	Noor Mohd.	Weaver	22	"
90.	Abdulla s/o Pir Baksh	Dhobi	15	"
91.	Isao s/o Lehna Singh	Jat	20	"
92.	Sundar Singh	"	19	"
93.	Bhag	Kamboh	19	"
94.	Sharaf Din s/o Sadr Din	Rajput	22	"
95.	Hira Singh s/o Nihal Singh	Sikh	24	"
96.	Basanta s/o Sarna	Sweeper	25	"

Sr. No.	Name and parentage	Caste	Age	Residence
97.	Hamid s/o Ahmad Din	Kashmiri	19	Amritsar City
98.	Ram Lal	Rajput	24	”
99.	Ghulam Rasul s/o Mohd. Shah	Kashmiri	30	”
100.	Ghulam Mohiud Din s/o Mohd. Joo	”	30	”
101.	Barkat s/o Behla	Sheikh	20	”
102.	Labhoo	Mohammedan	25	”
103.	Abdulla s/o Lal Mohamed	Lohar	20	”
104.	Dheru	Gujjar	40	”
105.	Harbhagwan s/o Jairam Das	Arora	50	”
106.	Bura s/o Arura Singh	Tarkhan	20	”
107.	Kala Singh	Hindu	40	”
108.	Ram Lal	Khatri	25	”
109.	Bua Das	”	25	”
110.	Kehar Singh	Saini	20	”
111.	Sobha Singh s/o Kharak Singh	Tarkhan	50	”
112.	Ram Lal s/o Moti Ram	”	22	”
113.	Kala Singh s/o Gulab Singh	”	50	”
114.	Bua Das s/o Fakir Chand	Khatri	22	”
115.	Kesar Singh s/o Gopal Singh	Hindu	15	”
116.	Nand Lal s/o Shiv Diyal	Brahmin	12	”
117.	Mohn Lal s/o Sham Das	Hindu	60	”
118.	Moti Ram	”	40	”
119.	Mohn Lal s/o Mani Khatri	Khatri	12	”

Sr. No.	Name and parentage	Caste	Age	Residence
120.	Balwant Singh s/o Arur Singh	Hindu	25	Amritsar City
121.	Harnam Singh s/o Gulab Singh	Tarkhan	15	"
122.	Budh Singh	Hindu	70	"
123.	Gopal Singh s/o Mehr Singh	"	30	Sathiala (Amritsar)
124.	Ram Chand s/o Saran Das	Kargar	34	"
125.	Narain singh s/o Diyal Singh	Arora	21	"
126.	Devi Diyal s/o Lachman Das	Hindu	25	"
127.	Thakur Singh	Arora	50	"
128.	Sundar Singh	Arora	30	"
129.	Kanshi	"	30	"
130.	Nathu	"	30	"
131.	Gopal Das s/o Prem Singh	Khatri	30	"
132.	Jwala Singh	Hindu	60	"
133.	Bhagat Ram s/o Hira Lal	"	60	Sialkot
134.	Bhangan Shah	"	50	Amritsar City
135.	Mohan Lal s/o Sham Das	"	60	Amritsar Raya Sansi
136.	Sobha Singh s/o Sant Singh	"	60	Amritsar City
137.	Bhagat Salig Ram s/o Sant Jawala Singh	Sadh	60	"
138.	Permanand s/o Dev Raj	Hindu	24	"
139.	Chanan	"	20	"
140.	Guru Brahman	Brahmin	15	"
141.	Murli Mal s/o Lakhu Mal	Arora	70	"
142.	Girdhari	Brahman	20	"
143.	Hira Lal s/o Bal Mukand	Khatri	30	"

Sr. No.	Name and parentage	Caste	Age	Residence
144.	Nikmu Mal s/o Girdhari	Khatri	14	Amritsar City
145.	Partapa	Arora	80	"
146.	Bhag s/o Sri Ram	Bhatia	40	"
147.	Sobha Singh	Tarkhan	55	"
148.	Gandoo s/o Nanak Chand	Khatri	18	"
149.	Chatroo	Sadhu	60	"
150.	Muni Lal s/o Devi Das	Brahmin	30	"
151.	Sojhan Singh s/o Sahib Singh	Arora	22	"
152.	Dass s/o Nand Lal	Brahmin	19	"
153.	Biroo s/o Gathoo	Khatri	50	"
154.	Harnam Singh	"	30	"
155.	Billa	"	18	"
156.	Hans Raj s/o Rohan Singh	"	23	"
157.	Dhani Ram s/o Lorin Chand	"	34	"
158.	Prabh Diyal s/o Ram Rattan	"	35	"
159.	Bal Mokand s/o Jai Ram Das	Arora	20	"
160.	Veshno Das s/o Chuni Lal	Brahmin	30	Tarn Taran
161.	Ahmad Villah s/o Karim Baksh	Kashmiri	35	Amritsar City
162.	Sant Ram s/o Shiv Ramdass	Brahmin	20	Amritsar, Varpal Village
163.	Daulat Ram s/o Brij Lal	Ahluwalia	27	Amritsar City
164.	Jagdish	Brahmin	20	"
165.	Bua Ditta s/o Nathu Mal	Khatri	20	Sarangdeo, Tehsil Ajnala

Sr. No.	Name and parentage	Caste	Age	Residence
166.	Sadhu Ram	Hindu	20	Sri Hargobindpur, Dt. Gurdaspur
167.	Lal Singh	Kamboh	35	Amritsar City
168.	Lalu s/o Sita	Arora	22	"
169.	Hari Ram s/o Hardiyal	Khatri	40	"
170.	Ram Singh s/o Jawahar Singh	Ramgarhia	21	"
171.	Faquir Chand s/o Hakim Rai	Khatri	30	"
172.	Bakshish Singh s/o Ishar Singh	Jat	—	Shamnagar, Distt. Amritsar
173.	Jhanda Singh	Jat	—	Kiampur, Distt. Amritsar
174.	Indar Singh	Jat	—	Begewala, Distt. Amritsar
175.	Hazari Lal s/o Dinna	Khatri	17	Amritsar City
176.	Charan Das s/o Ram Chand	Hindu	—	"
177.	Bhagwan Das Shawl Merchant	Bhatia	—	"
178.	Mehr Chand	Hindu	—	"
179.	Viroo Mall	"	—	"
180.	Kishan Das	"	—	"
181.	Guran Ditta	"	—	"
182	Chaju Ram	"	—	"
183.	Budha Singh	Sikh	—	"
184.	Bhagwan Das s/o Charan Das	Arora	—	"
185.	Mani Lal s/o Narsingh Das	Khatri	—	"
186.	Ram Nath s/o Lakhu	"	—	"
187.	Chuni Lal s/o Hira Lal	Arora	—	"

Sr. No.	Name and parentage	Caste	Age	Residence
188.	Kaniya Lal s/o Harbhagwan	Hindu	—	Amritsar City
189.	Pars Ram	Rajput	—	"
190.	Kirpal Singh s/o Partap Singh	Arora	—	"
191.	Kesar Singh s/o Chandumal	Hindu	—	"
192.	Sundar Singh s/o Giyan Singh	Tarkhan	15	"
193.	Sita Ram s/o Gobindram	Hindu	—	"
194.	Bhagat Singh s/o Kesar Singh	Jat	35	Jhugawan, Rupawali
195.	Natha Singh s/o Chet Singh	Jat	20	Jhetuwal
196.	Bhag Mal s/o Hari Ram	Arora	—	Amirtsar City
197.	Arur Singh s/o Roda Singh	Tarkhan	—	Vadala, Distt. Amritsar
198.	Ganga Singh s/o Lal Singh	Jat	—	Mahl, Distt. Amritsar
199.	Viroo s/o Mian	Jalaha	—	Makhanwind, Distt. Amritsar
200.	Gopal Singh	Jat	—	Vallah, Distt. Amritsar
201.	Kartar Singh s/o Ganda Singh	Arora	40	Amritsar City
202.	Gopal Singh	Khatri	—	Sobhala, Distt. Rawalpindi
203.	Hemraj s/o Khemraj	Banya	—	Amrit City
204.	Mul Singh s/o Kam Singh	Ramgarhia	—	"
205.	Sohan Singh s/o Chandasingh	Jat	—	Khorota, Distt. Rawalpindi
206.	Keher Singh s/o Ver Singh	Jat	—	Sultanwind
207.	Bibi Har Kaur w/o Hardit Singh	Jatni	—	Lopoke

Sr. No.	Name and parentage	Caste	Age	Residence
208.	Mangal Singh s/o Ishar Singh	Jat	—	Lohka, Distt. Amritsar
209.	Dhirt Ram s/o Bilas Mal	Hindu	29	Amritsar City
210.	Budha s/o Janni	Mohd. Sakka		Jhita Kalan, Distt. Amritsar
211.	Thakur Singh s/o Jawant Singh	Jat	—	Mehma, Distt. Amritsar
212.	Tehru s/o Asa Singh	Jat	—	Varpal, Distt. Amritsar
213.	Taroo s/o Jawala Singh	Jat	—	"
214.	Viroo s/o Nathu	Bharai	—	"
215.	Naina s/o Kunun	Mehra	—	Vanchari, Distt. Amritsar
216.	Vir Singh	Kamboh	—	Devidass Pura, Distt. Amritsar
217.	Bhagat Ram s/o Dhanni Ram	Khatri	17	Amritsar City
218.	Chet Singh s/o Diyalu	Jat	—	Kaler Guman, Distt. Amritsar
219.	Labhu Ram s/o Sitaram	Banya	27	Amritsar City
220.	Jawar Singh s/o Partap Singh	Arora	26	"
221.	Magalram s/o Gianimal	Hindu	—	"
222.	Bishan Das s/o Gurditta Mal	Khatri	30	"
223.	Harbhagwan	Hindu	—	Majith Mandi, Distt. Amritsar
224.	Khikamal *alias* Nikkamal c/o Dunichand Jairamdas	Hindu	—	Amritsar City
225.	Hukam Chand c/o Kalu Mal Shorimal	Hindu	—	"
226.	Harnam Singh c/o Kalumal Shori Mal	Hindu	—	"

Sr. No.	Name and parentage	Caste	Age	Residence
227.	Ram Chand	Hindu	—	Amritsar City
228.	Balmokand c/o Sitaram Mangal Chand	"	—	"
229.	Hari Ram Petition-writer	—	—	Amritsar
230.	Jagan Nath	Hindu	—	"
231.	Mohan Lal Broker	"	—	"
232.	Rakha Mal	Hindu	—	"
233.	Balmokand	"	—	"
234.	Tarachand, Woodseller	"	—	"
235.	Ramnath s/o Pagoomal	Khatri	—	"
236.	Thakardas	Hindu	—	"
237.	Mehrchand s/o Har Sahai	Hindu	—	Amritsar City
238.	Arura	Khatri	—	"
239.	Sundar Singh s/o Gurbax Singh	Arora	—	"
240.	Shafi, Kanjar	Mohammedan	—	"
241.	Nanak Chand s/o Chuttamal	Khatri	—	"
242.	Kashi Ram	Brahmin	—	"
243.	Sundar s/o Natha Singh	Arora	25	"
244.	Santa s/o Hariram	Brahmin	—	Varpal Distt. Amritsar
245.	Ilam Din	Mohammedan	—	Bhilowal Teh. Ajnala
246.	Mangal Singh	Sadh	—	Dhattal Tch. Ajnala
247.	Asa Singh s/o Ishar Singh	Jat	—	Ramoki Basarke Distt. Amritsar
248.	Harnam Singh s/o Tehal Singh	Kumhar	—	Gumanpura Distt. Amritsar
249.	Bishen Singh s/o Mitsingh	Jat	—	Chabba Distt. Amritsar
250.	Lachman Singh s/o Dyal Singh	Jat	60	"
251.	Rukn Din s/o Ilahi Bax	Mochi	—	Thanda Distt. Amritsar

Sr. No.	Name and parentage	Caste	Age	Residence
252.	Khushal Singh s/o Jiwan Singh	Jat	—	Fatehpur Distt. Amritsar
253.	Ujagar Singh s/o Budh Singh	Jat	—	Mehanpur Distt. Amritsar
254.	Sureina s/o Kharku	Sweeper	—	"
255.	Ujagar Singh s/o Wadhawa Singh	Jat	—	Dhand Teh. Tarn Taran
256.	Partap Singh s/o Tehl Singh	Jat	—	"
257.	Prem Singh s/o Nathasingh	"	—	Kaler Mangal Teh. Amritsar
258.	Chanan s/o Bhagat Ram	Hindu	—	Majitha Distt. Amritsar
259.	Karim Din	Lohar	—	Sohian Kalan Distt. Amritsar
260.	Tirlok Chand s/o Balmokand	Khatri	—	Amritsar City
261.	Bur Singh s/o Jhanda Singh	Jat	—	Jhamke Teh. Tarn Taran
262.	Madan Mohan s/o Dr. Mani Ram	Khatri	—	Amritsar City
263.	Ami Chand s/o Pirthi Nath	Brahmin	—	Muradpura Teh. Amritsar
264.	Ms. Bisso, sister of Jamadar Sher Singh	Jat	50	Sultanwind, Teh. Amritsar
265.	Budha Singh s/o Amar Singh	—	45	Tung, Distt. Gurdaspur
266.	Gulam Rasul s/o Dulla	Mohd.	—	Chabhal, Distt. Amritsar
267.	Ganda Singh s/o Sham Singh	Jat	—	Killa Jiwan Singh Distt. Amritsar
268.	Gauri Shankar s/o Kishan Diyal	Hindu	—	Batala, Distt. Gurdaspur
269.	Bhagat Ram	—	35	Gadi Guru Jawalasingh Distt. Montgomery

Sr. No.	Name and parentage	Caste	Age	Residence
270.	Hiranand, Petition writer	—	—	Ajnala
271.	Hansraj s/o Sohan	—	—	Pipli Teh. Batala
272.	Hukum Singh s/o Ganda Singh	—	30	Madoki Teh. Ajnala
273.	Diya Ram s/o Harichand	Arora		Miyali, Riya Distt. Sialkot
274.	Ditta Mal s/o Buta Mal	—	40	Jiwan Bhinder Riya, Distt. Gurdaspur
275.	Kartar Singh s/o Gandasingh	Arora	—	Mangat Bhim, Distt. Gujrat
276.	Kehar Singh s/o Sham Singh	—	40	Her Bhakna Distt. Amritsar
277.	Kahan Chand s/o Hem raj	—	—	Gurdaspur
278.	Bishan Singh s/o Lamburdar	—	—	Chabha Distt. Amritsar
279.	Kanshiram s/o Motiram	Saini	21	Bahlolpur, Dist.-Gurdaspur
280.	Kirpa Ram s/o Ganda Ram	Brahmin	26	Kot Karam Chand, Dist.-Gurdaspur
281.	Kanshi Ram s/o Mathuradas	"	53	Talwindi Phindran, Distt. Sialkot
282.	Lachman Singh s/o Harya Singh	—	28	Muradpura, Teh. Amritsar
283.	Mangal Dass s/o Diyaloo	Bairagi	25	Chabhal, Teh.Tarn Taran
284.	Madho s/o Raja	Barber	22	Narowal, Distt. Sialkot
285.	Nathoo s/o Jit Singh	Jat	22	Jethowal Teh. Amritsar
286.	Natha Singh s/o Jawala Singh	Jat	30	Jagatpur Teh. Tarn Taran
287.	Nanak Chand s/o Raja Singh	—	—	Kot Sadiqui, Dist. Kambelpur

Sr. No.	Name and parentage	Caste	Age	Residence
288.	Sundar Singh s/o Nathu	—	—	Khutra Kalan, Teh. Ajnala
289.	Surjan Singh	—	30	Chak Sikandar Distt. Amritsar
290.	Sohan Singh s/o Mohansingh	Carpenter	15	Lalo Ghuman Teh. Tarn Taran
291.	Thakur s/o Mula Singh	Jat	—	Pathan Nagar Teh. Ajnala
292.	Teja Singh's son	—	—	Bhala Pind Teh. Ajnala
293.	Tara Singh s/o Jhanda Singh	—	15	Musa Teh. Tarn Taran
294.	Arur Chand	Khatri	—	Amritsar City
295.	Abdul Hamid s/o Ahmaddin	Kashmiri	16	"
296.	Abdul Gafur	Carpet maker	—	"
297.	Amir	Ghumiar	—	"
298.	Veshno Das s/o Mohrajmal	—	—	"
299.	Bhag	Ghumair	—	Ladhewal Teh. Tarn Taran
300.	Bhagwan s/o Nihal Chand	Arora	45	Amirtsar City
301.	Chuni Lal	—	—	"
302.	Churanji Lal s/o Nathu Ram	—	—	"
303.	Charan Das s/o Rama Nand	—	—	"
304.	Dwarka Dass s/o Sitaram	Khatri	22	"
305.	Daulat Ram	Arora	—	"
306.	Diwan Chand s/o Dhani Ram	Khatri	35	"
307.	Dass s/o Damodar	Brahmin	25	"
308.	Datt Dabkai	Mohd.	40	"
309.	Data Mal s/o Narsingh Dass	—	—	"

Sr. No.	Name and parentage	Caste	Age	Residence
310.	Devi Ditta	Brahmin	—	Amirtsar City
311.	Dass Mall s/o Jametsingh	Zargar	—	”
312.	Faquir Chand s/o Nanakchand	Arora	45	”
313.	Harnam Singh s/o Bhagat Singh	—	17	”
314.	Hira Lal s/o Chamanlal	—	55	”
315.	Hukam Singh s/o Jagatsingh	Carpenter	—	”
316.	Har Narain	Khatri		”
317.	Harnam Singh s/o Chanda Singh	Arora	20	”
318.	Har Bhagwan s/o Kanahiya Lal	—	—	”
319.	Haru Mal s/o Labhumal Satawala	—	—	”
320.	Hira Nand s/o Wazira	—	—	”
321.	Hansraj, Postal Clerk	—	—	”
322.	Hussi s/o Sikkandar	Zargar	—	”
323.	Ismail s/o Miran Bux	”	22	”
324.	Ibrahim s/o Imam Din	—	25	”
325.	Jagan Nath s/o Bal Kishan Mehra			” ”
326.	Kashmir Singh	—	—	”
327.	Karam Chand *alias* Milla s/o Labhu	Arora	21	”
328.	Kishan Chand s/o Ami Chand	Khatri	40	”
329.	Kalu Mal s/o Veshno Dass	—	—	”
330.	Kaka Singh s/o Nihala	Chimba	23	”

Sr. No.	Name and parentage	Caste	Age	Residence
331.	Kadoo s/o Vashnodass	Brahmin	18	Amirtsar City
332.	Kashmiri Singh	—	—	"
333.	Labhu Ram s/o Chaju Ram	Khatri	14	"
334.	Lachman Kar	—	—	"
335.	Mohd. Shafi s/o Rahim Bux	Kashmiri	19	"
336.	Mangal Singh s/o Kanhia Mal	"	—	"
337.	Murli	—	—	"
338.	Miraj Din s/o Nabi Bux	Kharasi	18	"
339.	Manak Chand s/o Ataromal	—	—	"
340.	Mela Ram s/o Mathuradass	—	—	"
341.	Mehru Mal s/o Ramsahai	—	—	"
342.	Mullan s/o Rahim Bux	Kashmiri	40	"
343.	Mul Singh s/o Mana Singh	Carpenter	20	"
344.	Meva Singh s/o Hakim Singh	—	—	"
345.	Madho	Barber	—	"
346.	Mulak Raj s/o Nand Lal	Saraf	—	"
347.	Manon s/o Per Bux	Saka	—	"
348.	Mehr Chand	—	—	"
349.	Multani c/o L. Devki Nandan	—	—	"
350.	Mukhul c/o Phul Badshah	—	—	"
351.	Muni Lal s/o Ram Rakha Mal	Khatri	17	"
352.	Mela	—	—	"
353.	Mota Ram	Dalal		"

Sr. No.	Name and parentage	Caste	Age	Residence
354.	Mohan Lal s/o Ramsingh	Arora	19	Amirtsar City
355.	Musa s/o Jamal Din	Mohd.	16	"
356.	Nathu Ram s/o Mula Mal	Brahmin	30	"
357.	Nand s/o Karam Chand	"	—	"
358.	Narain Singh s/o Hardiyal Singh	Arora	—	"
359.	Murli Mal s/o Nathumal	—	12	"
360.	Nand Lal s/o Mela Ram	Brahmin	16	"
361.	Nathu s/o Govind Ram	—	—	"
362.	Palla Dalal s/o Nanakchand	—	—	"
363.	Puran Chand s/o Natha Singh	—	—	" "
364.	Prabh Diyal c/o L. Tirath Ram	Pleader	—	"
365.	Prabh Diyal s/o Sita Ram	Arora	19	"
366.	Ram Saran s/o Kaka Ram	Khatri	28	"
367.	Rura Ram s/o Kaka Ram	"	22	"
368.	Ram Gopal	"		"
369.	Ram Gopal s/o Sain Dass	"	30	"
370.	Ramzan Batt s/o Rahim Batt	Mohd.	40	"
371.	Sher Singh s/o Hira Singh	Arora	72	"
372.	Sant Ram s/o Prabh Diyal	—	23	"
373.	Sobha Singh	—	—	"

Sr. No.	Name and parentage	Caste	Age	Residence
374.	Sant Ram s/o Hari Ram	—	—	Amritsar City
375.	Sadiq s/o Miraj Bux	—	—	"
376.	Sher Singh s/o Hira Singh	—	17	"
377.	Sundar Singh s/o Nihal	Jat	35	"
378.	Umar Din s/o Din Mohd.	Mohd.	—	"
379.	Wassu Mal s/o Sitaram	Arora	32	"
380.	Warris s/o Allai Kasai	Mohd.	40	"
381.	Nihal Singh s/o Harnam Singh	Jat	35	"

APPENDIX II

TRIPURI 1939 CONGRESS SESSION

LECTURE OF SUBHASH CHANDRA BOSE

Comrade Chairman, sister and brother delegates I thank you from the bottom of my heart for the great honour you have done me by re-electing me to the presidential chair of the Indian National Congress, and also for the warm and cordial welcome you have given me here at Tripuri. It is true that at my request you have had to dispense with some of the pomp that is usual on such occasions. But I feel that this has not taken away one iota of the warmth and cordiality of your reception, and I hope that nobody will regret the curtailment of it on this occasion.

Friends, before I proceed any further I shall voice your feelings by expressing joy at the success of Mahatma Gandhi's mission to Rajkot and the termination of his fast in consequence thereof. The whole country now feels happy and tremendously relieved.

You are aware that the Wafdist delegation from Egypt have arrived in our midst as the guests of the Indian National Congress. You will join me in according the most hearty welcome to all of them. We are extremely happy that they found it possible to accept our invitation and make the voyage in India. We are only sorry that political exigencies in Egypt did not permit the President of the Wafd, Mustapha Nahas Pasha, personally to lead this delegation. Having had the privilege of knowing the President and leading members of the Wafdist Party, my joy today is all the greater. Once again I offer them, on behalf of our countrymen, a most hearty and cordial welcome.

Friends, this year promises to be an abnormal or extraordinary one in many ways. The presidential election this time was not of a humdrum type. The election was followed by sensational developments, culminating in the resignation of twelve out of the fifteen members of the Working Committee, headed by Sardar Patel, Maulana Azad and Mr. Rajendra Prasad. Another distinguished and eminent member of the Working Committee, Pandit Jawaharlal Nehru, though he did not formally resign, issued a statement which led everybody to believe that he had also resigned. On the eve of the Tripuri Congress the events at Rajkiot forced Mahatma Gandhi to undertake a vow of fast unto death. And then the President arrived at Tripuri a sick man. It will, wherefore, be in the fitness of things if the presidential address this year can claim to be a departure from precedent in the matter of its length.

Since we met at Haripura in February 1938, several significant events have taken place in the international sphere. The most important of these is the Munich Pact of September 1938, which implied an abject surrender to Nazi Germany on the part of the Western powers. France and Great Britain. As the result of this, France ceased to be a dominant power in Europe and the hegemony passed into the hands of Germany without a shot being fired. In more recent times. The gradual collapse of the Republican Government in Spain seems to have added to the strength and prestige of Fascist Italy and Nazi Germany. The socalled democratic powers, France and Great Britain, have joined Italy and Germany in conspiring to eliminate soviet Russia from European politics for the time being. But how long will that be possible? And what have France and Great Britain gained by trying to humiliate Russia?

There is no doubt that as the result of the recent international developments in Europe as well as in Asia, British and French Imperialism have received a considerable set-back in the matter of strength and prestige.

Coming to home politics, in view of my ill-health I shall content myself with referring to only a few important problems. In the first place, I must give clear and unequivocal expression to what I have been feeling for some time past, namely that the time has come for us to raise the issue of Swaraj and submit our national demand to the British Government in the form of an ultimatum. The time is long past when we could have adopted a passive attitude and waited for the Federal Scheme to be imposed on us. The problem is no longest as to when the Federal Scheme will be feireeddown our throats. The problems is as to what we should do if the Federal Scheme is conveniently shelved for a few years till peace is stabilized in Europe. There is no doubt that once there is stable peace in Europe, whether through a Four-Power pact or through some other means, Great Britain will adopt a strong Empire policy. She is now showing some signs of trying to conciliate the Arabs as against the Jews in Palestine, because she is feeling insecure in the international sperel. In my opinion therefore we should submit out national demand to the British Government in the form of an ultimatum and give a certain time-limit, if no reply is received with in this period or if an unsatisfactory reply is received, we should resort to such sanctions as we possess in order to enforce our national demand.

The sanction that we possess today is mass civil disobedience or Satyagrahs. And the British Government today are not in a position to face a major conflicts like an all-India Satyagrah for a long period. It grieves me to find that there are people in the Congress who are so pessimistic as to think that the time is not ripe for a major assault on British Imperialism. But looking at the situation in a thoroughly realistic manner, I do not see the slightest ground for pessimism. With the Congress in power in eight provinces, the strength and the prestige of our national organization have gone up. The mass movement has made considerable headway throughout British India. And last but not least, there is an unprecedented awakening in the Indian States. What more opportune moment could we find in our national history for a final advance in the direction of Swaraj, particularly when the international situation is favourable to us? Speaking as a cold-blooded realist, I may say that all the facts of the present-day situation are so much to our advantage that one should entertain the highest degree of optimism. If only we sink our differences, pool our resources and pull our full weight in the national struggle, we make the most of our present favourable position; or we shall miss this opportunity which is a rare opportunity is the life-time of a nation.

I have already referred to the awakening in India and to the awakening in the Indian States. I am definitely of the view that we should revise our attitude towards the State as defined by the Haripura Congress resolution. That resolution as you are aware, put a ban on certain forms of activity in the State being conducted in the name of the Congress. Under that resolution neither parliamentary work nor the struggle in the States should be carried on in the name of the Congress. But since Haripura much has happened. Today we find that the Paramount Power is in league with the State authorities in most places. In such circumstances should we of the Congress not draw closer to the people of the States? I have no doubt in my mind as to what our duty is today. Besides lifting the above ban. The work of guiding the popular movement is the States for civil liberty and responsible government should be conducted by the Working Committee on a comprehensive and systematic basis. The work so far done has been of a piecemeal nature, and there has hardly been any system or plan behind it. But the time has come when the Working Committee should assume this responsibility and discharge it in a comprehensive and systematic way and, if necessary, appoint a special Sub-Committee for the purpose. The fullest use should be made of the guidance and co-operation of Mahatama Gandhi and of the co-operation of the All-India State Peoples Conference.

I have referred earlier to the advisability of our making the final advance in the direction of Swaraj. That will need adequate preparation. In the first place, we shall have to take steps to remove ruthlessly whatever corruption, or weakness has entered into our ranks, largely due to the lure of power. Next we shall have to work in close cooperation with all anti-imperialist organizations in the country, particularly the Kisan movement and the trade union movement. All of the radical elements in the country must work in close harmony and co-operation, and the efforts of all anti-imperialist organizations must converge in the direction of a final assault on British Imperialism.

Friends, the atmosphere within the Congress today is clouded and dissensions have appeared. Many of our friends are consequently feeling depressed and dispirited. But I am an incorrigible optimist. The cloud that you see today is a passing one. I have faith in the patriotism of my countrymen and I am sure that before long we shall be able to tide over the present difficulties and restore unity within our ranks. A somewhat similar situation had arisen at the time of the Gaya Congress in 1922 and thereafter, when Deshbandhu Das and Pandit Motilal Nehru of hallowed memory started the Swaraj party. May the spirit of my late Guru, of the revered Motilal and of the other great sons of India inspire us in the present crisis, and may Mahatama Gandhi, who is still with us to guide and assist the nation, help the congress out of the present tangle. This is my earnest prayer, Vande Mataram!

■■■■